What People Are Saying About
Chicken Soup for the Preteen Soul 2 . . .

"When I read the stories, they did exactly what I expected a *Chicken Soup* story to do—they really provoked my thoughts. Some of them were happy/funny stories, and some of them were sad/tough-to-read stories. But all of them had one thing in common—they all showed how preteens get through the good times and the bad times."

Rosemary, thirteen

"One word . . . 'GREAT'!!! I loved the stories—some of them were happy, some sad—but they all teach a lesson. They are better than the mystery books I read (and I really like those). The stories are real and true . . . and that's what counts."

Brittany, twelve

"These stories have all helped me in their own way. Each one had benefits. They have touched my life, and as I get older I will remember these stories."

Nosylla, fourteen

"*Preteen Soul 2* is an amazing book. It has a story for everyone and they all are intriguing. You can feel the author's pain, happiness, frustration and laughter in every story. Every preteen's life will be improved reading a *Chicken Soup for the Preteen Soul* book."

Emily, twelve

"The stories in this book are even better than the first *Chicken Soup for the Preteen Soul* book. When you realize that someone is going through the same thing as you, it just makes you want to go back and read the story over and over again. Every preteen *must* get a copy of this book."

Katrisha, thirteen

"All of the stories were great! They encouraged me to go out and make new friends, try new experiences, and to defend my body as well as my mind. Thanks, *Chicken Soup!* You always know where to find the best stories—from the kids themselves!"

Erika, twelve

"I have read these stories over and over again! I think that every preteen needs to know they aren't alone."

Fabiola, eleven

"I just turned thirteen and I have been struggling with a lot of things lately. One of my friends read these stories and they changed her life forever. The stories help you learn what to do when you are in trouble. They teach you how to be yourself and not try to be somebody you're not."

Jessica, thirteen

"*Chicken Soup for the Preteen Soul 2* is very powerful stuff. These books mean a lot to me because when I read about the problems preteens in the stories have, it makes me realize that we all have the same problems between ages nine and thirteen."

Beverly, eleven

"When I read these stories I started to cry. They were so motivational and inspiring. Everyone should read *Preteen Soul 2*. These were the best stories I have ever read, and what I love about them is that they are true and they are stories from people my age."

Ahkeyah, ten

CHICKEN SOUP
FOR THE
PRETEEN SOUL 2

Stories About Facing Challenges, Realizing Dreams and Making a Difference

Jack Canfield
Mark Victor Hansen
Patty Hansen
Irene Dunlap

Health Communications, Inc.
Deerfield Beach, Florida

www.bcibooks.com
www.chickensoup.com

We would like to acknowledge the following publishers and individuals for permission to reprint the following material. (Note: The stories that penned are public domain or that were written by Jack Canfield, Mark Victor Hansen, Patty Hansen or Irene Dunlap are not included in this listing.)

Introduction. Reprinted by permission of Elisabeth Haney and Kenyon P. Haney. ©2003 Elisabeth Haney.

On Friends Chapter Opener. Reprinted by permission of Michele Davis and Laurie Davis. ©2003 Michele Davis.

Thanks Ya'll. Reprinted by permission of Michelle Strauss and Patricia Hartnett. ©1999 Michelle Strauss.

Story Opener. Reprinted by permission of Nicole Johnson and Raymond Johnson. ©2003 Nicole Johnson.

(Continued on page 397)

Library of Congress Cataloging-in-Publication Data

Chicken soup for the preteen soul 2 : stories about facing challenges, realizing dreams and making a difference / Jack Canfield . . . [et al.].
    p. cm.
ISBN-13: 978-0-7573-0150-6 (tp)
ISBN-10: 0-7573-0150-9 (tp)
    1. Preteens—Conduct of life—Juvenile literature.   I. Title: Chicken soup for the preteen soul two.   II. Canfield, Jack, 1944–

BJ1631.C4652 2004
158.1'083—dc22

                                                                2004047450

Publisher: Health Communications, Inc.
            3201 S.W. 15th Street
            Deerfield Beach, FL 33442-8190
R-10-07

Cover art by Danny Cannizzaro, nineteen
Cover art assembly by Peter Quintal
Formatting by Dawn Von Strolley Grove

We dedicate this book to the preteens
who are making our world a better place.
We salute you for not being afraid
to dream and for making a positive difference.
You are our heroes!

Contents

6. ON CHANGES

7. BUSTIN' DOWN WALLS

8. FAMILY TIES

12. ECLECTIC WISDOM

Acknowledgments

Once again, we are deeply grateful for the help and contributions of many who have made the process of creating *Chicken Soup for the Preteen Soul 2* a wonderful, fulfilling experience.

Our very special thanks to Gina Romanello, without whom this book would never have come together as well as it has. Thanks for your hard work. You are a blessing to us, Gina, and simply put—you ROCK!

Our heartfelt gratitude to our families, who have been Chicken Soup for our Souls!

To Jack Canfield's family: Inga, Travis, Riley, Christopher, Oran and Kyle for all your love and support.

To Mark and Patty's daughters, Elisabeth and Melanie Hansen, for once again sharing and lovingly supporting us in creating yet another book. To Eva Espinosa for keeping Patty's home life running smoothly while she was busy with this project.

To Kent, Marleigh and Weston Dunlap for helping see us through months of hard work by picking up the slack at home when needed. To Irene's mother, Angela Jack, for your unconditional love and support. And to Marcia Kirschbaum for helping Irene hold down the fort during book production and for your awesome friendship and support.

To Brittany Shaw and Joel Bakker for helping with whatever was needed to get us through different phases of production—you are a godsend. To Dena Jacobson, thanks for keeping Patty's office in order with grace and humor. To Dee Dee Romanello, for your friendship and ongoing support in so many ways.

To Danny Cannizzaro for another great cover design. We love working with you, Danny, and continue to be inspired by your artwork.

To Patty Aubery, president of Chicken Soup for the Soul Enterprises, Inc., for always looking out for us with love and support; Russ Kamalski, chief operating officer for Chicken Soup for the Soul Enterprises, for your professionalism and vision—you are awesome! Nancy Autio, Barbara Lomonaco, Leslie Riskin, Heather McNamara, Jesse Ianniello, Tasha Boucher, Veronica Romero, Robin Yerian, Theresa Esparza, D'ette Corona and Mike Foster at Chicken Soup for the Soul Enterprises—you are all wonderful.

Laurie Hartman, for being a precious guardian of the Chicken Soup brand.

Jody Emme, Debbie Lefever, Michelle Adams, Dee Dee Romanello, Shanna Vieyra, Lisa Williams, Tanya Jones, Dena Jacobson and Mary McKay, who support Mark's business with skill and love.

Peter Vegso at Health Communications, Inc., for recognizing the value of our books from the beginning and for getting them into the hands of millions of readers.

To our wonderful, easygoing and insightful editor, Allison Janse, at Health Communications, Inc. You are a true joy to work with and we feel blessed that you put your heart and soul into making this the best book that it could be.

Also, thanks to the rest of the editing team, Bret Witter, Kathy Grant and Elisabeth Rinaldi, for your devotion to excellence.

Terry Burke, Tom Sand, Lori Golden, Tom Galvin, Kelly Johnson Maragni, Randee Feldman, Patricia McConnell,

Kim Weiss, Paola Fernandez-Rana, Pat Holdsworth, and the rest of the marketing, sales, administration and PR departments at Health Communications, Inc., for doing such an incredible job supporting our books.

Claude Choquette and Luc Jutras, who manage year after year to get our books translated into thirty-six languages around the world.

The art department at Health Communications, Inc., for their talent, creativity and patience in producing book covers and inside designs that capture the essence of Chicken Soup: Larissa Hise Henoch, Lawna Patterson Oldfield, Andrea Perrine Brower, Anthony Clausi and Dawn Von Strolley Grove.

All the *Chicken Soup for the Soul* coauthors, who make it such a joy to be part of this Chicken Soup family.

To Joanna Stokes at Music World Entertainment for helping coordinate Michele William's story, to Courtney Myers in Lennox Lewis' office for your awesome assistance, and to Russ Riggins at Positively for Kids for helping coordinate logistics for Kristi Yamaguchi's story.

To our incredible panel of preteen readers and their teachers who read hundreds of stories in order to help us make the final selections—your input was invaluable and very much appreciated: the sixth-graders at Conrad Ball Middle School in Loveland, Colorado; teachers Marilyn Burns, Brooke LaFave, Alyssa Barnes and Pam Breitbarth. The students of Riverchase Middle School in Birmingham, Alabama; teacher Jean Estes, and especially Donna Thompson who has volunteered to help us from our very first book. We love you, Donna! The students and teachers of Robey Elementary School in Indianapolis, Indiana, and principal, Kyle Fessler. The students and teachers of Silvestri Junior High School in Las Vegas, Nevada; Jackie Soden and principal Steve Wood. We appreciate all of your hard work!

A special thanks to the awesome preteens of www.PreteenPlanet.com for reading and evaluating last-minute stories for us and endorsing the book; and to those who contributed to our compilation stories, "Preteen Wisdom" and "My Most Embarrassing Moment." We really couldn't have done it without you!

To Mary Beth Zaskoda, Maxine Dessler and Lisa Sourbrey who helped us locate young writers that we couldn't find. Thanks for going the extra mile.

Most of all, our gratitude goes out to everyone who submitted their heartfelt stories, poems, quotes and cartoons for possible inclusion in this book. We especially thank the Society of Children's Book Writers and Illustrators for always sending such well-written and age-appropriate material for us to consider.

Finally, thanks to all the preteens who took time to write to us just to say how much they loved *Chicken Soup for the Preteen Soul* and requested a second edition. It means the world to us to hear how our books have changed your lives for the better.

Because of the size of this project, we may have left out the names of some people who contributed along the way. If so, we are sorry, but please know that we really do appreciate you very much.

We are truly grateful and love you all!

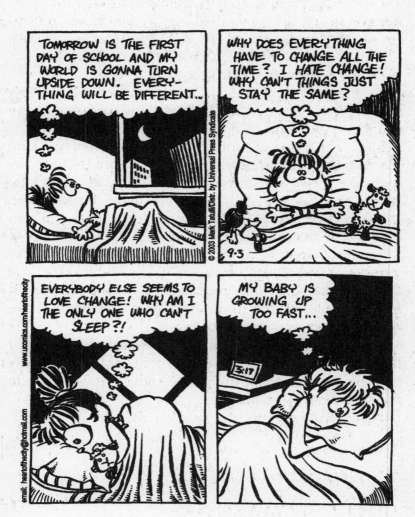

Introduction

Ever think that you'll have to wait to grow up to make a difference in the world? Well, *stop* thinking that! We've said it before and we'll say it again—YOU ARE UNSTOPPABLE! Preteens are continually stepping up and changing things for the better. To prove it, we have included inspiring stories about preteens like you who are making dreams come true while making life a little better for others.

As you make your way from being a kid to an adult, it seems that you're dealing with so many changes that sometimes it's tough just to keep your balance. *Chicken Soup for the Preteen Soul 2*, like *Preteen Soul*, addresses challenges that you face when it comes to friendships, first crushes, peer pressure, cliques, divorce, death and more, and how the choices you make—big and small—have a significant impact on your life and the lives of others.

We also recognize that there are moments in life that you can't change, can't take back and simply have to deal with. "That's life," as they say. So, we have added a new chapter called "Life Happens" that is designed to make you smile and think to yourself, *Hey, life ain't perfect, but it ain't so bad either.* We've also created a new compilation in this chapter titled "My Most Embarrassing Moment" that takes a lighthearted look at circumstances in which some people might have felt defeated, but chose to laugh or shrug it off instead.

And for when things get really tough—and sometimes they do—you may need some advice or information. To help you deal better, we've included Website information and an 800 number at the end of some of the stories.

Through *Preteen Soul 2* we really want you to get that you're not alone in the seemingly endless changes that you—and your body—are going through. Elizabeth Haney, eleven, describes it this way:

> *Being a preteen is harder than it looks. Your body is going through changes, so you have more emotions than you know what to do with. Sometimes you just want to cry and other times you feel like things are going your way.*
>
> *And then you have moms who just aren't ready for you to grow up yet. I mean, what are they going to do when we learn how to drive?*
>
> *And then there are dads. My dad is always there for me, especially when I need to talk about boys. He can always explain why they act so weird. (Sorry, boys!)*
>
> *There are millions of other kids going through the same things, although we are all slightly different. Like, you might be black, white or Hispanic or have red hair and you probably don't have a dog named Missy or an annoying neighbor. But you're not alone when it comes to what a preteen goes through.*

As the authors, we feel that we understand what issues are important to preteens, but we would never assume to know which stories will impact you the most. Once again, we have taken the best of the thousands of stories sent to us and asked preteens all over America to help us choose the best of the best. What you have in your hands is a book with the 101 stories and poems that your peers liked the most. How can you go wrong with that?

We hope that this book will show you that anything you put your mind and effort to is possible. You can—and will—recover from the stuff that messes with you, if you keep yourself open to all possibilities. Recognize that sometimes things just take time to heal or change for the better. Your attitude can make or break you. Whether you live with joy and happiness or allow the things that happen to you to defeat you is really up to you.

May these stories help you have better friendships, sort out your emotions and make good life decisions. Realize that you can make a difference right now. You don't have to wait to grow up to make your world a better place. You are powerful and able.

Above all, remember to enjoy your preteen years! And . . . never, *never* give up on your dreams.

Share with Us

We would like to know how these stories affected you and which ones were your favorites. Please write to us and let us know.

Also, please send us your nonfiction stories and poems that you would like us to consider for future books.

Send submissions to:

Chicken Soup for the Kid's/Preteen Soul
Attn: Patty Hansen and Irene Dunlap
P.O. Box 10879
Costa Mesa, CA 92627

E-mail us at: *mail@lifewriters.com*

Visit our Website at:
www.lifewriters.com
www.preteenplanet.com
www.chickensoup.com

1

ON FRIENDS

Someone to laugh with, perhaps to shed some tears
A person who's been with you all through the years.
Someone to shelter you from days that are cold
A shoulder to lean on, a warm hand to hold.
An arm to catch you if you slip and you fall
And an ear for your problems whenever you call.
Someone to share your giggles and your screams
A person to tell all your secrets and dreams.
Someone to hug you when you're happy or sad
To just be there in the good times or bad.
A person with whom you don't have to pretend
These are the jobs of a very best friend.

Michele Davis, fifteen

Thanks, Y'All!

We all take different paths in life, but no matter where we go, we take a little of each other everywhere.

Tim McGraw

I have distant friends, neighborhood friends, basketball friends and friends online. However, I have one group of friends that has really been special to me.

In the fifth grade, my twin sister, Monica, and I transferred to a new school. Without any hesitation, I went. I didn't argue. Since my mom taught there, I would no longer have to ride the bus with a bunch of rowdy boys and worry about stuff like getting kicked in the head. No kidding—they actually accidentally kicked me in the head one day!

At my old school, I hadn't made any real friends. I was treated like a complete dork because of the way I looked. I had glasses, baggy clothes, pimples and blemishes. I rarely smiled and hardly ever laughed, wore a belt and was overweight. I was also dealing with the reality of my parents getting a divorce.

So, on the first day at my new school, I just hoped that I would make friends. For a few weeks, I was always alone. Monica ended up having a different lunch period than I did, so I would just read during recess and lunch.

Then one day, a girl in my class named Cori came up to me at lunch and asked if she could sit by me. We began to talk, and since we both are twins, it gave us a lot to talk about. Soon, Cori introduced me to friends of hers—Adriane, Hannah and Toni—and I introduced them to Monica. Then Cori's twin, Cole, and his friends Matt and Ross started hanging around with us. We became one big inseparable group. At recess we played basketball and other games. We did everything together.

Ever since we've been together, my friends have always been there for me—even the boys. They liked me, for me. Having them in my life changed the way I felt about myself. Their friendship gave me a sky-high feeling. We barely ever argued! We were really tight. They seemed to understand how hard it was to change schools and have stuck with me through the tough times, like dealing with my parents' divorce.

One time, when Monica and I couldn't go outside with our friends after school, Toni supplied us with a pair of walkie-talkies to keep us all in touch!

I began being more outgoing, like getting involved in student council and entering writing contests—some that I even won! Then came the sixth grade, our last year of elementary school and the last year for all of us to be going to the same school together. Adriane, Hannah, Toni, Matt and Ross were going to Tison. Monica and I would at least still be seeing Cori and Cole since the four of us were all going to Hall Junior High.

I'd also be seeing my "old" classmates from the other elementary school, including some I had run into recently. Boys who had teased me in my old school, stood staring at me not even knowing who I was. The girls who previously had treated me like vapor now payed attention to me and called me by name. I couldn't figure it out. I didn't know why. I thought that I was the same old me. But then when I looked in the mirror, I realized that I was a lot different than I had been before.

I wasn't short and stubby anymore. I had grown tall and slender and my complexion had cleared up. The glasses were gone and my belts were pushed to the back of my closet. I realized then that my friends had done more than just make me feel good—they had made me feel confident because they had supported me, and slowly my appearance had changed.

With their help, I had pushed my weight off. Toni helped me with that by encouraging me not to eat some of the more fattening foods and telling me that I could do whatever I set my mind to. I had been trying to lose weight since I was nine, when the doctor had said to my mom, "Michelle has a weight problem."

I learned to properly wash my face with the help of my friend Hannah and her magical beauty tips. "Just wash your face every night, it doesn't take too long!" she instructed.

With the help of Cori, my belt was gone. "Believe me, it's a lot less painful on your stomach. I used to tuck *all* my clothes in, even sweaters!" she exclaimed.

Adriane suggested that I wear my glasses only when I really needed them. "If you can see how many fingers I'm holding up, you are okay," she said. "Just wear them when you need to see the homework assignment on the board."

My sister, Monica, loves clothes and helped me pay attention to how I dressed. She would give me feedback about what looked good and what didn't. It really helped to hear her say, "Wow, Michelle, that looks FANTASTIC on you! Man, why couldn't I have gotten that?"

With the help of Cole, I learned a little bit more about athletics. "No! No! The receiver receives the ball! No! No! The quarterback doesn't flip the quarter! That's the referee!" he explained.

With the help of Matt, I learned to smile. "It won't hurt you," he encouraged.

With help from Ross, I learned a laugh a day keeps the frown away.

"B in math? Awesome! That's not failing—it's just not perfect," expressed my friends.

As I gaze into the mirror, I turn to the left and then to the right. I smile at my reflection, because I now realize that these people, my true friends, never saw me as a dork. They saw the beauty in me. They brought my personality out.

The best friends that anyone in the world could ever have will be missed when we go to junior high. But I will cherish the memories that we have created, and whatever happens, I'll always remember that my friends helped me become who I am. In conclusion, I have to say . . . thanks, Cori, Cole, Hannah, Matt, Adriane, Ross, Toni and Monica. Y'ALL ARE THE BEST!!!

Michelle Strauss, twelve

Right in Front of Me

A friend will not talk bad about you
and will never lie.
Friends are always there for you
if you need to cry.
Friends will be there for you
through thick and through thin.
When the rest of the world walks out on you,
a friend will walk in.

Nicole Johnson, thirteen

When I was in the sixth grade, I met my new best friend. Her name was Courtney, and she was tall, pretty and smart. She was also one of the most popular girls in school. That same year, I met my worst enemy, this awful boy named David. Every day he would call me names and pull my hair. I couldn't stand him.

When we graduated to seventh grade, Courtney ran for student body president. One night, she invited me over to her house to make posters and buttons for her campaign.

When I arrived, I was horrified at what I saw. It was David! Apparently, Courtney and David had been friends for some time. David and I looked at each other as though we were two cowboys in an old Western movie ready for a showdown. Our eyes locked and each of us frowned at the other. After what seemed like an eternity, Courtney broke the stare by telling us to get to work on the posters. We sat in silence for a few moments, and then David said, "Hey, we haven't gotten along in the past, but let's call a truce for the sake of Courtney." I was stunned at his suggestion, and I also couldn't refuse.

Once we decided to stop being enemies, we hit it off almost immediately. David and I found out that we had the same sense of humor and laughed at the same jokes. We both loved the same music and going to the same movies. We could talk about anything. I couldn't believe that a few hours before, I couldn't stand to be near David, and now here we were, covered in glue and glitter and laughing so hard our stomachs hurt. I never even had this much fun with Courtney. But even after I realized that I had this connection with David, when I went home, I kind of dismissed it. After all, he was a boy and Courtney was my best friend.

A couple of months later, my grandfather died. A week after his funeral, my parents decided that we should move. I was terribly upset because I loved my school and my friends, especially Courtney. But she promised me she would call me at least once a week and we would get together as often as possible. There was no doubt in my mind that we would stay friends through this difficult time in my life—dealing with my grandfather's death and, on top of that, moving to a new town. I gave David my new phone number, too, and told him to call me.

A couple of weeks went by, but I never even got one

phone call from Courtney. On the other hand, David had already called me several times to ask how I was doing and tell me what was happening at my old school. I was so upset that I hadn't heard from Courtney that I finally decided to call her. When she answered the phone, she apologized for not calling me and told me that she was going to be in a play and that I should come and see it with David. Courtney said we would all go out to dinner afterward. I was so excited that I was going to see my best friend again.

My mom dropped me off at the theater, and I ran into David right away. We had been talking so much on the phone that I felt like I had just seen him the day before; it was a great feeling. After the play, David and I waited for Courtney to come meet us so that we could go to dinner. But Courtney never showed up. She left without even saying hello or good-bye. I was heartbroken and I started to cry. I had wanted to see and speak with my best friend, who hadn't even called me since I had moved. I needed her to be there for me, to ask me how I was holding up, and she wasn't even interested.

After I had finished bawling my eyes out, I looked up and there was David. I realized something at that moment; my true friend wasn't at all who I had thought. During a rough transition in my life, the person that I had thought was my best friend couldn't even make time for me, and the person who was once my enemy became my closest friend in the world.

I have never spoken to Courtney again. But every week, David and I talk on the phone. To this very day, David is my best friend.

Heather Comeau

The Mysterious Book Bag

The homemade book bag was sprawled across my bed. It appeared to have taken over the entire room. I hovered in the doorway just staring at it, a little afraid to move toward it. I closed my eyes for a second, trying to imagine the large shoulder bag gone. I carefully visualized a nice, normal store-bought backpack in navy blue or black.

I opened my eyes again. It was still there. The large sack was the color of rust, and fuzzy, like a stuffed animal. I knew that my mom had spent all day happily sewing as she envisioned me proudly walking from class to class with it flung over my shoulder.

To make matters worse, I realized that the fabric was actually left over from a toy horse that my mom made for me when I was a baby. Now there was sentiment attached to it. I entered the room and picked up the gift. My mother had even quilted little running horses along each side. And, just to make certain that no one would be confused as to who owned this furry monstrosity, Mom had embroidered my name on one side.

If I had been eight and not twelve, I would have been thrilled. The book bag was huge, with numerous pockets. The thing would easily hold all of my school supplies, and it was sturdy, too. It would last, so I couldn't hope that it would soon fall apart, giving me the perfect excuse to be rid of it.

"Do you like it?" my mother asked.

"Yes," I said in a halting voice. "Thank you."

"Well, if you don't like it, you don't have to use it," Mom said sadly.

"Oh no, Mom, I love it," I lied, picking the bag up and rubbing the soft fabric against my face. The last thing I wanted to do was to hurt her feelings. "You used the same fabric from Flaming Star," I said with a smile, letting her know that I understood the connection to my childhood stuffed animal. "Thanks," I muttered again and hugged her.

After a while, I got up the nerve to load the new bag with notebooks, pens and other school supplies. *It is kind of cute*, I tried to convince myself.

The next day I was to start seventh grade at a new school, in a new state, in the middle of the school year. I was nervous and excited all rolled into one.

That first day at school I heard the whispers. "Have you seen the new girl? She's from California. Did you see that big furry bag?" Then there were giggles.

Because I started school in the middle of the year, all of the lockers had been assigned to other kids. There was no storage available for me, so I was forced to haul all my stuff around in the oversized fuzzy bag, making me seem suspicious.

I soon became known as "the weird girl with the huge, fluffy horse bag."

Wild stories flew back and forth about what I kept in the bag that never left my side. *Drugs?* some kids wondered. *Clothes? Is she homeless?*

There was nothing interesting in that bag, just my coat during cold weather, school books, papers and pens. Eventually, most students pretty much ignored me, but some of the kids teased me about the fuzzy horse bag. People grabbed at it, pretended to pat it like a dog and tried to toss their trash into it. My teachers didn't seem to notice, probably because I didn't ever complain or ask for help.

As the year progressed, I started to hate that bag. I blamed all my problems on it. I felt helpless and alone, miserable, and homesick for California and my old friends.

One day toward the end of the school year, my math teacher assigned each student a partner to work with on word problems. I was told to work with Debbie, a popular redheaded girl who was in several of my classes. She smiled and waved me over toward her desk, so I grabbed my notorious bag and quietly moved toward her. As I sat down, I realized that I had never spoken to her before.

"So, what's in the bag?" Debbie asked loudly with a grin. The students working at the table next to us turned to hear my answer.

"Um, just books and stuff," I stammered, caught totally off guard.

"Can I see?" she boldly asked.

Then she held out a hand for my bag. I was so shocked that I simply handed it over without a word.

By this time, numerous other kids were watching us.

"So, why do you have clothes in there sometimes?" Debbie asked.

"Just my coat or a sweater or whatever I wore to school." I replied.

"But why?" Debbie tilted her head with the question. "And, why on earth do you cart around *everything,* for *all* of your classes? Do they do that in California?"

"No, in California I had a locker!" Then I explained.

"They were all out of lockers when I got here this year."

Then Debbie started to laugh—not at me, but at the situation. "You mean, you've just been carrying your stuff around all this time because the school didn't have enough lockers?"

I nodded.

"This happens every year. The school doesn't have enough lockers, so lots of us have to share." She started giggling again. So did I. "There's, what, a week left of school," Debbie said through spurts of laughter. "But, you can share with me if you want. That bag is kind of funky—very chic when you think about it. One of a kind."

Then Debbie stood up, still grinning. "Hey everyone. Guess what? Laura's bag is just full of school stuff!" she exclaimed. "No locker," she said with her hands up and shoulders scrunched, as if to say, "What was she supposed to do?"

"All right, Debbie, that's enough," the teacher said loudly. "I'm glad that's settled. Now get back to math!"

Debbie rolled her eyes and handed me a piece of paper with her locker combination scrawled on it. "Wish I'd asked you about that bag months ago," she whispered. Then she asked me something I never thought I'd hear. "Do you think your mom would make *me* one?" When I nodded, bewildered, she started laughing again. "I think we're gonna be friends," she declared, loudly enough for the whole class to hear.

And we still are.

Laura Andrade

A Friendship to Remember

For some, life lasts a short while, but the memories it holds last forever.

Laura Swenson

Her name was Emma. She was the new girl in school. I remember feeling very sorry for her because every student was staring, pointing and whispering about her. She was extremely small, very thin and, worst of all, she was a twelve-year-old girl who had no hair.

Emma ended up in my homeroom. She was introduced to everyone that first day and was then told to find an empty seat. Emma took a seat two rows away from me, one chair up. She lay her head down on her new desk, crossed her legs and put her hands over her face. She tried to conceal her embarrassment but everyone could sense it.

At lunch, Emma sat at a table alone. I think she was too frightened to approach anyone, while at the same time everyone was too frightened to approach her. About ten minutes into lunch, I decided to leave my table and walk over to her. I pulled out a chair and sat down. I said, "Hi, my name is Veneta. Do you mind if I sit with you?" Emma didn't answer, but nodded, never picking her head up or raising her eyes to see me. Trying to make her feel more comfortable, I began talking just like I had known her forever. I told her stories about our teachers, the principal, and some of my friends. By the end of the twenty minutes that we sat together, she was actually looking at me right in the eyes, but there was still no expression on her face. She simply looked at me with a blank stare.

When the bell rang and it was time to go to our next class, I stood up, told her it was nice to get to talk to her and went on my way. I felt terrible walking away, as I had been unable to get her to talk or even smile. My heart was aching for this girl because her pain was so obvious to me.

It wasn't until about three days later, when I was at my locker getting things ready for class that Emma finally said hi to me. "I just wanted to say thank you for talking to me the other day," she said. "I appreciate you trying to be nice to me." When she began to walk away, I gathered my things and chased her. From that day on, we were inseparable.

This girl just captured my heart. She was loving and caring, compassionate and honest, but most of all, she was lonely. We became best friends, and in doing so, I set my twelve-year-old self up for the most devastating thing I would ever experience. I found out that Emma had cancer and was not given a very good chance of beating her disease.

For five months, Emma and I were the best of friends. We were together at school every day and then together almost every night to study or just hang out—and, of course, every weekend. We talked, we laughed, we joked about boys and we fantasized about our futures. I wanted to be her friend forever but I knew that it was not to be the case. After five months of being best friends, Emma became very, very sick.

I spent all my free time with her. I would go to the hospital when she was there and sleep over at her house whenever she was home. I knew in my heart I had to make sure she understood that she had become my best friend in the whole world—the sister I never had.

I was at home one Sunday, sitting with my dad watching football. The phone rang and my mom answered it. I could hear her mumbling and then she hung up. She walked into the room, her eyes red and tears streaming down her face. I knew instantly what had happened.

"Is Emma all right?" I asked. Mom's inability to reply answered it all.

Emma had been rushed to the hospital. She had gotten a very high fever. The news was not good. Her cancer was not responding to any treatments—it was spreading. Emma was losing her battle to stay alive.

Three days later, Emma passed away at home, in bed. She was just twelve years old. I remember feeling numb, knowing that she had passed on, but not quite understanding the finality of it all. Over the next couple of weeks, I quickly learned the hardest lesson I have ever had to learn in life.

Not only did I have to learn to deal with death, mentally and emotionally, I had to learn to grieve. I hadn't yet been able to do that. Then one day, her mom came over and handed me a box. She said she had found it in Emma's things. There was a note on it, saying to give the box to me when she was no longer here. I took it up to my room, stared at it for an hour or more, and then finally got up the courage to open it.

Inside, I once again found my best friend.

Emma had put several pictures of her and me in the

box, some of her favorite jewelry and, most important, a note to me. I began to sob but I managed to read it.

"I never thought I would ever know true friendship," she began. "I was always treated like an outsider, a circus freak. If anyone talked to me, it was usually to ask what was wrong with me or, even worse, to ask me if I was going to die.

"You are my very best friend in the whole world and I will never forget you. If you are reading this, I am in heaven. Please don't cry. I'm happy now, and I'm no longer sick or bald. I'm a beautiful, perfect angel.

"I'll watch over you every day of your life. I will be there for you during your first heartbreak and I'll watch with joy on your wedding day. You deserve the best, Veneta. Never change and never forget our friendship. I'm so grateful God allowed me to know you. I will be waiting to see you again. Love, Emma."

Reading that letter changed my life. Although she was the one who was sick and losing her life, she had taken the time to make sure I would be okay. She wanted to make sure I could cope with losing her.

Her death was the hardest thing I've ever had to experience. But I believe that God put our lives and our hearts together for a reason. We needed each other. Emma needed a friend, and I needed her strength and courage. Even to this day I thank God for Emma. I also still talk to Emma every day. I know she hears me and I know she looks out for me. Our friendship will never fade or die away. People may come and go, lives may change in an instant, but love and friendship will last forever.

Veneta Leonard

Friends at First Sight

Remember, the greatest gift is not found in a store nor under a tree, but in the hearts of true friends.

Cindy Lew

Bam! The car door closed as I ran to the gate. There was Jesse, waiting for me. He was the only kid who was tall enough to reach the lever on the gate at our daycare sitter's, Mrs. Rogers. He greeted me with a smile and we ran inside. After my mom signed me in, she called me back over to give me a kiss good-bye. I kissed her as usual and said, "See ya later, alligator!" She replied as usual, "After a while, crocodile!"

Jesse and I always wanted to play outside. I was about four or five when Jesse and I discovered how to dig perfect tunnels; we even planned to sneak away down the tunnel to my house and then to China.

One day, while starting one of our digs, we lifted up

this old rock and found two scorpions. It was very frightening, so we ran straight inside screaming, "It's Scorpion
Invaders! They just arrived!" All the other kids followed
us in, and until the "invaders" were gone, we played
inside.

Just before lunchtime, Jesse jumped up and down on
Mrs. Rogers' couch—something that we were forbidden
to do. He got in so much trouble! During his time out, I sat
by him. I wasn't supposed to but I did anyway. Then, at
lunchtime, as usual, I pulled the sticker off my apple and
gave it to Jesse. It was a tradition to give the sticker to
your friend, so I always gave mine to Jesse and he always
gave his to me.

After lunch, we finally got to go outside, since Mrs.
Rogers' husband killed the two scorpions. Jesse got on the
swing and I pushed him back and forth until it was time
for our naps.

After what seemed to be the longest naps ever, Jesse
and I stayed inside and played a game that we had just
made up. It was called Kitty Transporters. We were small
enough to fit under an old chest-of-drawers where we
pretended like we were in a time travel shuttle that was
transporting us to our newest location. We were kitties
following our instincts as to which way to go and when to
get ready to fight. We played and played all through
snack time and when everyone else left, Jesse and I went
outside and played our game in the sandbox until my
mom arrived to pick me up.

That was a typical day for us at Mrs. Rogers'. Somehow,
Jesse and I always got along. We never got bored, because
we used our imagination and we just loved playing
together.

Flash forward: Jesse's in the seventh grade at the same
school where I'm now in sixth grade. We usually don't get
to see each other except in passing period or at lunch. I

think I embarrass him a little by always saying hi and bye, but he never shows it.

As you can see, Jesse and I have always been friends. We went to the same baby-sitter every day since, well, forever. We know each other so well that I could tell you just about anything about him. For one thing, he's smart. He can build a whole computer in one day, so whenever I'm stuck on the computer I always call him for help and advice. Jesse loves jokes and he always has a joke that will cheer me up whenever I'm down. He's truly the most kind and generous friend anyone could ask for.

I thought it was really, really nice of him to show up at my twelfth birthday party this year. Except for Jesse, it was all girls, but he didn't seem to mind. Ever since I was three or four, I've always invited him and he's never missed one single birthday party of mine. He has always gotten me a Barbie *every* year. I love Barbies. I collect them still today, so he got me one this year. His face turned bright red when I opened his gift and said, "I got a Barbie!" After the party, I said, "Thank you. I can't believe you came!" He replied, "Hey, that's what friends are for." Then he grinned, gave me a hug and said, "Happy birthday!"

I know that some friends just come and go—but not Jesse. Even though he's a guy and I'm a girl and we're definitely growing up, we are friends to the core. Our friendship was meant to be from the first time we met.

Because of Jesse, I truly believe in friends at first sight!

Stephanie Caffall, twelve

Tears in the Bathroom Stall

The only real mistake is the one from which we learn nothing.

John Powell

As a sixth-grader, I began noticing how other kids were separating into cliques. There were the geeks, the jocks and the popular cool kids. I wasn't sure where I belonged. And I think that was the problem.

Our teacher had assigned "secret buddies" for the coming week. The purpose of this assignment was to do nice things for your buddy without letting them know who was doing it. We could leave encouraging notes on their desk or mysteriously leave a card in their backpack or book. Our teacher wrote each kid's name on a piece of paper and threw them into a bucket, then we each closed our eyes and drew the name of the classmate who we were to secretly befriend and support over the next five school days.

By the middle of the week, everyone, including me, had

turned this assignment into a contest to see whose secret buddy could leave the best gift. Instead of encouraging notes, we left stationery sets on our buddy's desk. Instead of giving compliments, we were giving bubble gum, lollipops and even money. It seemed that everyone was getting cool presents from their buddy. Everyone except me, that is.

My buddy followed our teacher's directions without a fault. I received handmade cards, notes with nice thoughts and countless smiley-face pictures proclaiming that I was one of the nicest girls in the class. My buddy seemed to think highly of me from the notes that were left, but the lack of gifts made me wonder what was up with whoever had pulled my name.

On the last morning of our assignment, I walked into my classroom and noticed that there was a package on my desk. At last, my buddy had grasped the idea that everyone else had! I ripped open the tissue paper and just stared down at my desk. There sat a canister of perfumed powder. The girls sitting near me giggled and went off about the "old lady" gift I had received. And to make matters worse, the powder had already been opened. I felt my face turn red as I shoved it into my desk.

I tried to forget about the embarrassing gift, but when I was in the bathroom before recess, the same girls who had seen me open the powder started talking trash about my secret buddy for giving it to me. I quickly joined in. "How lame," I heard myself saying. "What could my buddy be thinking by giving me such a stupid gift? My grandmother wouldn't even want it."

The girls laughed at my remarks and filed out of the bathroom. I stayed to wash my hands and let the water run through my fingers as I thought about what I had just said. It wasn't normally like me to say mean things like that about someone.

As I turned off the water, I heard a creak. I turned around to see one of the bathroom stall doors open. A girl from my class took two steps out of the stall and looked up at me. There were tears streaming down her face.

"I'm your secret buddy," she whispered to me. "I'm sorry about the gift." Then she ran out of the bathroom. Her sobs stayed with me long after the door had closed.

My secret buddy was a girl named Rochelle, a girl who came from a poor family. She and her siblings were targets at school for those who felt they were better just because their parents had money. Yet through all the teasing and harassment, Rochelle never had a bad word to say back to anyone. She just took the horrible treatment silently.

I was sick to my stomach as my cruel words ran through my mind. She had heard every single thing that had been said. And, once again, she silently took it in. How could I have been so mean?

It took me a few days, but I finally found the courage to face up to Rochelle and apologize. She told me that she had felt bad all week about not being able to leave any cool gifts for me. Her family could not afford it. So finally, her mother had given up the one thing that was a luxury to her so that Rochelle would have something to give. Her mother had assured her that the nice girl Rochelle had talked about would like the powder. Rochelle couldn't wait to get to school that morning and put it on my desk.

And I had ruined everything for her.

What could I say to Rochelle? How could she ever forgive me for making fun of her? Along with my apologies, I told her the truth. I admitted that I had only said those things to be cool, to try to fit in. I didn't know where I belonged, I explained.

Rochelle looked me in the eyes and said that she understood. She had been trying to fit in, too. "We aren't that different from each other, are we?" she smiled. Her simple words, spoken from her heart, found their way straight into mine.

Up until then, like everyone else, I had avoided the "Rochelles" of the world. But after that day, I gained respect and admiration for people like Rochelle—people who give from the heart.

Cheryl Kremer

The Cool Girls

I sat in my living room staring out of the bay window. I didn't want to wait outside for the school bus—no, that would seem too anxious. I had decided that I would wait until I could see it coming down the street, and then casually walk out the front door. After all, I was cool now. I was entering the fifth grade.

Much to my dismay, the sight of the bright yellow bus coming toward my house sent me into a knee-jerk reaction, and I found myself running into the driveway—running and tripping. My backpack went flying and I landed on my hands and knees. Luckily, there were no major scrapes and I was able to return to a standing position almost immediately. The only thing I felt was the intense rush of heat to my red cheeks.

As I climbed the bus steps, the driver asked if I was okay. "Uh . . . yeah," I quietly replied. "It's nothing." I quickly examined all the kids' faces for any type of reaction. Most seemed to be staring out the window. Maybe no one had seen my spill.

I slowly moved toward the back of the bus to find two girls staring at me. As I sat down in front of them, I heard one of them burst out into a full-blown laugh, while the other quietly chuckled. They were whispering—about me, I was sure. I crossed my hands on my lap and pretended not to care.

I felt them watching me, even though my back was to them. They were definitely older—maybe seventh-graders—I wasn't sure. I sat frozen in my seat, feeling like the dorkiest kid in the world, as tears formed in my eyes. This was not the impression I had been hoping to make, especially to the older kids. Then, much to my surprise, one of them tapped me on my shoulder and introduced herself.

"Hi, I'm Jessica!" she exclaimed. "Are you going into sixth?" In my mind, I quickly went from dork to super cool. Maybe they thought I was older. Wow! I shyly replied, "No, fifth," as I turned around and smiled. "Oh," the other girl giggled, "Fifth grade!"

I suddenly felt accepted. They knew how old I was, they had seen me fall—and yet they still wanted to talk to me. I had already made two friends and hadn't even arrived at school yet! I was already seeing in my mind how cool it would be, to be walking through the halls and saying hi to my new seventh-grade buddies.

As it turned out, I rarely saw them in school, but I was happy enough to just be bus pals. I sat in the same seat every day on the bus, just in front of them, and waited for them to talk to me. One day, they asked to see my lunch box. "Wow, it's really cool," they both commented as they took my pink-and-white-checkered box from my hands. I couldn't *believe* how much they liked me. They returned my lunch box and thanked me for letting them see it. "Oh, no problem," I giggled, filled with smiles both inside and out.

When I opened my box at lunch that afternoon, *my lunch was gone.* The empty box resembled my heart, as it sank to the pit of my stomach. I never even paused to think of another possibility. In one single moment, everything made such painful sense. They were never interested in me, they were not my friends, and this whole time I was some kind of joke to them. I felt like a fool—right back to the moment I tripped in my driveway. That was how they saw me; that's who I *really* was. Some little dorky fifth-grader thinking she was actually fitting in with the older kids.

I never cried. I never said a word. I didn't tell my teacher because I didn't want to get them in trouble. They already thought I was a dork. I didn't want to add "tattletale" to the list. I simply closed the box and sat in silence for the rest of the lunch period. I had no appetite anyway from the thought of having to face them on the bus that afternoon.

When I stepped onto the bus, I only saw Jessica sitting quietly alone in the back seat. I slipped into a seat in the front without making any eye contact with her. There was no sign of Jessica's partner in crime. I held my empty lunch box tightly against my legs and quickly got off the bus as it reached my house. When I got to my room, I finally burst into tears.

The next morning I vowed not to even look to the back seat, which of course I did anyway. It was only Jessica alone once again, not looking quite as cool and confident without her friend. As I sat once again in the front seat, I suddenly felt a presence behind me. "Hey," Jessica quietly muttered as she tapped me on the shoulder. I turned around and managed a slight smile. "Look," she proceeded, "I'm really sorry about the lunch thing." I wanted to just say it was okay, but I couldn't manage to speak. She went on to tell me that Cory had been getting in a lot of trouble lately and had gotten kicked out of school. Her parents were sending her to boarding school and she wouldn't be on the bus anymore. With that, Jessica handed me a brown paper bag filled with a freshly made lunch, as well as some cookies her mom had made. "I hope this makes up for it," she told me, and returned to her seat. So, Cory had been the troublemaker, because when she wasn't around, Jessica was really pretty nice.

Jessica and I sat in silence for the rest of the ride. When we arrived at school, I waited for her as she stepped off the bus. "Thanks for the lunch," I said. We smiled at each other, and then walked to our own classrooms.

Eventually, Jessica and I became real friends. Sometimes we hung out at each other's houses after school, and there was never a mention of Cory. We had a lot of fun together and the age difference seemed to disappear. I never even thought much about the lunch incident again. All I could think about was how Cory had gotten some free food but, in the process, lost two really nice people as friends.

Mel Caro

Being There

If you make it plain you like people, it's hard for them to resist liking you back.

Lois McMaster Bujold

I wish that everyone could see friendship the way that I see it.

Friendship is not just based on the type of music that someone listens to. Friendship is not just based on the type of clothing that you wear. Friendship is not even based on the sports teams that you prefer. It's not based on age, skin color, religious beliefs or gender.

Due to problems before my birth, I was born with cerebral palsy. I have been in an electronic wheelchair since I started school. I'm now in the ninth grade and have made friends all over the area near where I live. I have friends from all different age groups, young and old alike. There are friendly people everywhere I turn and so I gather friends very easily.

One of the ways that I experience friendship is through my own family. My cousin Chaz is a good example. Since I have limited use of my hands, I can't always do things myself. One time, while eating at McDonald's, we decided to eat at a table away from the adults. A Quarter Pounder is too big for me to pick up, so Chaz just picked it up and fed it to me. He didn't even think about doing it, he just picked it up and did it. That's friendship.

One time I went to a sleepover at my cousin Sky's house and he had about eight other guys there, too. In the middle of the night, after his parents were asleep, as you can guess, we were still awake. We were all lying on the floor talking our heads off when we decided to get up and go outside. Because I can't put myself in my wheelchair, all the boys grabbed my arms and legs and placed me in it. No adults were needed for the amazing feat. Sometimes, it's handy to have a lot of friends.

Then there's my grandpa. He's seventy-nine years old. Whenever I get time off from school, we take a day and go to the mall. First we go eat breakfast and he helps feed it to me. I play video games, and he helps to insert the coins. That's what I would call a really friendly grandpa.

I have another friend—a guy in his early thirties named Steve who went to summer camp with me for several years in a row. Without his help, I couldn't have participated in a lot of the activities. He totally didn't have to do that, but because he did, he showed me that that's what friendship is all about.

My church youth group plays basketball at the church gym a lot. Whenever I go to these events, they allow me to play on one of the teams. Have you ever played against a team with a kid in a one hundred-pound wheelchair? I'd say that's friendship.

Have you ever thought about where wheelchair ramps are located? They are sometimes in locations that are inconvenient to get to. Most people take the fastest route to the door, but when you're in a wheelchair, it's a little different. One of the coolest things that my friends do is walk the long way to the ramp with me. They could easily run up the stairs and leave me behind, but they don't.

If you've never really thought about the true meaning of friendship, I hope that reading this little piece of my life has given you something to think about. I have many friends who like the same sports teams that I do and even friends that wear the same style of clothes that I wear. I have friends who are part of my family and friends who are older and even younger than I am. My friends are as different as people can be from one another, but they all have something in common. Each of them recognizes that being a friend means being there for your friends. And, as you can see, they've all been there for me.

Jared Garrett, fourteen

[EDITORS' NOTE: *To find out more about cerebral palsy, log on to* www.ucp.org.]

An Unexpected Reaction

Darkness cannot drive out darkness;
only light can do that.
Hate cannot drive out hate;
only love can do that.

Martin Luther King Jr.

I hated my parents' divorce. Because of it, my mom could no longer afford to send me to private school and now everything was ruined. Instead of graduating from the eighth grade with all the friends that I'd had since I was six years old, this year I had to go to public school with strangers. I felt like life was against me, nothing was fair, and I was determined to hate the new school and everybody there.

My vow dissolved on the first day of my new school when I met Ally. She was pretty and popular. Ally wore cool clothes while I, on the other hand, had to make do with much less. But the difference in our backgrounds never made a difference to our friendship. Ally and I had many common interests; we giggled and talked and even sang in the school choir together. We became so close, that in a way I felt like I had known her even longer than my old friends. Ally's popularity helped open doors that might have remained firmly shut to me in the preteen world of cliques. Because of her, I felt as if I had always attended this junior high.

One day, Ally announced that she was having a slumber birthday party. I was informed that I needed to bring my sleeping bag, a pillow and other stuff like make-up. My mom even let me buy a brand new pair of pajamas to wear at the party.

Finally, the momentous Friday evening arrived. I chattered nonstop to my mom as she drove me over to Ally's house. When we arrived, I bounced out of our old car and, clutching my sleeping bag to my chest, I scrambled up the long walkway to ring the bell. *This is sure going to be one great party,* I thought, as I waited impatiently for the door to open.

Ally's mom, who always radiated perfection, opened the door. As usual, her dress was flawless and every blonde hair was in place. At our school concert, when Ally had introduced me to her, her mom had smiled at me and even commented on my lovely voice. Tonight however, something was different. I was surprised by her lack of warmth and I saw that the smile on her lips did not quite reach her eyes. A sickening silence descended as her pinched smile faded and was replaced with a cold, questioning stare.

Then, she told me to go home. She said that I could come over and visit Allison tomorrow, but not tonight. I couldn't understand what she was talking about. Had I imagined Ally's friendship and the invitation? I started to cry. A queasy stomach followed my unstoppable tears.

"Mom, Mom, where are you?" Ally called from beyond the door. Before her mother could answer, Ally had rounded the corner and stood in the doorway. She had only to look at my tearful expression to see that there was a problem.

"Mom, what's wrong?" she asked. Ally's exasperated sigh and the gripping of her fists told me that this was not the first time that mother and daughter had had a run-in.

"Carmen is here to visit," Ally's mother explained. "I told her to come back tomorrow because you're having a party."

Ally's face flooded with crimson as she nervously glanced at me. "I invited Carmen to my party, Mom. She's my friend, and I want her here." Mortified, I stood quietly as the discussion continued.

"This is a sleepover," replied her mother in hushed tones. "I can't have a colored girl sleep in our home." I couldn't believe what I was hearing. *A colored girl!* I had never heard of such a term (except maybe in old movies) and certainly not in reference to me. And why would the color of my skin matter anyway?

In an act of ultimate defiance and unparalleled friend-ship, Ally firmly stood her ground. "Carmen is my friend. If she can't stay, no one stays. I won't have my party with-out her."

Was I hearing correctly? She was willing to cancel her birthday party on my behalf? A look of agitated confusion passed over her mother's face, and then I saw her face harden. "All right. If that's the way you want it, go tell the other girls they have to go home."

There are times when words are pointless. I was chok-ing with gratitude at this display of friendship. Then, I became suddenly nervous that the blame for the cata-strophic end to the party would fall on my fragile shoul-ders. One by one, the girls came out of the house and quietly assembled under the cold, moonless sky to wait for their parents to come and pick them up. As Ally and her mother argued inside their home, I sat alone, while the other girls spoke in whispers and glanced my way from time to time.

On Monday, the canceled birthday party was the main topic of conversation at our school. Some of my new so-called "friends" looked right through me, ignored me and generally acted as if I didn't exist—except for Ally.

Even with her support, the intense hurt took a long time to heal. As junior high ended and we went on to high school, Ally and I remained close—despite her mother. Ally's living example of true friendship exhibited a maturity far beyond her age and taught me, as probably nothing else ever could, the value of a friend.

I hope that I have learned my lesson well, that I have returned her friendship in kind, and that I have been the same kind of true friend to others. After all, wasn't it Emerson who said, "The only way to have a friend is to be one"?

Carmen Leal

2

ON CRUSHES

I've never felt this way before
It's all brand new to me
My head is spinning, I can't breathe
You are all I see.

I long for you to notice me
I wish you'd ask me out
So this is what first love is like,
And what a crush is all about.

Amanda Beatty, twelve

Tasting the Moment

When I was twelve, I wanted to have a summer romance more than anything I had ever wanted before—more than being able to drive a car and more than having big boobs—I wanted to fall in love.

I had no idea what falling in love meant though. I thought that a romance would make me feel different—older and experienced. My friends all had experience with boys. They knew how it felt to have someone else's hand squeezing their hand or to have somebody smile at them for no apparent reason. I was starting to feel certain I never would. And then I met Erik.

Every summer my parents and I would go on vacation to the same RV campground. The campground was a haven for potential summer romances. My friends and I would check out all the new campers, hoping there might be some new love interest. We would talk about romance and imagine what we would do when we did have a boyfriend.

"I'd sit with him at the campfire," Trish would say.

"We'd go for walks, holding hands," Kelly said.

And I never said anything. I didn't know what I would do if I met a boy I liked. I never had much to say to boys. I couldn't remember the punch lines to jokes and didn't know what kind of questions to ask to get a conversation started. Whenever I did meet a new boy, I'd stammer and mumble, tripping over my tongue as often as I tripped over my own feet.

Then that summer, three baseball teams with twenty fifteen-year-old boys on each team camped at our park.

Everyone was in heaven!

Everyone . . . except my father.

"You are to be inside at ten o'clock tonight," he said. In all those previous years, I never had a curfew at the campground. Neither had my brother. Except this time. My brother was still allowed out and I, like Rapunzel, was locked in my tower while the rest of the world (my friends) were being swept off their feet. Unlike Rapunzel however, I knew what I was missing. They were all going to have another romance while I, once again, was not.

"Oh Andrea," Kelly had said the next morning. "It was so amazing! The guys on this team are so cute!"

My stomach crashed to the floor as she listed off their names. *Taylor, Matt, Anton, Erik* . . . I had missed it again.

"And we're going to their game this afternoon!"

I was allowed to go to the game. The game itself wasn't great—they weren't the best players and they weren't even playing on a very good ball field. It was out in the country and it didn't have any bleachers. We had to sit under this old, wooden canopy that had a few picnic tables. It was sunny and hot and we were dying of thirst, but I LOVED it.

My friends pointed out each of the players that they had met the night before. We were sitting pretty far away, so it was hard to tell what they looked like, but I felt that this was what having a romance was all about—going to watch your guy play baseball and cheering him on.

"And that's Erik," Kelly pointed out this guy who was

kind of skinny with a few loose curls that stuck out from underneath his baseball cap. He looked over at us girls, waved and smiled. My stomach was flopping around like a fish on dry land.

They lost their game and the tournament. We spent the rest of the day swimming and hanging out on the beach. Erik and I went for a walk on a road just outside our campground. He held my hand as soon as we were outside of the park. I hadn't thought about what a guy's hand would feel like holding mine.

It was fun walking with him, holding hands. We walked along a dirt road leading to a hill through a grove of poplar trees. In the midst of the trees, at the top of a hill, was a giant rock. We sat there for a few minutes, still holding hands. He kept smiling. His teeth were so white they were glowing in the early darkness. I could smell him— sort of a mixture of bug repellent and lake water. He slowly leaned his head closer to mine.

This has to be what falling in love feels like, I thought. I was so totally nervous that my stomach was doing flip-flops.

His face was just inches away and then his lips pressed against mine. His lips opened just a little and I followed his lead, opening my own lips just a little. As I did, I felt this odd little gurgle creeping up in my throat. The next thing I knew, I let out this tremendous burp right into his mouth!

Mortified, I excused myself and looked away. I wanted to run away but he was still holding my hand.

Then, weirdly enough, he laughed. Then I laughed too, and the "romance" of my first kiss was over. We walked back to the campfire holding hands.

Finally tasting a kiss didn't change me, make me feel older or more self-confident around boys. But I discovered that sometimes people like Erik come into your life and can help make an embarrassing moment a little easier.

Andrea Adair

Ditched

Whether joy or sorrowful, the heart needs a double, because a joy shared is doubled and a pain that is shared is divided.

Ruckett

When I was in the sixth grade, I met this boy named Grayson Mitchell who was in the seventh grade. All I could do was think about him and talk about him and dream about him. He was the first boy I had ever felt this way about. I thought I might be in love!

Days went by, then weeks and pretty soon months and I still hadn't gotten up the courage to speak to him. I was so sure he was the one that I didn't pay attention to how rude or snobby or stuck-up he was. I just thought it made him even cooler.

Pretty soon I started changing my hair, my clothes and my personality for him. I wanted to be like all the girls he spoke to and liked all put together. After a while, he started to notice the changes and I thought he was starting to like me. Then a few days later, I got on the bus and there was Grayson, looking cooler than I had ever seen him before.

After a while, he started whispering to his friends and glancing over at me. A moment later, he turned and said to me, "I gotta ask you something. Everyone is sayin' you like me. I was just wondering if it's true."

I looked down at the floor and nodded. "Really, you do?" he asked. I nodded again. "So, uh, you wanna go out Saturday? I really like you." I looked back up and nodded again. I was so excited, I couldn't speak! He named a little restaurant near my house and a time that I should be ready.

That Saturday, I went to the beauty salon and got my hair straightened and then my nails manicured and polished bright pink to match my new skirt. I went home and put on my new outfit and heels. My best friend, Nicky, was with me all the way. I then realized that Grayson hadn't told me if he was going to pick me up or meet me at the restaurant since I was so caught up in the moment on the bus. So, I quickly called him up, and he said that he would have to meet me there. "I'm so sorry. I wanted to pick you up. I really did," he apologized. I said it was no big deal for the millionth time and told him I'd see him there.

"Do you need a ride?" my mother asked, when I was ready to go. I thanked her for offering but told her that Nicky and I were going to walk, and the two of us headed for the restaurant.

"I can't believe he asked you on a date! You are the luckiest girl in the world. Oh, my gosh! I can't believe it—Grayson Mitchell . . ." Nicky kept talking the whole way to the restaurant.

When we finally got there, I said, "Well, here it is. The first date with the man I'm *definitely* going to marry!"

"Well, go already," Nicky said, as excited as I was. "Are you gonna go home or wait?" I asked her. She practically yelled, "Wait, of course!" I looked at her with the biggest smile on my face and headed inside. As I approached the front door, I felt happy and scared at the same time. "Mitchell, please," I said to the man at the counter. He started rummaging through the list of reservations. When he finally looked up he said, "There is no Mitchell." I looked at him astonished and asked him if he could please look again. He again looked through his papers and came back with the same answer. *I must have gone to the wrong restaurant,* I thought. I went back outside and told Nicky what happened and how I might have gotten the wrong restaurant, and she agreed.

We walked back to my house and I tried to call Grayson, but there was no answer. *He must be waiting for me at the restaurant,* I thought. *The right restaurant.*

Nicky and I waited for his call, but it never came. At school on Monday, I looked around for him everywhere, but I couldn't find him. Then, finally at lunch, I spotted him outside and went over to talk to him. He saw me and started whispering to his friends. I thought he was talking about how much he liked me or something. When I finally reached him I said, "What happened last night? There was no Mitchell on the list at the restaurant. I think I got the wrong one."

"You didn't get the wrong restaurant," he said with a mean look.

"I don't understand," I said.

"Does she understand anything?" he asked his friends in a sarcastic voice.

I just stared at him waiting for an explanation.

Suddenly, he started laughing and laughing and wouldn't stop. "What an idiot!" he said between laughs. Finally, after he stopped laughing, he said, "You don't get it, do you? I don't go out with people like *you*. You're a sixth-grader." My eyes started getting watery as the nightmare became true. I turned and ran away. Nicky had seen the whole thing and started to run after me.

I got to the girls' washroom and went inside one of the stalls hoping no one would see me or hear me crying. A few moments later, Nicky was in the washroom, too, trying to get me to come out. Right when I thought she was going to leave, she asked me something that at the time seemed like the stupidest question you could ever ask. "Do you still like him?" I was so astonished!

"Of course not!" I answered. "He ditched me on what seemed like the most important night of my life! How could I still like him?"

Then she said something else I couldn't believe.

"Then why do you care so much?"

"Whadda ya mean?" I questioned her.

"If you don't like him, why do you care so much that he burned you? Now you know how he really is, and you don't have to worry about him anymore."

She was right. I shouldn't care! I opened the stall door and stepped outside and hugged my friend as hard as I could. She looked at me with big eyes and a weirded-out look. Then, after a while, she smiled at me, and I smiled back.

"Let's go to lunch," Nicky said. And that's just what we did, not caring who saw me or what all the whispers were about. I just kept on smiling—knowing that it was a good thing Grayson didn't show up so I didn't have to have dinner with that creep. I didn't need Grayson or anyone else.

That is, except Nicky, my best friend!

Colleen Mahoney, twelve

Clueless

A person wrapped up in himself makes a small package.

Harry Emerson Fosdick

I fell in love with him because he was the most popular guy in school.

He was the new boy in town, and he and his brothers had become the rage of the whole school. Not only were they all the most handsome hunks we'd ever set our eyes on, they were also musicians. And Peter—he was the lead singer. How cool is that!

I was at home, sick, when he joined our school. My friends would call me up and rave about this great new guy that I just *had* to see. My curiosity rose even higher when they told me stories of how he'd play the guitar in class, never have any homework done and didn't care about anyone or anything. When his trips to the principal's office had beaten the school record, I was intrigued. This was one guy I just had to meet.

I had gotten sick at the beginning of the school year, so when I came back to school fifteen days later, all the seats in our class had already been assigned—except to Peter and me. Our teacher set up two chairs and a table on the side of the class—a temporary arrangement until she could fit us in.

Our first day was a complete disaster. Not only was he stubborn, selfish and immature, but he made it a point to argue with me about everything.

"What's the circumference of a circle?"

"It's not *that!*"

"World War II started in 1939, right?"

"Yeah, if history textbooks are all correct."

"What's the capital of Finland?"

"Why? You planning on going there?"

Soon, we were in each other's faces all day long. I swear, if it hadn't been for his hazel eyes, I'd have killed him. Finally, one day our teacher warned us that we better start getting along or she'd make us sit together through the entire semester. Not wanting to spend a moment with him longer than was necessary, I decided to give it a try.

Being nice to him wasn't as hard as I had imagined. It was *impossible!* His atrocious attitude, sarcastic comments and blatant disrespect for everyone around him was more than I could take. But once he'd start to sing, you'd forget everything in the room. The only thing you'd hear was his voice, the only thing you'd see—his eyes.

With each passing day, we became closer. His atrocious attitude now seemed pretty cool, and the sarcastic comments were kind of funny. It was hard not to like him after getting to know him. Then I went a step ahead and fell utterly head-over-heels in love with him. Little did I know a spark had hit both sides.

A common friend, who'd noticed the change of

attitude, decided to play Cupid. So, he asked Peter out for me, without asking me! Then asked me out on behalf of Peter, without asking him! We ended up going out and laughing over what had happened!

A week later, we were officially a couple. I felt so lucky to be with the guy all the girls were literally drooling over. He was charming. He was funny. Best of all, he was popular. I could feel other girls' eyes piercing into my skin as I sat with him and laughed at the latest escapade in his life.

Popularity has its consequences, though. About a week after we'd started going out, I discovered a secret. He'd been going out with another girl, too. And another. He was leading us all along the same sweet path, with none of us having the slightest clue of what was going on. As soon as I found out, I decided to dump him. I wasn't about to take any of this.

The so-called relationship ended in the drain. With so many girls running around trying to impress him, he found it very convenient to play with each one's emotions.

For him, it was a popularity game. The one with the most girlfriends wins. Me, I don't work like that. I wanted exclusivity. In the end, we finished where we had started—detesting each other's guts.

I fell in love with him because he was the most popular guy in school. I fell out of love for pretty much the same reason.

Mridu Khullar

Teasing Tami

I didn't have the best self-image in junior high, and there were two things that I fell back on in order to be accepted: athletics and humor. I've always been a decent athlete and I have always been able to make people laugh. Unfortunately, sometimes the laughter came at someone else's expense. At the time I didn't fully realize what I was doing to other people around me, especially Tami.

When I found out that she had a crush on me, I did everything possible to get her to stop liking me. While some of the boys in my class were starting to be interested in girls, I just wasn't there yet—in fact, the whole thing kind of freaked me out. Instead of trying to let her know that I wasn't ready for a relationship with a girl yet, I went out of my way to make things miserable for her. I wrote stupid songs about her that made my friends laugh whenever they saw her, and loudly told crazy stories about having to save the world from "Tami, the Evil Villain."

Everything all changed about halfway through the year

though, when Mr. Greer, my favorite P.E. teacher, stopped me in the hall one day.

"Hey, Michael, you got a second?"

"Sure, Mr. Greer!" I said. Everybody loved Mr. Greer, and I looked up to him like a father.

"Michael, I heard a rumor that you've been teasing Tami and making her life miserable." He paused and looked me straight in the eye. It seemed like an eternity before he continued. "Do you know what I told him? I told him it couldn't possibly be true. The Michael Powers that I know would never treat another person like that—especially a young lady."

I gulped, but said nothing.

He gently put his hand on my shoulder and said, "I just thought you should know that." Then he turned and walked away without a backward glance, leaving me to my thoughts.

That very day I stopped picking on Tami.

I knew that the rumor was true and that I had let Mr. Greer down with my actions. More important, though, it made me realize how badly I must have hurt Tami for Mr. Greer to want to talk to me about it. He not only made me realize the seriousness of my actions, but he did it in a way that helped me to save some of my pride. My respect for him grew even stronger after that.

Even though I did stop teasing her, I never was brave enough to apologize to Tami for being so mean to her. She moved away the next year, and I never saw her again.

Just because I didn't know how to deal with Tami liking me, I still should have known better than to handle it the way I did. I think I actually did know better, but it took my favorite teacher's gentle guidance to help me change my ways.

Michael T. Powers

The Note

Kind words do not cost much. Yet they accomplish much.

Blaise Pascal

When I was in the fifth grade, I fell in love—real love—for the very first time. It only took about a week into the school year for it to happen, and I was completely, head-over-heels crushing on Mike Daniels. No one ever called him just Mike; it was always one word—Mike Daniels. Blond hair that stuck up in every direction and blue eyes that crinkled in the corners when he laughed—visions of Mike Daniels occupied my every dream.

To say I wasn't the most popular or prettiest girl in our class would be an understatement. In fact, I think I must have been the original geek. I was so skinny that I still had to wear days-of-the-week panties and dorky undershirts when most of my friends were starting to wear bras and more grown-up undergarments. My mom made me wear brown orthopedic lace-up shoes to school every day, because I had a foot that turned in and my parents wanted to "correct it before it was too late." Right smack dab in the middle of my two front teeth was this giant space that even gum surgery the year before hadn't fixed, and the two teeth on either side of my front teeth over-lapped, making me look like I had fangs. Add a pair of thick glasses, thin baby-fine hair (with a home permanent from my mom—help!), knobby skinned-up knees and elbows—and what do you get? A kid that only a parent could love.

I wouldn't—couldn't—tell my friends that I was in love with Mike Daniels. It was my secret to write about in my journal. In my dreams, Mike Daniels would all of a sudden grasp what a beautiful soul was hiding inside of my gawky body and realize that he loved me for who I *really* was. I spent hours writing poetry for him and stories about him, until one day I got up the nerve to actually write to him about how I felt.

Our teacher, Miss Finkelor, was really awesome about most things, but the one thing she was majorly serious about was not writing notes to each other during class. Everyone did it anyway. Except me. My only shot at self-esteem was being teacher's pet, and I excelled at it. I loved it so much it didn't even bother me when kids teased me about being the teacher's favorite.

It was a huge decision for me to go against the one thing that Miss Finkelor detested—note passing. But I knew that there was no other way to tell Mike Daniels about how I felt—and I also knew that if I never told him, I was going to burst . . . or maybe even freak out. I vowed to do it on Monday morning.

So, first thing Monday morning, in my very best print-ing, I wrote, "I love you." That was it. Nothing else—no flowers, no poetry—just, "I love you." I passed it to Dianne, who sat between me and Mike Daniels, and whispered,

"Give this to Mike Daniels," trying to look really casual, like it was a request to borrow a book from him or something. I held my breath as I watched him open and read it—then read it again. Then he folded it up and put it into his pocket. *Oh my God, what have I done? What if he shows it to his buds at recess? They'll all laugh their heads off. I'm a fool. An idiot. Why did I tell him?* I felt like I was going to throw up.

I was so involved in feeling like I was going to hurl, that I didn't even feel Dianne punching me in the arm. Then she shoved a note in my hand. Slowly, I opened it. It was my own note. *Great, he thought it was so stupid that he sent it back to me,* I thought. Then it dawned on me—he had written something on the back of it. "I like you, too. I'm glad we're friends."

I didn't know whether to laugh or cry. I was so relieved that he didn't trash me—that could have easily happened if Mike Daniels hadn't been a really nice guy. With that one little gesture of kindness, Mike Daniels made me feel special—and, not only that, but I felt that somehow, he *had* seen the real me hidden in the body of a fifth-grade geek.

I kept that note for years—all the way through the eighth grade. Whenever I felt bad about myself, I would reread Mike Daniels' note and remember that act of kindness. It didn't matter to me what inspired him—if it was pity, or the recognition of things to come—that note gave me strength to go through the challenges of the tough years that followed fifth grade.

Patty Hansen

Not My Boyfriend

That's the penalty we have to pay for our acts of foolishness—someone else always suffers for them.

Alfred Sutro

"Jason likes you," Kellie said, as she sat down next to me on the bus. "He wants to know if you'll go out with him."

"Jason?" I said, surprised. After all, I knew who he was since we rode the same bus to and from school, but I didn't really know him. He was in seventh grade—a year younger than me—and we had never even talked to each other. I had certainly never thought of him as a boyfriend or anything.

"I'll have to think about it," I said. I really couldn't imagine being his girlfriend. But, on the other hand, some of my friends had boyfriends and others had guys who liked them. I wanted one, too.

When the bus reached my stop, I practically danced

down the street to my house. "You must have had a good day," my mother smiled when she saw me.

"I did!" I said. "Jason likes me! He wants to be my boyfriend!"

After explaining to my mother who Jason was and reassuring her that, no, I wasn't too young to have a boyfriend, I decided to say yes to Jason. *It will be the most romantic day of my life,* I said to myself.

The next morning, I spent extra time on my hair and put on my favorite perfume. Kellie and Jason were both already in their seats when I got on the bus.

"Well?" Kellie asked, leaning over the back of her seat. I wondered why she, another seventh-grader I knew only as someone on my bus, suddenly had such an interest in my love life.

"Yeah, I guess I'll go out with him," I responded, trying not to sound too excited.

She got up and headed to the back of the bus, where Jason sat with some other seventh-grade guys. "She said yes," she told him. Suddenly, the bus erupted with chants of, "Whooooo . . . Carol and Jason." I didn't pay any attention. *I have a boyfriend,* I thought to myself all the way to school. *I'm going out with someone!*

Before going into school, I stood talking to some of my friends. Of course, the topic of conversation was my new boyfriend. Every few minutes, I glanced over at Jason who was talking to his friends at the other end of the sidewalk.

I wasn't sure if I should go over and talk to him. I wanted to, but the only thing I could think of to say was "So, you're my boyfriend," and since I didn't want to sound stupid, I stayed put.

Finally, I saw him walking over. He was looking right at me, so I broke from my friends and smiled at him. He didn't smile back, though. Instead, he stopped and said, "I don't want to go out with you."

"You don't?" I choked out, trying to catch my breath.

"No," he replied. "Kellie was bugging me yesterday. She kept asking me who I like, so when she asked if I liked you, I said yes just to shut her up. Sorry if you thought I was serious."

Then the bell rang and everyone headed inside. I felt as if someone had punched me in the stomach. All the guys snickered as they walked by me and I wanted to just crawl into a hole—to go home, get into bed and never leave my room again. I walked slowly into my classroom, wondering why the day that was supposed to be the most romantic of my life had turned into the most humiliating.

I couldn't concentrate all day, and I stared into space through most of my classes, but none of my teachers seemed to mind. The story had gotten around, so they probably all knew what was wrong.

When I got home I slammed the door of my room and cried for hours, not because that particular guy didn't want to go out with me, but because I felt so stupid to have created an entire romance with Jason based on a conversation with Kellie. When I realized that I wasn't upset about Jason not being my boyfriend, I stopped crying.

In the six months that remained until I graduated from eighth grade and moved on to high school, I never talked to Jason again. In fact, if we hadn't been on the same bus, I probably would have forgotten all about him. I'm glad I didn't, though. The next year, a girl I knew slightly told me that she knew a guy who liked me.

"If he likes me, he'll have to tell me himself," I replied. And he did.

Carol Miller

Without the Kisses

There is never a better measure of what a person is than what he does when he is absolutely free to choose.

William M. Bulger

In the eighth grade, all I wanted was to be alone with my first boyfriend, Mark. His family had just moved to our town and I barely knew him, but he had a nice smile, and my friend Victoria thought he was cute, too. The second week after he started at our school, he asked me to go out, and I said yes.

Mark and I didn't talk much, but he gave me his navy blue and white jacket to wear and waited for me at my locker each day after sixth period drama class.

Over the next few weeks, we went to each other's house a few times, but our parents would never leave us alone. At Mark's house, we made popcorn and watched family movies with his mom and dad. His mom called our

movie nights "double dates," which made Mark blush and
then roll his eyes when she wasn't looking. My parents
were just as paranoid, and even more embarrassing. My
dad was so weird about me going with a guy that he had
a mental block against Mark's name. My mother was so
sure we shouldn't be alone together that she once
decided to rearrange the kitchen cabinets at nine o'clock
on a Saturday night, just so she could keep an eye on us
in the adjacent family room.

It seemed like my older brother, Dirk, was always
allowed to be alone with his girlfriend, Maggie. I could only
imagine what they were doing and I thought, *If Dirk gets to
be alone with his girlfriend then I should get to be alone with Mark.*

At Mark's locker the next day, I told him what I had
been thinking about, and his brown eyes bulged from his
head. He told me he would come up with a plan to get us
alone that weekend. The rest of the week seemed like a
month. I kept imagining how his lips would feel when
they touched mine. I had watched actors kiss on TV practically every day, but wished I had paid better attention
to how they did it. I worried that my lips would get dry,
that my braces would cut him and that my tongue
wouldn't know what to do. The more I thought about it,
the more the whole thing grossed me out. But my friends
Victoria and Shauna had both been kissing boys since the
seventh grade, and I felt like a prude around them. It was
all they ever talked about, it seemed. I figured I should
just get it over with once and for all.

That Saturday, Mark told his parents we were going for
"an evening stroll" to feed the ducks at the lake a block
from his house. In preparation for the big night, I took
forever to curl my long hair, but I didn't use a lot of hair
spray just in case he wanted to run his fingers through
my hair. I wasn't sure why he'd do that, but people were
always doing that in the movies.

The sun had just set when we made our way down his street, pretend-balancing on the center white line in the road. Three houses down from Mark's on the corner sat a pitch dark, vacant house under construction. That house was at the center of his plan, which I thought was brilliant until we got there and saw how creepy it was. Mark quietly led me through the side gate and across a pile of dirt that must have been part of the construction. I could feel dirt slipping into my sandals, grinding between my heel and sandal as we made our way to the back of the empty house. Mark yanked the chrome handle on the sliding glass door and pulled it open easily. I looked down to swat a mosquito dining on my leg and saw my heartbeat through my shirt.

Inside, the music from a single cricket echoed around us, making the house seem bigger than it looked from the street. At first I wanted to go back to his house, but then Mark gently placed his hand on my shoulder and led me to a spot near the fireplace. Mark pulled two cement blocks across the floor, making a screeching noise so loud I could still hear it after it stopped. He placed the two blocks next to the fireplace and we sat. And sat. The amber light from the neighbor's back porch placed a halo around Mark's eager yet fearful face. He raised his eyebrows higher each time he looked over at me. I fidgeted with my pink and green friendship bracelet and tried to push the sand out of my sandals with my toes. Mark tapped out a drumbeat on his knee, but I could barely hear it because the cricket was so loud. It sounded like the cricket was sitting on my lap.

How long are we going to just sit here? I thought. It seemed like forever until finally, Mark spoke. I nearly jumped when he turned toward me. He made such a quick move on the cement block that it sounded like he ripped a hole in his shorts. Then he looked deep into my eyes and whispered, "Is Mr. Bergman hard for Algebra One?"

"Uh," I looked down at my hands and realized that I'd tied a knot in the end of my friendship bracelet. "He's hard, but he warns us about pop quizzes."

It turned out, he liked Mrs. Fir for English but thought Mr. Wright was an idiot with his horn-rimmed glasses and bad jokes. That started a long conversation about all of our teachers and their crazy quirks, and by the time we left that empty house, we were laughing so hard that we couldn't hear the cricket anymore. I must have licked my lips a thousand times that night, thinking, *At any moment, he'll kiss me.* But after all the anticipation, I'm glad he didn't. Even with all the pressure from our friends at school, we managed to skip the kissing and just get to know one another. At least for that night.

When it came down to it, we were too young for soap opera love scenes or swollen lips from kissing with braces on our teeth. That night, as we walked back to his house holding hands, I wondered if it was my hand or his that was so warm.

Jennifer O'Neil

3

ON ACHIEVING DREAMS

Inside of us there lives a light
Burning like fire in the night.
Gleaming down and lighting the way
For hopes and dreams to shine someday.
It gives a brilliance to our lives
And sparkles like diamonds
With a glowing light.
So hold out your light
For all to see,
And never let go
Your dreams are the key.

Hannah A. Heninger, fourteen

Reprinted by permission of Leigh Rubin and Creators Syndicate, Inc.

Head-Butting the Wall

Every action we take, everything we do, is either a victory or defeat in the struggle to become what we want to be.

                                                    Anne Byrhhe

I grew up in a small town in New Jersey where I felt bored and trapped. My family life was all about, "Mom works, Dad works and kids are expected to go to school." My parents didn't have the money to buy me stuff I got interested in, and we didn't have any time to spend together except during meals. That didn't cost anything or take up any extra time.

I was angry and frustrated most of the time—it seemed that no matter what I did or said, I felt like I was head-butting the wall and getting nowhere. No one could get through—not my parents, my teachers or my guidance counselor. No one could help me.

Then I started high school, and a lot of the people I

knew began using drugs and alcohol. Because I wasn't interested in that, I found myself on the outside of my peer group. I was totally alone and I hated the world.

I started roaming the streets looking for trouble. I fought older, tougher guys around town and gained a reputation for being crazy. I'd take any dare. If someone said to me, "Smash your head on this rock for five bucks!" I would.

I was well on my way to prison or the morgue when I stumbled on punk rock music. The whole idea of a punk lifestyle sounded cool. So, I spiked my hair and took on a whole new identity until, one day, some *real* punkers came up to me in the hall at school.

"Hey, man, are you punk?"

"Yeah, yeah, man, I'm punk," I fumbled.

"Oh, yeah? What bands do you like?"

I didn't know any bands—none.

"Who do you listen to?" I didn't know one band from the other. Then my eyes landed on their band-logo T-shirts.

"Dead Kennedys, Black Flag, The Misfits . . ." I thought I had them fooled. But I was pretty much busted.

"Stop looking at our shirts. You don't really know any punk bands, do you?"

Totally busted. *Where do I go with this?* I thought to myself. Before I could come up with a strategy, one of them dared me to come home with them to his house. We went down into his basement and they shaved my spikes off. Then they said I was really punk. The next thing I knew, I was meeting up with them after school and hanging out.

Some of my new friends would occasionally get a hold of a skateboarding magazine, and they'd show me pictures of some decks. When I saw the boards, I connected. I became obsessed. I wanted to get my hands on a board and more of those magazines. One kid, the younger brother of one of my friends, had a stash. I cruised over to his house and knocked on the door.

"Hey, man, can I take a look at some of your skateboard magazines?" I asked.

This guy was hardcore. He wasn't about to let me *touch* his prized possessions, but he let me stand on his back porch and look at them through his screen door as he turned the pages, one by one. That's when I saw an article about street skating and a photo of a guy jumping off a car.

"I can do that! I can totally do that," I tried to convince him. He looked at me, doubting every word, but he got his board out and challenged me right then and there. I took the dare, grabbed the board and got up on his grandpa's car. Slam! I hit the ground. I got back up. I went through the same thing over and over—biting dust every time. Then finally . . . I landed it!

He screamed, "You did it! You're a skateboarder!"

I was hooked, rushing on adrenaline. I wanted to experience it again and again.

I began to follow a group of guys in my neighborhood that had boards. I'd beg them to let me skate. They treated me like dirt, but because they had boards, I took it.

I *had* to figure out how I could get my own board. I finally conned my mom into giving me money for a board by promising her that it would be my one and only Christmas present. I ordered a board and when it arrived, I was totally stoked. Then my mom made me hand it over. Her words, "Sorry. You can't have it until Christmas, Mike," were torture.

Weeks later, Christmas came and *finally* I got my board. I skated every spare second I could. I went from skating a few minutes a day to hours a day. I'd skate to and from school, after school, after dinner and after homework. When I started trying to skate the half pipe, I'd get nothing but grief about my style. I was doing everything I could just to gain the speed needed to get up the other side of the ramp. I'd flap my arms to get momentum. "Look at the chicken-man," guys would taunt. I didn't care—whatever it took, I'd try it. I lived and breathed skateboarding. It was my sanctuary and my salvation; it was my "thing."

I easily navigated the traps and pitfalls of high school and adolescence by just getting on my board and riding. But it wasn't just the physical act of skateboarding that made an immediate and lasting impact on me; it was the entire subculture of doing your own thing. Instead of following the crowd, I had discovered my individuality. My small town that once felt full of dead-end streets suddenly opened up. I found a wide-open country of possibilities. At fourteen, that's some vital stuff.

I truly believe everyone needs to find something to help them discover their identity and give them a sense of purpose, meaning and direction. For me . . . it just happened to be skateboarding. Skateboarding saved my life. It gave me the ability to express myself, connect to a passion and offer something unique back to the world. Now, as a professional, I travel the world, skateboarding and sharing my life story.

I'm still head-butting the wall, the difference is that now I'm fighting to keep the sport of skateboarding open to everyone and anyone—regardless of how good they are, what they look like or where they live. I want everyone to know that if they just believe in themselves and have a passion for the sport, anything is possible.

Mike Vallely

[EDITORS' NOTE: *To find out more about Mike, log on to* www.mikevallely.com.]

The Idea

Getting an idea should be like sitting down on a pin. It should make you jump up and do something.

E. L. Simpson

When you're in fifth grade, you're pretty much into what is going on in your own world. Your friends, the sport you play or things you're interested in seem to be all you think about.

But my fifth grade teacher thought that we should know more about what is going on outside our own lives. So each week, we would read articles from the newspaper about what was happening all around the world. Most of the time, I thought the articles were interesting, but none of them meant much to me, until the day that we read about Afghanistan and how the Taliban government had not allowed girls to go to school. When the Taliban lost their power, the girls were going to be able to get an education just like the boys did. Still, the boys and girls would not be able to go to school together, so they would need to have separate supplies for the girls.

Because the country had just been through a terrible war and things were pretty bad there, the country was too poor to get new school supplies. I wondered how those girls were going to go to school if they didn't have basic things like pencils, paper, desks and books.

That same year, our school received new desks. The old ones were hauled out and put into storage, in case the school ever needed an old desk for anything. I thought that was a waste. That's when I got the idea. *If my school didn't really need the desks, why not send them to the girls in Afghanistan?*

When I told my idea to my teacher, she told me she wasn't sure that could happen. Desks are very heavy and it would cost a lot to ship them.

So I told my stepmom about the old desks at my school and what I thought should be done with them. She loved the idea. She said it would take a lot to get the desks halfway around the world but she believed that with help from the right people, it could happen.

We began e-mailing organizations like the United Nations Children's Fund (UNICEF) that works for children's rights. We found out that UNICEF is really into making sure that girls around the world can get a good education. We were hoping that they would want to help. My stepmom's friend Julie and some people that she worked with also helped us by e-mailing moving companies and shipping companies like UPS hoping that they would agree to ship the desks to Afghanistan. Even my brother got in on it and designed a T-shirt for the project, which I named "The Idea."

Pretty soon, we got an e-mail back from UNICEF telling me that they liked my plan, but that it was still hard to get into Afghanistan because of the war. They said that they would try, though.

We also were contacted by a reporter from the *New York Times* who was on location in Afghanistan, covering the war. He e-mailed us, telling us all about what was going on in the area where we wanted the desks to go. Things were still pretty bad there. It made me feel even worse, knowing that the kids who lived there had to be so afraid all the time.

Knowing that UNICEF and others were going to try and help us find a way to get the desks overseas, we went to my school principal to ask if she could arrange to have the desks donated. She said she'd try. Then one day, she gave us the answer. It was yes!

A moving company said they'd let us use one of their big containers to ship the desks overseas. Then UPS said they would let us use a truck to get the desks to the container. So my stepmom, her friend, Julie, and other friends of ours came to help load the desks onto the UPS truck. It was hard to fit them all in, but we did it. The best part was getting to ride in the truck to the shipping container. There, we took all the desks off of the truck and put them into the container that would finally take them to Afghanistan. It was hard work, and we were all exhausted that night, but I felt good inside.

Then we learned that the desks would be sitting in the container for at least a few weeks. UNICEF still couldn't get into Afghanistan because of the war.

While we were waiting to hear from UNICEF again, someone told us about some more desks that were just sitting in storage at a nearby college. We asked the college if they would donate them and they said yes. So we let UNICEF know about those desks, too. The next thing we heard was that there were schools down in Haiti and Jamaica that needed desks for their schoolchildren. So about fifty of those desks were shipped to help the kids there. I was happy that we were finally able to help someone—even if it wasn't the girls that I had originally hoped to help.

Finally one day, UNICEF called to let us know that about one hundred of the desks that my school donated had made it into Afghanistan. It was an amazing feeling to know that I had accomplished something that many people thought could never happen.

All of a sudden, I began getting calls from organizations that wanted to give me awards for all I did to help the Afghani girls. I was nominated to receive the Clara Barton Red Cross Award and I was given a Humanitarian Award that was actually created in my honor from the Pop Warner Football League! I received a painting from the families in Jamaica that I had helped. Even George Bush, President of the United States, sent me a Student Service Award along with a pin and a letter telling me how proud he was of what I had done.

It was all very exciting and fun. But to me, the best part was imagining how happy the girls in Afghanistan were to finally have a desk of their own to sit at while they are in school.

Having that dream come true gave me a whole new thing to dream about. One day, I hope that I can go to Afghanistan to meet the girls that I helped. I may have to save up all of my allowance to do it, but just to see their smiles for myself will make it all worthwhile.

Sydney Milucky, thirteen

Deep Inside

Standing on the beach,
Sand between my toes,
What lies in my future?
Who will come and go?
The sun beams down upon me,
As I raise my head and look
At the vast ocean before me,
Its size, which I mistook.
I feel so insignificant,
Compared to this great expanse.
What difference can I make?
Will I even be given a chance?
I realize then while standing there,
That all I have to do,
Is listen to my heart,
And it will pull me through.
For strength and inspiration,
Are not material things,
They come from deep inside of you,

They give your soul its wings.
So whenever you're in doubt,
And you begin to stray,
Take a look down deep inside,
And the answer will come your way.
If you only believe in yourself,
You can make your dreams come true,
For no one else can do it,
The power must come from you.

Stephanie Ives, fourteen

More Than I Had Dreamed Of

If at first you don't succeed, try, try again.

American Proverb

From the time I was seven, I had a dream of becoming a member of my school cabinet. I always admired my school leaders for taking responsibility for all of us. They gave instructions, conducted school activities, proudly wore their cabinet badges and carried our school flag for parades. They represented us and gave speeches on school issues. Our school cabinet members were our role models.

So, for the next few years, I dreamed—dreamed of being a leader. Dreamed of being the person addressing issues of students. Finding solutions. Making a difference.

Years flew by, and soon I was eligible to participate in the elections. When I was twelve, I entered my name as a junior member. I prepared my election speech and then, on the afternoon that we all gave our speeches, everybody voted. My close friends pledged their votes for me. I was hopeful and I prayed that I would win.

The next morning, we all assembled at the school grounds and our principal announced the results. I waited anxiously for my name to be announced. I was all set to fulfill my dream.

One by one, the names were announced and the whole school cheered as the girls with the highest votes walked up to the stage. I closed my eyes and waited for my name to be called. The last name was read and my name wasn't among them. I was totally brokenhearted. My dream had been shattered, and I just wanted to run home and cry my heart out.

And then the reality struck that I hadn't had a chance to win. I wasn't well known, flamboyant or stylish. I wore braces and wasn't too pretty. Girls across the school hardly knew me. I just did not have what it took to win a school election.

I was depressed because I had nurtured this dream for a long time. I went through something that a huge majority of preteens face—rejection. My whole world began to cave in and suddenly it seemed as if I had no friends.

As I cried in my room that evening, I suddenly took a deep breath and decided I was going to stop seeing myself as a failure. So what if I had lost an election? There were many more things in life to accomplish. I would work hard to make my dreams a reality. I wouldn't stop dreaming.

It didn't matter if I wore braces or if I wasn't too pretty. That didn't give me a reason to give up. I decided that I would stand for elections again in my final year at school—and I would win. I sat at my study table and began to write down my thoughts.

I recognized that my competitors had a lot of things in

their favor. Their flamboyant personalities were their biggest strength. What were the points that would work in my favor? I had good grades, and I was friendly and helpful. And my biggest strength was the faith I had in myself to be a good leader. I would not allow my plain appearance or my braces to hold me back from putting my best foot forward. That evening, I began my election plans a whole year in advance.

First, I realized that I would have to work for each vote. Girls would have to get to know me as a person and recognize that I had the ability to represent them. I loved making friends and I liked being helpful, so I decided that perhaps I could use these qualities to work to my advantage. I began to make new friends and help them out in different ways. Slowly and steadily during the year, I made friends across the school. When my official campaign began, they helped drum up support for me.

In order to learn how to present a great election speech, I attended a course on effective public speaking. At twelve, I was the youngest participant in the course. By the time the election rolled around, I had a good speech and was well prepared as I delivered it with more confidence than I had the year before.

The day after the election took place, every minute seemed like an hour while I waited for the results. Would my efforts pay off? Would I accomplish my goal? Would I be one of the five senior school leaders?

During the assembly, when the principal announced, "Lin Rajan has been elected to the school cabinet with the second highest number of votes in the school," the students cheered as I walked up to the stage. The joy on the faces of all my friends showed me that my victory was also *their* victory.

Suddenly, I realized that I had accomplished much more than I had dreamed of. The path I had chosen had given me more than the cabinet badge; I had made many new friends and had helped people along the way. I had won the acceptance and love of my schoolmates and they knew me as somebody who would stand by them. I was able to put a smile on their faces and brighten up their day.

I realized that just by being me and going for my dream, I had *already* made a difference.

Lin Rajan

"When I said, 'If at first you don't succeed, try, try again,' I wasn't talking about video games."

Welcome to New Hope, Pennsylvania

Sometimes you gotta create what you want to be a part of.

Geri Weitzman

The idea actually came to me during my *Harriet the Spy* phase. I ran around town with my notebook and pen permanently glued to my hand, jotting down descriptions of "suspicious characters" and "fishy situations." I wanted desperately to solve a crime . . . but instead, I wrote a book!

New Hope, Pennsylvania—my hometown and favorite place to spend a sunny Saturday afternoon. What's not to love? Wacky toy stores, a mule barge, great food and gorgeous views of the historic Delaware River (the same one that George Washington crossed!). I saw all that New Hope had to offer, but it seemed to me that many other kids didn't get the same opportunity. As I walked through our quaint town, I realized that the visitors were mostly adults. This disappointed me, because I knew that New

Hope had great potential in the kid-friendly department. So, I decided to do something about it. My notebook of prospective cases became a guidebook of interesting places. I morphed from detective to investigative reporter, searching for the most kid-pleasing sites in the New Hope area. I wrote small segments about what made them so appealing and even interviewed our local town historian to include some interesting facts.

I borrowed my dad's camera and began snapping away, capturing the essence of New Hope in photographs. Finally, when I had all of my information, I sat down at the computer and began formatting all of my writings and pictures inside brightly colored borders. I even created the cover using my own drawings of New Hope landmarks. I called it *The Kid's Guide to New Hope*. I was thrilled at the product of my labors. I was so proud of my vibrant creation. But I wasn't sure what to do next.

I submitted the book to many publishing companies, including the guidebook legend, *Fodor's*. Everyone wrote back saying the book was incredible, but unfortunately, it wasn't their type of book. I was starting to think that all of my efforts would end up unrewarded.

Then one day, my family and I were eating in a local restaurant and my book came up in a conversation with the manager. She thought it was a great idea, and being actively involved in town politics, asked me to give her a copy to present at the next town council meeting. I brought her the book the next day and she took it to the meeting. The response was incredible. The borough council wanted me to come to a meeting and share my book with the town! I even spoke in front of the mayor.

It was because of that experience that things really began to take off for *The Kid's Guide*. I gained many mentors, such as Paul and Jan Witte, members of the community who wanted to lend me a hand. They started

The Julia Fund, trying to raise enough money to self-publish the book. Another mentor, Nancy Wolfe, who was an author herself, talked to the local printing company she used to produce her books and was able to secure a discount for the printings. It was the spirit of New Hope at work. The entire town worked together to help me make my publishing dreams come true.

Soon, enough money had been raised to print thousands of copies of *The Kid's Guide to New Hope*. And to top it all off, I became the owner and founder of Simply Kids Publishing. And I was only ten years old!

Next, I had to find stores that would be willing to sell the guides. I also had to be able to get them to be willing to sell them pretty inexpensively and not take much of a profit, because I wanted the books to be cost effective for kids. I went to Farley's, the town bookstore, and they eagerly accepted my proposal. Books were also placed in the New Hope Library and in the Visitor's Center. But my big break came when the local Barnes & Noble said that they would carry *The Kid's Guide*. They also asked me to hold a book signing. It was incredible!

That experience made me realize just how many other wannabe kid writers there probably were out there, so I began sending sample copies of the book to local schools. Many of the local school principals asked if I would come and talk about my experiences and give advice.

As the word spread about *The Kid's Guide to New Hope*, our phone started to ring off the hook with requests for interviews with our newspapers. I even appeared on local television shows as a positive role model for other students. It's no wonder that copies of the book flew off the shelves! I began to receive checks from the bookstores, and I made a profit on every book sold. I knew exactly what to do with the money. I donated almost all of the profit from the book sales directly back to town organizations such as the Chamber of Commerce, the local library, and the police and fire stations.

Earning money wasn't my reason for writing *The Kid's Guide to New Hope*. People started visiting New Hope . . . with their children. That's what I had wanted to happen. Families were visiting our town once they realized how many exciting things there were for kids to see and do. New Hope was flourishing again, and that was the greatest reward I could ever have asked for.

Julia Yorks, fifteen

Better Off

In helping others, we shall help ourselves, for whatever good we give out completes the circle and comes back to us.

Flora Edwards

A lazy summer's day found me cleaning out my room and sorting through boxes. I picked up a newspaper article that I had almost forgotten about—one my mom cut out for me to read. I began to throw it aside, but I started feeling uneasy. The article was about a local woman with two kids who had fled an abusive relationship where the man she lived with had flicked hot ravioli on her two-year-old child's face, among other things. The woman's job brought in barely enough to keep them living in a week-to-week hotel room. Her seventeen-year-old son worked a janitorial job after school to help prevent them from becoming homeless. The article said that the boy was in need of a jacket and some pants that fit his tall frame.

I had seen pictures of homeless adults, but never of any kids my age. I imagined how cold and embarrassed he must have felt at school. I've been fortunate to always have a roof over my head, clean clothes that fit and a loving family. My mom always taught me to share what I have and to see God in everyone. I decided right then that I would give him some of my clothes.

I began sorting through my closet. That can be emotional—especially when you decide to give away one of your favorite shirts because you know somebody else needs it more than you do. Things like the clothes you wear play a huge part in acceptance in high school.

I started thinking that so many kids like me have more clothes than they need—or even want. That gave me an idea for a bigger solution. The kids in my area usually either donated the clothes they no longer wanted to a thrift store or threw them away. I wanted to educate them about the suffering some of their peers were going through and offer them a simple way to make another teen's life a little better.

I thought that this would be a good project for earning my rank as an Eagle Scout because it would involve a lot of planning and the help of many people. The local volunteer center seemed like a good place to start, so I asked to meet with the youth coordinator there. When I told her what I was thinking, she fell in love with the idea, but cautioned me not to be overly optimistic about the amount of donations I would receive. I had a vision in my head of enormous piles of clothing coming in. She suggested that I might need someplace to store the clothes and a way to clean and deliver them.

After hours of brainstorming, she recruited me for the Youth Volunteer Corps, whose members were enthusiastic teen leaders from schools around our county. I presented my idea to them, which I decided to call, "Teens Dressing Teens," and asked for their help. I was amazed by how they dug right in, quickly deciding that they could present the project at their schools and bring back what they collected to one of the meetings. And that's exactly what they did.

At the next meeting, donated clothes were piled five feet high and five feet wide against the walls of the room!

So, my simple gesture to help one teenager evolved into a countywide clothing drive. Over the next four months, students from seven high schools and two middle schools cleaned out their closets of nice clothes and donated them to foster kids and homeless teenagers in the area. Clothing began piling up around school and I'd see collection boxes and signs I didn't even make. The issue changed from obtaining enough clothing to finding somewhere to store it! The large shed for storing donations at the Catholic Charities Homeless Services Center soon filled up, causing them to halt all clothing donations from anyone for almost a month!

Generous stores answered my request for gift certificates for new socks and underwear. My church helped, and my family pitched in. A shoe store collected used and new running shoes and attire for a running program at a children's home. Suits and work clothes were donated. It got to be so overwhelming that we began accepting only clean clothing because we didn't have the people to wash so many items.

All was going pretty smoothly. Then one day, I got a note to go to the office immediately. I was told to call home. My heart raced, wondering what was going on. My mom answered the phone.

"Kirk, your dad is in critical condition. He's going into surgery. They say that he has a fifty-fifty chance of living."

I was speechless, and at the same time, I felt strongly that he would survive. I thought that maybe this would convince him that he should finally make the decision to quit smoking cigarettes and stop drinking. That illusionary bubble burst that evening at the hospital, when he was pronounced dead at 6:03 P.M. I put off my much-anticipated race in the Footlocker Cross County Championships and did some serious praying. I was shocked because my father was not overweight though he did smoke and have a lot of stress. The doctor said that it was an aortic aneurysm and that, "it just happens without cause." I guess it goes to show how quickly life can change.

Everyone in my family was grieving. I sought comfort in them and in my faith. I was tempted to just shut down completely and withdraw from life and the activities I had become involved in. But that's not my style. I also knew that my father would want me to be happy and continue living my life fully. That would be what would make him proud. I decided to go on.

Although I miss him, I know he is looking over me. His death changed me, no doubt about it. It made me realize even more how precious life is and the importance of using my god-given talents and abilities to help others. So, I finished leading the clothing drive with the help of many wonderful people. Together, we made it possible to help *many* people in need—not just teens.

I never met any of the kids that received the clothing. I respected their dignity and just wanted them to know that people care.

Although I also never met the boy in the newspaper article, I obtained a $50 gift certificate and delivered it to his teacher. A few months later, while waiting at a traffic light, I'm almost certain that I saw him sitting in the back seat of an older car. Our eyes locked for just for a few seconds. In that moment, I felt that we conveyed a sense of respect and understanding of each other.

Then the light turned green and off we went, still never having personally met, but definitely better off because of each other.

Kirk Brandt

No Place I'd Rather Be

All our dreams can come true, if we have the courage to pursue them.

Walt Disney

Growing up, I always dreamed of being a professional figure skater. After years of hard work, support from my family and good coaching, I am living proof that dreams can come true.

When I was born, my parents immediately noticed something wrong. My feet were deformed, pointing inward and curling under. I wore casts and foot braces my first two years to correct the problem. My casts were changed every two weeks. I teetered at first, yet I learned to balance and walk in casts. Soon after the last set of casts came off, Mom enrolled me in dance classes as therapy for my feet.

I, however, quickly decided to try something else. Not far from my house was an ice rink in the mall. There, local skaters would perform ice shows. I remember seeing the glittery costumes, the dazzling spotlight, and their graceful movements. I wanted to try skating.

I started taking group skating lessons, but I'd cry before class because going into a group scared me. Performing on ice came naturally, but I have always been shy and afraid to speak in group settings.

One thing I've never been afraid of is competition. I get nervous, like everyone else, but never fearful. For me, skating has never been about beating others. It's been about being my personal best. I progressed through various levels rapidly and gave my first ice performance at age seven. Soon I started winning local and regional competitions. That's because being on the ice has always been the one place I can truly express my emotions. The ice is like home.

I began seriously training when I was nine years old. Mom and I would wake up at four o'clock in the morning, six days a week. I'd skate for five hours. Then I'd go to school. Since education has always been important in my family, I had to find creative ways to fit in school studies throughout my amateur career.

Twenty-four hours after graduating from high school, I moved to Canada. Saying good-bye to my family and friends made me homesick before I even left, but I knew deep down that I had to leave and train full-time to give my dreams a chance at reality.

I went to compete in the Olympic Games in 1992. No one, not my coach or even my family, ever talked to me about winning a gold medal. In fact, I wouldn't even allow myself to think about it. I thought that would jinx me. So, I went with the attitude that I wanted to enjoy the Olympic spirit.

My practice sessions felt great leading up to the competition. Finally, the day arrived. I remember stepping onto the ice and thinking, *I can't do this. How am I going to keep myself from freaking out?* I took a deep breath and eased into a solid performance that placed me first going into the finals.

Two days later, I was the first of the final six skaters on the ice. My long performance started well, but I slipped while landing one of my easiest triple jumps, and my hand touched the ice. I didn't want to make two mistakes in a row, so next I did a jump with just two spins to play it safe. As I neared the end, I had one more jump, the triple Lutz. *Okay, this is it. You have to do this,* I told myself. I landed it perfectly.

When medals were awarded, I found myself on the top step, the gold hanging around my neck and America's national anthem playing. Words can't describe the overwhelming mixture of emotions I felt.

Little did I know how much that one night would change my life. Interviews. TV shows. Magazine covers. Dignitaries. Celebrities. Parades. Fans. Endorsements. My big dream came true when I signed a contract to skate professionally with the Stars on Ice tour. I thought life as a pro would be easy. It's not. It takes as much training now as before.

Throughout the tour, special children visit us at practice. Their courage in the face of incredible challenges teaches so much to all who meet them. It has helped me see that we all have the opportunity to make a difference in someone's life. That's why I started the Always Dream Foundation. Our goal is to make a positive difference in the lives of children.

How can anyone love ice? Frozen water can be so painfully hard and oh so cold—just as life can be. Ice doesn't care who skates across its surface. It doesn't care who loses balance and falls on its slippery back. Still, when the lights go on and the crowd roars its welcome, there's no place I'd rather be.

For me, the ice is a warm world of beauty and grace. Being on the ice is being alive. I encourage you to pursue the things that make you feel alive. And, as you glide your way along life, remember . . . always dream.

Kristi Yamaguchi

[EDITORS' NOTE: *To find out more about the Always Dream Foundation, log on to* www.alwaysdream.org. *Check out* www.positivelyforkids.com *for cool books featuring the life stories of star athletes and celebrities.*]

4

ON TOUGH STUFF

Grasping into thin air,
We reach but cannot touch
Things we wish would go away
Things that hurt too much

Why do we face such tough times
While others go unscathed
Where do we find a shelter
When it rains on our parade

Life will give us roses
But every petal falls
Leaving joy and sadness
From the memories we recall

So if time's our greatest treasure
And love is all we need
Let's give each other all we have
Nothing else is guaranteed

Irene Dunlap

Stay with Me

You were so full of life, always smiling and
*   carefree.*
Life loved you being a part of it, and I loved you
*   being part of me.*

Brittany L. Hielckert, fourteen

I was the new kid in the neighborhood. My family had just moved from the country to a bigger city, so I had to start over making friends. I wasn't sure how I was going to do that, even though I had moved many times before that. It was just never easy introducing myself to total strangers with the hopes that they'd like me enough to become my friend.

So, I was really lonely until the day that this boy named Brandon came up to me and asked if I wanted to play with him and his friends. After that, we were like best friends. He was a few years older than I was so he always treated me like a little sister. If he wasn't at school, he was playing with me.

A few months passed and then a whole year went by. We were closer than ever, even though Brandon began making more friends at school, and they would come over, too. Still, he let me play with him, even when they were around. Brandon never let anyone push me around or pick on me. He was *always* there for me.

When my mom would call me in for dinner, I would always beg her to let me play for a few more minutes. He would say, "No, go ahead. I'll wait right here for you." I would sometimes think that he would not be there waiting when I was done, but he was always still there.

A lot of times, Brandon would help me with my homework and tell me more about what a certain subject was about. Afterwards, we would ride bikes or skate around our neighborhood together. The most important thing that he ever taught me, though, was to be my own person. He always used to say, "Who cares what others think about you? You should only care about how you feel about yourself." That saying got me through a lot of hard times.

One weekend, I had to go to my grandmother's. A new kid, named Lance, had moved to our neighborhood a few weeks before, and he seemed cool. The day I left, Brandon said he was going over to Lance's house to play video games. I said, "Okay, I'll see ya Sunday afternoon."

Well, things changed forever after that. Brandon spent the night over at Lance's and they played video games and watched movies. That Saturday, they went into Lance's parents' room to play Nintendo 64. Lance noticed that there was a little gun by his dad's bed, so he picked it up to check it out. Just joking around, he pointed the gun at Brandon and pulled the trigger. He thought it wasn't loaded. Well, he thought wrong.

I didn't get back until late Sunday night. I came in to find everyone in my family crying. I was scared because I didn't know what had happened. My mom took me into her room and said there had been an accident. From that moment on, I knew nothing would ever be the same. She finally told me that Lance had accidentally shot Brandon with a gun and that Brandon didn't make it. My mom wouldn't tell me where he had gotten shot but I had a good idea of it.

I started crying, and I ran to my room and hid my face in my pillow. I didn't want to talk to or see anyone.

A few days later, we went to his funeral. I couldn't help but cry. I went up to see him and I realized he was in a better place, because I knew that Brandon knew God, and that was comforting to me. All this happened about six years ago. I am now thirteen. Still, there isn't a day that goes by that I don't think about him. I cry whenever I pass by the cemetery. My best friend is gone, but the friendship that he showed me—the new kid in the neighborhood—will stay with me forever.

Jaime Fisher, thirteen

[EDITORS' NOTE: *For information about gun safety, go to* www.kidshealth.org, *keyword search: "gun safety".*]

A Loving Mother

The best things in life are never rationed.
Friendship, loyalty and love.
They do not require coupons.

George T. Hewitt

I'm a girl with bipolar disorder. That's when your moods go up or down way too far. Sometimes with bipolar, you feel so happy that you get kind of hyperactive, bouncing off the walls and jumping for joy. Then, within minutes, bipolar can make you feel really sad or so mad that you start throwing stuff around, screaming and stomping.

With bipolar, when a person gets either really, really happy or really, really sad or mad, they have no idea why they feel that way. They can think of nothing that caused their mood to be so extreme one way or the other.

When I was seven years old, I got mad at my mom for no reason. We got into a fight over nothing, and I got so mad that I threw my glass piggy bank at her. Pretty bad, huh?

Maybe some of my anger was due to the fact that my parents had recently divorced and my mom and dad were not getting along well. My dad had been following my mom around. Then one night, he came into our house and attempted to hurt her, and she ran outside to call the police. At that point, he started to go up the stairs to find me. I was asleep and my stepdad kept him from getting to me. He ran away before the police got there, but the next day, the police arrested him for harassing our family.

That next day, I was supposed be with my dad but, of course, he didn't show up. That's when I knew something was wrong. My mom tried to protect me from finding out why he didn't come. She just told me that he had done something wrong and couldn't be with me. I cried every night because I missed him, and I became really depressed. Finally, I bugged my mom enough that she told me what had happened that night. In a way, it just made me more upset because everyone had kept the truth from me.

Around that time, I also began experiencing these extreme mood shifts. First I'd be really, really happy and then the next minute I'd be really, really mad. Then I couldn't stop myself from crying. It was very confusing, and I felt like I had no control over my emotions anymore. When I would get into trouble, I couldn't understand why I was behaving so badly. I would later come back to my mom and apologize to her for being so out of control, and she would always say, "It's okay, Holly. You're forgiven. Tomorrow will be a better day." It was hard on her, I'm sure, but she tried to deal with it by giving me love and understanding. She somehow knew that I couldn't help myself and suspected something more was wrong with me when one day I got so depressed that I asked her,

"Why don't you just get rid of me?" I had been so down that I didn't even want to live anymore.

She didn't think that my behavior was all because of what was happening between her and my dad. So, she took me to see a doctor who helps kids that have the same kind of issues that I was dealing with. It helped to know that there was someone out there who could understand me. It didn't seem like my family was able to do that at that time.

The day I threw the piggy bank my mom realized that I had gotten so out of control of my emotions that I could be a danger to myself and others. So, she and the doctor agreed that putting me in the hospital would help keep me safe while they ran some tests. It was there that I was diagnosed with bipolar disorder. The good news was, once they knew what I had, they could find the right medication to help me balance out. While in the hospital, I also learned about bipolar and the challenges of living with this illness.

I felt so much better after I got out of the hospital. I stopped feeling so sad and then suddenly totally happy. Finally, I felt normal for the first time in a long time.

Still, when I had some bad mood swings after I got out of the hospital, I thought that Mom would want to send me back there as punishment for my actions. But my mom never wanted to punish me for doing something that I couldn't control. She explained to me that she never wanted to be away from me, she only wanted to find the help that I needed to get better and stay better.

Sometimes I would think about how my mother could have given me away because it was so hard to deal with me when my bipolar was going on, but she is too much of a loving mother to ever do that. Instead, she was always behind me, supporting me with tons of love and patience. When I begin to get a little out of hand, my mom watches to see if I continue the behavior. If I do, it usually means that I need to change medications because the one I'm on has stopped working. That's part of the challenge of living with bipolar. Sometimes, body chemistry can change, causing the medications to act differently or the body just simply stops working with the medication and you have to change it.

Not long ago, I began hearing voices telling me to do stuff. I had to go into the hospital again to get off of the medication that I was on and start a new one. It was hard to face going into the hospital and going through another adjustment, but after being there for a few days and getting a new medication, the voices went away and I felt more like myself again—more balanced.

It's been five years now since I was diagnosed with bipolar. For the most part, I am doing well, and my emotions are more in the middle now and less "way too up" or "way too down." I can thank my mom for helping me make sure that I don't get sick and out of control. No matter what, she's there for me. Knowing that, I can cope with having an illness that I'll always have to work at managing.

With her there, I can get through another day.

Holly Howard, twelve

The Worst Day of My Life

*I no longer feel anger, I sometimes feel pain,
I will cry in the night for you, I will love you
forever.*

Kristina Taskova-Zeese, ten

I was sitting in class with about twenty-five other first-graders, listening to our teacher go on and on about the kind of words that sound alike. The only thing I could think about was getting out of class for recess.

Then my name was called over the intercom to go to the school office.

When I got there, my brother, William, was waiting for me with my dad.

That's when I really started to wonder. Dad never picked me up early and it wasn't even his weekend to have me since my parents were divorced and I lived with my mother. I started to get little butterflies in my stomach warning me that something was definitely wrong.

We got in the car and there was my grandfather from my mother's side of the family and my uncle from my father's side of the family. That also was weird. I kept hearing Dad say to my grandfather, "Don't worry, Ray, everything will be all right, I promise." I wondered why he was saying these things. *What was going on?* Then I started thinking that maybe I really didn't want to know what they were talking about.

We finally got to my grandparents' house and Dad told us to come on inside; we all needed to talk. Right then, William and I looked at each other, both thinking that we were in trouble.

We got inside and no one knew how to bring bad news to a nine-year old and a six-year old. With tears coming to his eyes, my dad said, "Kids, first we want you both to know that we will all get through this together. It will all be okay. Things happen, and a family must help each other and work through it."

Finally after what seemed like hours, but was actually only a few minutes, Dad said, "Kids, your mother has been in a very bad car accident."

"Well, is she okay?" I asked.

"No, I'm sorry. It killed her. The accident took your mother's life!"

I was so upset that I ran outside crying. I sat on the porch with my face in my hands sobbing. So many things were going through my mind. *What will happen? Where will I go? What will happen with William?*

At that time I had no idea what the things my dad had said meant, like God doesn't take people from earth unless he believes they are prepared for heaven. I was so angry with God though! He had taken the person who had brought me into this world—one of the most important people in my young life.

Now that I am older I understand what my dad had

meant. Losing someone you truly love makes you value life a lot more. After my mother died, I went to live with my father, and he and I became very close. He remarried and we are very happy.

My brother, William, has had a terrible time though. We had different fathers, and he went to live with his own father. Not too long after our mom was killed, his father was run over by a train cart and killed. William now lives with our grandparents and I try to see him as much as possible.

Now I know why people say your life can change with each breath you take. I do regret a few things. I regret being angry with my mother that morning and not telling her that I loved her. One thing I do know is that at her funeral she did hear me tell her I was sorry. I asked her to help me with each day.

I know she heard me because every morning when I wake up I hear my mother in my heart. She tells me to make the best of my life with my new mother. People hear this and say it's weird but I can hear her and I can understand everything that she tells me. I still think about her all the time and I miss her a lot, but I have to live my life and do the things she didn't get to.

I also know God has a reason for everything that he does. You may not understand these things now but when someone this close to you dies it all starts to come together. Hold on to what you love and make the best of it. With life, there aren't second chances.

Jennifer Kerperien, fourteen

Luann. *Reprinted by permission of United Feature Syndicate, Inc.*

Lucky

When you're a preteen, a *huge* problem might be like when you just have to have this new rock-rap CD that you don't even like, but everybody else says is cool, but your parents won't give you the twenty bucks for it.

Or having this gigantic zit and desperately needing to see a dermatologist right away when nobody else can even see the zit.

I thought life was so unfair when things like this happened—until September 11, 2001.

I was in P.E. when the planes hit the World Trade Center and the Pentagon. As soon as I got home and for weeks after, I saw the disaster unfold on TV. Seeing the innocent people running for their lives as the debris started coming down and the fire and smoke billowed out of the buildings brought tears to my eyes. I couldn't help imagining what the people on the planes and in the buildings were thinking and going through, not knowing what was going on. I admired the courage of the firefighters who rushed in and risked their own lives to save others.

It tore my heart apart to watch the desperate looks on the faces of so many people who didn't know if their loved ones were dead or alive while trapped in all the rubble. I felt so sorry for the people whose loved ones were killed and wished that I could help ease the pain of those families whose family members died.

Then it hit me: All my life I had thought mainly of myself. I had it easy in life and had been taking it all for granted.

A cold chill ran down my back, and I cried just thinking of the possibility that it could have easily happened to my family. My mom or dad, or both, could have been killed like that, and I would never, ever see them again. I began to evaluate what a real problem in life was.

This tragedy taught me that awful things can happen to anyone at any time. I know now that I have it made compared to others. Now when my mom or dad or sister go somewhere, even if it's just to the store, I try to remember to tell them that I love them because I know there is a chance that I may never get to tell them that again.

Not getting a new CD or having a zit is not going to make or break my life. I can live with those kinds of problems. But losing someone I love would truly make my life miserable.

9/11 showed me just what I am.

Lucky.

Very lucky.

Molly McAfee, thirteen

Maddy

As I opened the front door of my house, I heard a dog bark. My older sister, Amanda, was holding up a chew toy, as a furry, brown and white puppy tried to bite it. "Molly!" my sister cried, as soon as she saw my face. "Guess what!" I didn't have an interest in dogs at the time and I didn't understand what was so great about them. I didn't answer Amanda.

"Where's Mom?" I asked. Amanda said that she was upstairs, so I rushed up. "Mommy?"

"Hi, Honey," Mom said, excitedly. "Did you see her? We have a new puppy."

I immediately grabbed the neck of my mom's dog, Emily, and squeezed it. Emily growled. Emily had never liked me. "Why does Amanda get to have a dog?" I grumbled.

Mom sighed, and sat me down on her lap. "You can have your own dog when you're older," Mom started, "But right now you are too young to take care of a dog."

"Ugh!" I cried. "I'm going to call Sam." Samantha was

my friend. My mother had known her mother for a long time. Later that evening, Sam and her mom, Alexis, came over to see our new dog. I wouldn't go downstairs. I stayed in my mom's room, watching a movie. Later, Sam came upstairs, grinning. "Your puppy's name is Maddy," she said. "Your mom and dad and sister all agreed on it."

"Maddy!" I cried. "I don't want to own a dog named Maddy!"

"Come downstairs, Mol. Maddy's cute!" Sam said. I was stubborn, though, and refused.

That night, while I was in bed, I felt something furry cuddle up next to me. "Maddy?" I said. Maddy looked up at me. I looked down at her. From that moment on, I realized that I loved her.

Maddy and I did a lot of things together. My mom let me take her for walks, and sometimes Maddy and I would gang up on our old dog, Emily. Maddy gave me love, love that no human can give. The kind of love that they can't tell you, they just show it—and you just feel that love when they do.

A few years later, my parents separated. Then they got a divorce. Maddy stuck by my side through the whole thing. My dad moved to an apartment downtown. Amanda and I would be with my dad on Saturdays.

On one Saturday, Amanda suggested that we bring Maddy along with us to Dad's. When we got to Dad's apartment we decided to take her for a walk. We were all hungry, so Dad tied Maddy to a large pole outside of a restaurant. When we finished eating, it was dark, and we started to walk home. While walking down the sidewalk, I stroked Maddy's fur. Her soft, warm fur. Suddenly, Maddy spotted another dog on the other side of the street. Breaking free from Amanda's grip, Maddy ran across the street. Because it was late at night, and the drivers in the cars couldn't see Maddy, she almost got hit by a blue Jeep, but she got away. As she was about to reach the other side of the street, a car hit Maddy.

"Maddy!" my sister cried and dodged into the street with my dad. I just stood there, alone on the sidewalk, crying, replaying the scene over and over in my head. My love for Maddy was unbearable; I didn't know what to do. About fifteen minutes later, Amanda came back, tears streaming down her face.

"We couldn't find her," she sobbed. "But I think she'll be okay." I didn't believe her because she was crying, but I nodded my head.

"I'm s-scared," I stuttered. I didn't know what to think anymore. Was Maddy dead or was she going to be okay? We had raised Maddy since she was a puppy, and I couldn't imagine all of the awful possibilities that could happen. My dad came back, looking very sad and discouraged. "Come on," he said. "We're going to find her. She couldn't have gone far, if she is hurt."

He called the police, asking about reports. Finally, after over an hour of searching, my dad got a phone call, saying that they got an injured sheltie. We zoomed to the pound. There was Maddy, inside a cage, covered in a blanket. I couldn't look at her. I was too scared and frightened. My sister and dad thanked the people at the pound, and the people who brought her in, and Amanda carefully sat in the back seat of the car, Maddy on her lap. I crawled into the front, crying and moaning. Maddy was bleeding badly, and she was suffering.

When we got to the vet, my sister charged out with Maddy in her hands, and handed her to my dad. I still refused to look. I sat down in a waiting room chair, and after my dad had given Maddy to the vet, he came and sat with me. He dialed my home phone number. My mom answered sleepily, and my dad explained the whole thing to her.

My dad told me that this was too much for me, and that my mom was coming to pick me up. When Mom got to the vet's, I burst into her arms. "Molly, come on—let's go home. She'll be okay." And then my mom started crying, too.

The car ride was silent. When I got home, I felt too afraid and lonely to sleep alone. So, I climbed into bed with my mom, as she prayed a million times for Maddy. The next morning, I woke up and climbed into my own bed. About an hour after I was awake, my mom came into my room, sobbing. "I'm so sorry!" she wailed. "Oh Molly—I'm so sorry! She's gone!" And she wouldn't stop hugging me.

I didn't cry. I couldn't. I felt like I needed to, but it just wouldn't come out. More than anything else, I felt anger. But, I was sort of glad for Maddy. She wasn't suffering anymore.

About four weeks later, we got a new dog, and I named her Baylee. She was very shy at first, but once she got used to the house, she was very happy. At first, I didn't want another dog. I wanted Maddy. I finally learned to love Baylee—but nothing can replace how much I loved Maddy. It's always hard to lose someone you love. I realize that if I hadn't gotten Baylee, I probably would have kept feeling angry and mad. Everyone dies sometime—and it was just Maddy's turn to die. She may not be with me physically, but she will always be with me in my heart . . . and in my soul.

Molly Miller, ten

A Halloween
No One Will Forget

There are no rewards or punishments—only consequences.

Dean William R. Inge

When I was seven, my friend Sarah and I went to a horse show to compete in a barrel-racing event. That's where we both met Caleb. Caleb's mom is a barrel racer and horse trainer, and Caleb was helping his mom at the show by loading and unloading her equipment for her.

Even though he was older than us, Sarah and I both thought Caleb was really nice and a lot of fun to be around. Everyone liked him. We got to be good friends with him and we would hang out together whenever we would see him.

The year after we met Caleb, I had a Halloween party at my house. The morning after my party, my mom and dad were listening to the news and heard that a boy had accidentally hanged himself the night before. I didn't think too much about it until I heard who it was. It was Caleb.

One of the horse farms in our area had a Halloween haunted hayride and Caleb had gotten a job working there with about fourteen other kids who were supposed to scare the people who went on the hayride. For instance, a guy would open and close the lid of a coffin and this girl would jump out at the people. Caleb's job was to jump out of the woods as the hayride passed him.

I guess that just jumping out of the woods and saying, "Boo!" wasn't enough for Caleb. He always loved to get a rise out of people. Right next to Caleb there was a skeleton hanging from a tree. Just before the wagon got to him, Caleb took the rope from around the skeleton's neck and put it around his own neck because he thought that would scare people more than the skeleton did. What he didn't realize was that, even though his feet were touching the ground, he didn't weigh enough to keep the branch that the rope was tied to, from whipping back up, making the rope tight enough to choke him. When he started choking, the other kids thought he was just goofing around like he always did, trying to put on a big act. Caleb couldn't get the rope off by himself from around his neck because he had double-knotted it. By the time everyone realized that he wasn't kidding around, it was too late. Even though they tried to save him with CPR, Caleb died. He was only fourteen.

When I heard this I couldn't believe it. Caleb had his whole life ahead of him. Our whole town was shocked and everyone was so sad. It took everyone several months to just get over it. Sarah and I would talk about all of the good times we had and we comforted each other. But even now, I don't feel like I'm completely over it.

I think about Caleb and how everything would be

different if only he hadn't put that noose around his neck. I guess he didn't think it was dangerous, but now we all know that it was. I realize now that you really have to think about the things that you do, before you do them. Even though you may think nothing can ever happen to you, you can prevent accidents before they happen simply by realizing there can be dangerous consequences from your actions. I hope that everyone who reads Caleb's story will think before they act and think twice before they *ever* put *anything* around their necks.

Heather Hutson, nine

The Sandals That Saved My Life

*Though no one can go back and make a
brand new start, anyone can start from now
and make a brand new ending.*

Carl Bard

My junior high days were the darkest and the hardest
time in my life. During that time, I didn't feel like I had
any friends, except for this one person. This "friend" used
to tell me that we would always be "friends forever."
Friends are people who care for you and who are there for
you whenever you need them. They nurture you when
you're down. I never felt that way about her.

We only had one class together, so I didn't see her
very often. She was all wrapped up in her own thing—
her boyfriend, her social life, all her other friends.
When I would walk the halls of junior high by myself,
I would see her hand-in-hand with other people and
she would just stare at me as I walked by. She never

came over to talk to me except in that one class.

One rainy day, I got on the Internet and instant-messaged her. I thought it was the greatest thing in the world that we could talk on the Internet back and forth; it was so cool. We started chatting about school, boys, everything that two normal preteen girls would talk about. I brought up that I had gotten a new movie, and I wanted her to come over and watch it with me. I waited and waited for her reply, and when it came it was like daggers in my heart with unbearable pain.

She said, "Why would I want to come and watch it with you? Every time you get something new, you always have to brag about it to me and it makes me sick. You brag about everything all the time." I apologized to her up and down, that that's not what I meant, and I kept on apologizing.

Then she wrote back, "I am not going to sit here and fight with you about it, even though it is true," and she signed off.

I sat in my chair for ten minutes in a daze, wondering how a person who said she was my friend could say something like that to me. I went into the living room and sat down next to my mom, then burst out crying. She comforted me and reassured me that whatever it was, everything would be okay.

When I went to bed that night, I couldn't sleep. I felt so alone; like no one really loved me and like I was just some person that other people could just use whenever they felt like it. I felt almost invisible. I cried and cried until I finally fell asleep.

The next morning, I woke up around 8:00. My mom came into my room and said that she and my dad had doctor's appointments and that they would be back in a couple of hours. After they left, I sat on my bed and wondered what would be a good way out of this. Then, something came to my mind.

I would kill myself and put everyone out of their misery. That way, they wouldn't have to pretend that they like me, or that they are my friends. My social life wasn't the only reason that I decided to do this. Other things, too, were really bothering me—my grades, for one.

I sat and thought about how I would do it. *Should I shoot myself or take pills, or should I cut my wrists?* I settled on pills. I put the pills on the table next to my bed while I sat and wrote my final words to my family and friends.

I was ready to pop the pills for my final minutes on Earth.

Then the phone rang.

It was my mom calling to see what my shoe size is because she had found the cutest pair of sandals at Old Navy. I said, "Oh . . . yeah, okay, I wear an eleven."

Then she went on, "What's wrong? Are you feeling okay?"

I was like, "Yeah, Mom, I'm fine."

Then the words that I had longed to hear from *anyone* came out, "I LOVE YOU, and I'll be home in an hour." I hung up the phone. I sat in a daze, with the pills in my hand, thinking, *How could I have forgotten that someone actually does love me?*

When my mom came home, she hugged me and kissed me and said that she loved me a lot. I never told her what I had been thinking about doing.

The next day my "friend" called and said, "I was only kidding about the whole thing." I never told her about it, either. I kept it to myself. To this day, I still haven't told anyone about what I almost did. I have never actually blamed anyone but myself.

I am so blessed that my mom's phone call got through to me. Not only did it make me realize that I really am loved and cared about, but that suicide is never the answer. Maybe I just needed to hear the words "I love you" more often. Maybe we all do. Even when I have problems at school, my family is always there for me and I needed to remember to value that support. I know that I have to be there for them, too.

According to my definition of friendship, my mom's the best friend I'll ever have. My mom doesn't know how really special she is and how much of a hero she is. Thank you, Mom, for loving me so much—and saving me—without even knowing it. You're my forever friend.

Mallorie Cuevas, sixteen

[EDITORS' NOTE: *If you, or someone you know, is thinking about suicide, call 1-800-SUICIDE or log on to* www.save.org.]

65 Roses

To accomplish great things, we must not only act, but also dream; not only plan, but also believe.

Anatole France

I have always wanted to be normal. Or at least to know what it is like.

I have cystic fibrosis—often nicknamed "65 roses," because it is hard for some people to say. But I think that's a pretty cover-up name for a horrible disease. It is a respiratory disease, which means that it affects the lungs and a person's breathing.

When I was little, I didn't care if I had it or not. I always took my medicine and never worried about it. That's all changed since I learned something. My mom denies it, but according to my doctors, I might die from it.

This is the one thing I have kept from all my friends. My friends say they understand, or think they do—but they don't. I was reading a story out loud to them, and I had to stop because the next words were about death from cystic fibrosis. I feel like I can't let them know because I don't want them to treat me differently and think I am fragile or something.

Recently, I have been thinking a lot about death. I believe in God, but what if . . . ? Thinking that there is even a slight possibility that there isn't a God, or a Heaven, gives me a horrible feeling. I finally told my mom about being afraid of dying, but I just couldn't tell her about how I was questioning what happens after death.

I always used to ask God why he gave me this. Then I found the answer after reading a story in a book. I believe he gave it to me so I will keep my head up no matter what and to realize that others have diseases a lot worse than mine. Every time I start to feel sorry for myself, I either hang out with my friends, read books, or play with my pets—because they always love me.

I play hockey a lot with my friends. Sports are a little harder for me than for others. It is harder for me to breathe. Still, I have always dreamed of being an Olympian in hockey. I just want one medal no matter what color and I won't stop until I get it. My friends and family help me, because they believe in me all the way.

So for today, I try as hard as I can because I really don't know what my future will bring. But I believe, in my lifetime there could be a cure for cystic fibrosis. With God anything is possible.

Denise Marsh, eleven

[EDITORS' NOTE: *To find out more about cystic fibrosis, log on to* www.cff.org.]

READER/CUSTOMER CARE SURVEY

REFT

We care about your opinions! Please take a moment to fill out our online Reader Survey at **http://survey.hcibooks.com**.

As a **"THANK YOU"** you will receive a **VALUABLE INSTANT COUPON** towards future book purchases

as well as a **SPECIAL GIFT** available only online! Or, you may mail this card back to us.

(PLEASE PRINT IN ALL CAPS)

First Name		MI.		Last Name

Address			City

State	Zip		Email

1. Gender
☐ Female ☐ Male

2. Age
☐ 8 or younger
☐ 9-12 ☐ 13-16
☐ 17-20 ☐ 21-30
☐ 31+

3. Did you receive this book as a gift?
☐ Yes ☐ No

4. How did you find out about the book?
☐ Friend
☐ School
☐ Parent

☐ Online
☐ Store Display
☐ Teen Magazine
☐ Interview/Review

5. Where do you usually buy books?
(please choose one)
☐ Bookstore
☐ Online
☐ Book Club/Mail Order
☐ Price Club (Sam's Club, Costco's, etc.)
☐ Retail Store (Target, Wal-Mart, etc.)

6. What magazines do you like to read? *(please choose one)*
☐ Teen Vogue
☐ Seventeen
☐ CosmoGirl
☐ Rolling Stone
☐ Teen Ink
☐ Christian Magazines
☐ Other

7. What books do you like to read? *(please choose one)*
☐ Fiction
☐ Self-help
☐ Reality Stories/Memoirs
☐ Sports

8. What attracts you most to a book?
(please choose one)
☐ Title
☐ Cover Design
☐ Author
☐ Content

TAPE IN MIDDLE; DO NOT STAPLE

FOLD HERE

Books for Life

Do you have your own Chicken Soup story that you would like to send us? Please submit at: **www.chickensoup.com**

Comments

5

LIFE HAPPENS

Bad hair days and mixed up romance
Told that there's gooey stuff stuck to your pants
Getting a sister when you wanted a brother
Finding that "Life Skills" is taught by your mother
Slipping and falling and ripping your jeans
Discovering your sister has ruined your things.

Sometimes life gives us days full of laughter
And then we have some that are filled with disaster
Some things that happen aren't part of our plans
We have to roll with it and just throw up our hands
What life will bring next is predicted by none
Which makes it exciting and often more fun.

Irene Dunlap and Patty Hansen

Klutz Dust and Puberty

Life is a roller coaster. Try to eat a light lunch.

David A. Schmaltz

Have you ever had one of those days that seem normal at first, but little by little, you realize that you're out of sync with the world around you? On the way to the bus I tripped over a crack in the sidewalk, making me drop my English report onto the road, just in time for it to be run over by the bus, then it hit me! (No, not the bus.) The realization that this was one of those days.

In math, I found my little brother's homework folded neatly inside my book, instead of my own. Try explaining *that* to a teacher who already knows that math is not your best subject.

"Let's not make this a habit," Mr. Barner said, tapping his pencil on his grading book for emphasis. *Like I could even think up this excuse for not doing my homework.*

"Since you claim to have already done this assignment,

you shouldn't have any difficulty reproducing the answers for me during your lunch hour." *What? No trouble reproducing the answers? It took me one hour and all my dad's patience to produce them the first time.*

My English teacher accepted my crumpled and tire-treaded report, but not without delivering a lecture on the importance of the proper presentation of my work. "I do expect better from you in the future." *Future? What future?*

I re-did my math homework and made it to the cafeteria with a few minutes to spare. A lot of good that did me. The only food choices left were liver and onions (like onions are supposed to be some big bonus) and spinach.

All through my geography speech on "The Greening of the Earth," my best friend, Kara, kept showing me her teeth. I thought she meant for me to smile more, so I grinned bigger.

It wasn't until I sat down after my presentation, in front of the whole class, that Kara told me I had spinach stuck in my teeth.

"I know," I joked, trying to sound like I wasn't humiliated, "it was a visual aid for extra credit."

I got unstoppable hiccups in science, started out on the wrong note in choir . . . well, actually, it was the right note—but, for the wrong song, and I slammed my finger in my locker.

When the final school hour came, I thought for sure that I had it made. My mother was the trained volunteer presenter for the Life Skills unit that month. I knew at least she had to be kind to me.

Laughing and talking as we took our seats, my mother asked for our attention.

"Welcome class," she smiled, "our subject during this unit is puberty." She paused and looked around the table.

WHAT!!!!! No, no, no, no, NO! Not that! Not here! Not my mom talking about puberty and hormones in front of my friends! With diagrams! And boys in the room!!!!

She calmly stood there as though she was only discussing the weather. I guess in a way she was discussing the weather—whether or not I'd live through this.

What if I accidentally made eye contact with someone? What if it was a boy? I safely stared at the floor. The hands on the clock moved in slow motion. I tried to force time along by thinking of places that I would rather be.

Allergy shots. Detention. At home cleaning the bathroom. Tick... tock... Tick... tock. *Does she have to tell us absolutely everything she knows? Does she know absolutely EVERYTHING?*

My mother finally wrapped it up. "Are there any questions? Don't be afraid to ask!"

Right! And don't be afraid to walk through a tornado, or tease a hungry pit bull or jump out of an airplane with a hole in your parachute.

Silence.

"Go to my happy place. Go to my happy place," I said under my breath, frantically trying to calm myself.

Tick... tock. Tick... tock. Tick... tock.

My mother just kept smiling, "Well, next week you will have a chance to write your questions on a piece of paper and we will go over them together."

Next week! Maybe if I slept without covers and left my windows open all night I could be in the hospital with pneumonia by this time next week. Would it be wrong to pray for something to happen to prevent my mother from being here? Nothing bad or anything. How hard can a flat tire be for God?

It was only when the bell rang that I could breathe again. The class hurried out before I dared to look up. My mother was smiling down at me.

"Sweetheart, you handled yourself very well. I realized by your reaction that I should have made sure that you understood what our topic would be today." We pushed the chairs back under the table. "I was so concerned about

Kara's mother this morning that I wasn't as sensitive as I should have been."

"Kara's mother? What's wrong? Kara didn't say anything."

"Kara doesn't know. She had already left for school when her mother was rushed by ambulance to the hospital with severe diabetic shock."

My heart froze. "Diabetics can die from shock, can't they?"

"Yes. It was very serious but she made it through." My heart beat with relief.

We headed out the door into the golden light of late afternoon filtering through the autumn-colored trees that umbrella the sidewalk. My mother seemed to glow with the light around her.

"How was your day, Sweetie?"

"Well, Mom, it was a rough one," I paused, "but now, after knowing that Kara almost lost her mother today, little things don't seem to matter all that much."

My mother put her arm around my shoulders and we headed off for the car. "Sweetie, there's something that I have wanted to tell you since you came into class."

"Yes," I answered, feeling the near magic of our closeness.

"Sweetheart, you have a big wad of gum stuck to the seat of your pants."

"I what?" I twisted and turned, but I couldn't see behind me. I gave up.

What's a little klutz dust in the grand scheme of things? Life is beautiful, after all.

Cynthia M. Hamond

Jimmy, Jimmy

Mistakes are the usual bridge between inexperience and wisdom.

Phyllis Therous

When I was in the seventh grade, I broke my leg skiing. The doctor described my injury as serious—a spiral fracture of the tibia that was fragmented in three places—and just barely spared me the surgery to put pins in my leg. The tradeoff was that I had to wear a cast from hip to toe for four months, the first of them in a wheelchair. The weather that winter alternated between snowy blizzards and mucus-freezing-in-your-nose cold, so Mom or Dad had to drive me anywhere I wanted to go. Since sledding, skating, going to the local McDonald's and hanging out were my friends' favorite pastimes, I didn't get out much.

That left plenty of alone time for me to daydream and develop the biggest crush on a new boy in my class. His name was Jimmy, and he was *gorgeous*. He had thick brown hair, dreamy dark eyes, a perfect complexion and a great body. His slight Texas accent could charm anyone, and he was *sooooo* nice. *If only he would notice me!* But how could he? I hardly ever got to see him outside of the classroom, and he seemed to like one of my girlfriends, Kim. Besides, boys tended not to "like me" like me, because I was taller than all of them. I hoped Jimmy wouldn't notice my height thing since I was sitting in a wheelchair or slouching over crutches all the time. I didn't dare tell anyone about my crush, not even my best friend. I wanted to spare myself the misery of being teased. The crush on Jimmy was my big secret.

Then one Saturday evening, I got the phone call of my life. It was my best friend, Jodie, calling to say that someone in our class liked me and wanted to ask me out, but he wanted to know if I liked him first.

"Well, who is it?" I asked Jodie.

"Jimmy," was the unbelievable reply.

I felt goose bumps crawl up the back of my neck to the top of my head. I nearly dropped the phone.

"Well, do you like him? Would you go out with him if he asked you?"

Then doubt quickly crept its way into my thoughts. Paranoia set in. Perhaps this was some cruel trick by my friends to find out who I liked. After all, how could Jimmy like *me*? We'd never even spoken so much as a word to one another.

"I guess so," I tentatively replied. My stomach was getting queasy. I waited for the teasing to begin.

"You guess so? Well, do you or don't you like him? It's got to be one or the other," Jodie pressed.

"Yes, I like him," I replied with a little more enthusiasm this time, my secret finally out.

"Great! Can we come over now? Jimmy wants to ask you out tonight!" gushed Jodie.

"Uh . . . sure. Come on over."

When the doorbell rang about fifteen minutes later—an absolute eternity—I answered the door to find my friends on the front porch. The guys were around the corner, waiting to send Jimmy over. I stepped out on the porch with the aid of my crutches and closed the front door behind me. My friends were smiling at each other, celebrating their roles as matchmaker, so excited to be a part of getting me together with my first boyfriend.

The girls left me alone on the porch so that Jimmy could ask me to go out in private. I waited there for him. I was anxious, nervous and excited. My stomach uneasy, part of me still wondered if this could be some big joke. For the first time since I broke my leg, I was thankful to have crutches to support me.

I was as white as a ghost, more nervous than I had ever been. Jimmy rounded the corner and stepped up onto the front porch. *Oh, no.* I wanted to hobble back inside and shut the door behind me. *What have I gotten myself into? How could I be so stupid?* I was so caught up in Jimmy dreamland that I had neglected to ask Jodie, "Jimmy who?"

There stood Jimmy, so sweet, with a nervous smile and a love-struck look. His red-freckled face seemed a little redder than usual. This wasn't *my* Jimmy. Not my big-crush Jimmy. Not Jimmy of my dreams and daytime fantasies. It was the *other* Jimmy in my class, who I liked as a friend but most definitely did not "like" like.

I heard myself mutter a feeble, "I guess so," when he asked me to go out with him. *What else could I do? How could I turn him down after he had prescreened his proposal through Jodie?*

We didn't hang around very long on the front porch. As soon as I could, I made some lame excuse about how I had to go back inside the house because my parents would wonder where I was.

Once alone inside the house, I worried about what to do next. I certainly couldn't tell anyone about the mix-up. I'd never live it down. I decided to hide behind the excuse of my broken leg and my life as a social recluse, until I could figure things out. And there was the solution! I would only have to see Jimmy in school, and only in the classroom where we couldn't really talk, and most definitely could not kiss. How on earth could we go out under those circumstances?

I waited what seemed to be an appropriate length of time (about three days), offered my excuse to my girlfriend, Jodie, and asked her to break up with Jimmy on my behalf. I figured that since she helped me get into this mess, she should help me get out of it. Jimmy confronted me, flushed with anger, to confirm the breakup after Jodie told him. Slouching down lower on my crutches, I said something like, "Sorry. I hope that's okay with you." *Lame. Lame. Lame.*

Rumors floated around about me only agreeing to go out with Jimmy so I could say I had had a boyfriend . . . and about me breaking up with Jimmy because I was too afraid to kiss a boy. I suffered their laughter in silence and never told anyone about the case of mistaken Jimmy. My big crush remained my big secret, my first true love.

Karen Lombard

The Mummy Returns

Let there be more joy and laughter in your living.

Eileen Caddy

Here we were, standing at the entrance of the ride, "The Mummy Returns," at Universal Studios, in Hollywood. My mom, dad, brother, and best friend, Stephanie, were there with me. My heart started beating fast and as we walked in, I began thinking about what crazy things might happen in there.

The shadows crept silently over us as we glanced at ancient Egyptian artifacts. A chill of excitement immediately ran up my spine. We walked deeper and deeper into the mazelike cave, entering a world of the unknown. The creepy walls started narrowing into a small hallway, where we were spinning and turning in circles. We timidly approached the aisle, dizzily grabbing the railing on either side of us.

As we walked on and on, things started popping out at Stephanie and me. Scared to death of this place from the beginning, Stephanie started frantically running in the opposite direction, back the way we came in. Wanting to pull me along with her, and not realizing what she was doing, she grabbed some lady's purse thinking that it was mine. When she realized that it wasn't mine, she returned it to the person then ran to catch up with us.

Looking at the spidery cobwebs and dead bodies all over the place, we were led to a vast bridge. Dangling from a rope was a man! (Fake, of course!) Stephanie got the living daylights scared out of her again, and literally threw my mom completely off the bridge because she was so scared.

Worse things started to happen. As I was holding on to Stephanie frantically, in the rush of people on the bridge, my brother Gianni tried desperately to get my attention.

"Turn around, turn around," Gianni yelled repeatedly. Finally realizing what he was saying, I turned around. There, to my surprise, was a big mummy standing right there! He was covered in a white wrap from head to toe. He looked at me through those ancient eyes of his, staring at me and giving me a dirty look. As he went past me, he walked impatiently, sternly, strictly and seriously, like an army general. He must have been trying to get past me to get to Stephanie, but he couldn't. I have a feeling that he radioed his other mummy friends to watch out for our group after that, because worse things started to happen, like scary things jumping out at us from the walls.

Stephanie and I screamed, yelled, pushed, shoved, and dodged everyone and everything in our way, to get out of there. In the process of doing so, we created a domino effect—Stephanie pushed into me, I shoved into Gianni, and Gianni rammed into my dad—which was a big mistake! Losing his balance, my dad desperately flayed and waved his hands in the air, trying to grasp onto something—anything—in the pitch-black darkness. Yes, my dad did catch his fall, but with something very peculiar. His hand touched a gushy, blubbery thing, and he grabbed on to it for support. It turned out to be some lady's left boob! The lady must have been too embarrassed to respond, because she didn't even scream.

Trying not to laugh too hard and make any other accidents happen, Stephanie and I calmly walked on. As we did, another mummy popped out at us. We couldn't help but scream our brains out again. It happened to Gianni, too. "Aaaawww!" The mummy screamed at Gianni. Then Gianni screamed back. The confused mummy attempted to try to scare my brother one last time. He came at it a different way. "You need to brush your teeth," the mummy commented. My brother quickly responded, "You need a shower!"

Later on, mummies were falling out of the walls, and one just happened to bump into my mom. The ridiculously haunting mummy got my mom so freaked out, she screamed and peed her pants!

We all piled out of the haunted house, out of breath, laughing hysterically and holding our stomachs tightly. We all had the same thought running through our minds: *We had just experienced the funniest moments of our lives!* A lot of crazy things can happen in one little haunted house.

Chiara Cabiglio, thirteen

Whose Room Is It, Anyway?

Who could deny that privacy is a jewel?
In each civilization, as it advanced, those
who could afford it chose the luxury of a
withdrawing-place.

Phyllis McGinley

I dreaded coming home from school and going into my room. Every day it was something different. The hours away at school were long enough to cause a drastic, terrible change to my peaceful haven. Today was no different.

As I entered the house, Mom called out a cheerful, "Hello!" and greeted me with a smile. It seemed like nothing was wrong. She asked me how my day had been, if I had any homework. . . blah, blah, blah. I was still suspicious. Mom could be so unaware! Yesterday, I discovered a chocolate chip cookie smeared around the mouth of my favorite figurine, a porcelain angel with glittering gold wings and beautiful long blonde hair. She had the prettiest pink lips, which were now covered in chocolate.

Obviously, Callie had enjoyed the cookie so much she wanted to share it with my angel. *Not funny.*

I looked around for my little sister, Callie, who had just turned three. I didn't see her, but I heard the TV blaring in the other room. She loved to sit and watch the afternoon cartoons, turning the volume up and then back down, up and down. As I scanned the family room, I noticed it was pretty messy. There were toys all over the floor, but none of them seemed to be mine. There were a few headless dolls, some blocks, a few juice-stained stuffed animals, the remains of a green grape crushed into the carpet and videos strewn all over the floor. My hopes were slowly rising. If Callie had focused on destroying only the family room, well, maybe . . .

I peeked around the corner into the extra room, and there she was, sitting on the couch with her chubby legs stretched out in front of her, clutching the remote with sticky hands. Her long, thick blonde hair was all tangled, and it looked as though she had specks of sand or crumbs in it. Her pink and blue outfit was still remarkably clean— that was truly amazing. I figured that Callie must have gotten her clothes so dirty that Mom had recently put a clean outfit on her. That seemed much more reasonable than assuming that she had kept this outfit clean all day. No way. Not my sister, the destroyer. Not my sister, the three-year-old terror. Not my sister, the menace of my life.

She looked up from gazing at the TV and saw me. A huge grin broke out on her face, and she laughed in delight, clapping her hands. I was surprised that they didn't stick together.

"Sissy!!" She leaped off the couch and ran to me, squeezing my knees and almost tipping me over.

"Hi, Callie," I said, with the slightest hint of a smile. I ruffled her hair, and white crumbs drifted like dust to the floor. "Yucky, Callie," I said, pointing to the crumbs that had settled onto the carpet. I turned around and started the dreaded climb to my room.

Up the stairs I trudged. *What was it going to be today? Grapes shoved into my CD player? My treasured collection of ceramic bear figurines colored with Magic Markers? Or maybe smashed into a million bits and shoved into the CD player?* My door was still closed, which was a good sign. Maybe she hadn't been in here today after all. Maybe Mom had been able to keep her out. I was so hopeful that I breathed a sigh of relief.

I pushed open the door . . . .

And saw destruction! Covering the floor was more of the same substance that I had just seen in Callie's hair! It was *everywhere*—on my bed, on the floor, on my bookshelves and desk, and yes, even coming out of my CD player! I bent down and touched it, wondering what it was. Then I saw an empty can thrown in the corner. *Parmesan cheese!* She had poured Parmesan cheese all over my room! I ran downstairs as fast as I could, almost tripping a few times, and came face to face with my bewildered mother.

"She did it again!" I screamed, my face red and hot with rage.

"Oh no, now what?" My mother covered her face with her hands, as if dreading what I was going to say.

"Parmesan cheese," I replied through clenched teeth.

"What? How . . ." And then Mom's face registered understanding. "I made spaghetti for her lunch and I must have forgotten to put the cheese away," Mom sighed. "Don't worry," she said, "I'll clean it up, and then we'll get your dad to put a Callie-proof lock on your door tonight."

I felt better, now that I knew that soon my room would truly belong to me once again. But I was still angry at my little sister so I went into the family room to tell her how bad she had been.

"Callie . . ." I started.

"Sissy!" she cried, her big brown eyes lighting up with joy. "Hooray!" She leaped off the couch once again, and hugged my knees with such happiness that I could only look down at her and smile. After all, she was only three and experimenting with the world. It was sort of nice to feel so loved by someone younger than me and I guess that's why she always chooses my room to explore and destroy—because she looks up to me, her big sister.

Mom kept her promise and cleaned my room so that it was spotless. Dad put a lock on my door that very evening. And . . . they bought me a new CD player that was even better than the old one Callie had jammed with Parmesan cheese!

Aidan Trenn, eight
As told by Melinda Fausey

Gabriella

Life is 10 percent what you make it and 90 percent how you take it.

Irving Berlin

I was so excited when I found out that my mother was pregnant. The sonogram showed that she was going to have a little girl.

I was five years old, and all I could think about was having a little sister who looked up to me. In my mind, I formed the image of what my perfect little sister was going to look like. She was going to have curly gold hair that cascaded down her perfect little shoulders like a waterfall and perfect heart-shaped, berry-stained lips that were always smiling. Her cheeks were going to be a rosy red color, she was going to have eyes that looked as if they came from the heavens because they were such a bright, beautiful shade of blue, and her skin was going to look like it was carved from porcelain because it was so pale and flawless. She would be quick-witted and always fun to be around. I couldn't wait until she was born.

My mama and daddy even let me choose her name. She was going to be called Gabriella. I thought that was the most beautiful name in the whole world. I went clothes shopping for Gabriella with my mama and I picked out the tiniest and most beautiful clothes I could find, all sorts of pink, fluffy dresses and outfits. I didn't think that I could wait nine whole months until she was born! Nine months is an eternity to a five-year-old.

Well, finally the day came. I rode to the hospital with my grandma. We were both so excited! I chattered nonstop about how Gabriella and I were going to be inseparable.

When we got to the hospital, I wasn't allowed to go into the labor room, so I sat outside and waited, forever . . . it seemed. Finally my grandma came out. She was smiling from ear to ear. She said, "Tiffany, come and meet your brother, Christopher."

BROTHER!?! What!! I didn't want a brother—I was going to have a sister! They were just going to have to put him back because I didn't want any smelly little brother. I followed my grandma into a little room, crying because I didn't want to see him.

She placed him in my arms, and I looked at him. He had scrunched-up little blue eyes that were sparkling with happiness. His nose was perfectly rounded. He opened his mouth and stuck out his tiny pink tongue, tasting the air. *He was beautiful.* Then I knew, right when I looked into his eyes from heaven, that I loved him just as much as I would have loved Gabriella.

Thirteen years later, I still love Christopher with all my heart—even though he can be a pest sometimes. He has grown up to be tall and good-looking. At thirteen, he is becoming a young man. The best part? He looks up to me—just like I had wanted my little sister to.

Tiffany Clifton

The Big Slip

I was getting ready to walk out the door after my usual morning routine when my mother yelled for me to get out to the car—as she often had to do just to get me moving. I grabbed my book bag, threw on some shoes, and walked through the door to the garage with no idea what was going to happen that day.

The morning went off without a hitch: math class, English, social studies. Finally it was 11:30, time for lunch.

I went to my locker, grabbed my lunch, and walked to our gym/cafeteria with the rest of my friends. The lunchroom was always a mess when it was our turn, because we were the last ones in the school to eat—after the kindergarten through fifth-grade kids were done. We had a very small school and it was used as both a cafeteria and a gym. Dust and dirt often collected on the floor from students' shoes—not to mention spilled milk, drinks and dropped food.

I sat down at a table with my friends, ate my lunch and sat back to talk with them for the remainder of the lunch period. We got up when it was finally time for recess. During recess there was never anyone eating in the gym, so we had the option of using it. We started playing a game of half-court basketball.

The game was about halfway through, and my team had the lead. I was outside of the key, guarding an opponent, when he shot the ball over my head. I jumped to block but missed. Michael, a teammate, got the rebound and was immediately covered by Andrew. Seeing that I was open and that he had a clear passing lane, he threw the ball to the ground for a bounce pass. I remember the ball hitting the floor only to come back up and hit me in the chest. Then my memory just goes blank. Just like when you fall asleep. You never see it coming—it just happens and there is a gap of memory between that instant and when you wake up.

It turns out that I caught the ball, slipped and bounced on my head. Maybe it was the wet floor or the shoes I was wearing. But either way, I was headed to the hospital.

The next part of this story is a little sketchy because I don't remember it at all. What you are reading now is what I've heard from various sources. I was lying on the ground with blood coming out of my nose, and Jarred asked me, "Are you all right?" There was no reply. The lunch aides ran to my side as I suddenly sat up and began hitting away or waving my arms at anyone who came close to me. I said that I had a really bad headache and the aides suggested that I lie down on the couch in the teachers' lounge. Our principal came into the gym and started to ask me questions. When I hit her with my fist, she realized I wasn't myself and yelled for someone to call an ambulance.

The paramedics arrived and took me to St. Luke's. The doctors, noticing I was going to need an emergency CAT scan, called and told them to rush the person out to make it available for me. Such a call is uncommon. Usually they simply rush the patient up there, hoping it's open. They rushed me to the CAT scan and took the pictures of my brain. The doctors found that I had ruptured a blood vessel inside my skull. I was bleeding inside my head, and the growing amount of blood was applying a lot of pressure to my brain.

The doctors had to surgically relieve the pressure, so I was rushed to surgery where Dr. Shinko would operate. He told my mother that there was a 75 percent chance he could relieve the pressure. My father, who was away in Chicago on business, was frantically awaiting a flight home after hearing about what had happened to me. As I headed into surgery, I have a vague memory of saying to my mother, "Tell everyone that I love them."

Inside the operating room, I have another vague memory of about six people around me, very busy doing things. I remember yelling, "My head hurts like heck, my head hurts like heck!" Then a female nurse kindly said to me, "We're doing everything we can." That's where the memory ceases.

Dr. Shinko had to shave the side of my head to make a clean incision, which begins at the front side of my ear and ends about a centimeter away from my left eye. He cut through a lot of nerves, but he knew they would grow back. He was able to relieve the pressure and close the incision using staples instead of stitches. Then I was taken to a hospital room where the doctors and my parents awaited my awakening.

I remember slowly raising my eyelids. My eyes half open, I heard someone whispering, "He's awake." Then another person saying the same thing. I remember thinking, *What is going on?* There was a machine to my right displaying my heart rate and other information. To my left was an IV bag hanging on a rack. Sitting on a chair to my left was my mother and standing behind her was my father. I asked in a soft voice, "What happened?"

They explained what had happened, and they asked me if I remembered the basketball game. I remembered every detail of it—even who was on my team and who was on the opposing one—everything, that is, except the accident. I stayed in the hospital for about a week, really groggy most of the time. I did more sleeping than anything else.

I woke up one day to find my room showered with cards. A few of my friends visited me to tell me how all the girls cried after it happened. And they asked if I could play in our upcoming tournament basketball game. I knew I wouldn't be able to, no matter how much I wanted to.

After some more tests, I finally left the hospital in a wheelchair, all the while insisting I didn't need one. But I didn't get my way.

It was weird going to church the following Sunday and hearing my name on the sick list to be prayed for. My punishment, as I call it, was that I couldn't run for two months and worse, couldn't play contact sports for six months. It stunk having to be tied down like that, but I got through it.

Dr. Shinko say he fixxxed everythiiing but for ssomme eason me dont realllly belive himm.

Scott Allen, eleven

Confessions of a Four-Eyes

Assumptions allow the best in life to pass you by.

John Sales

I made it all the way to fifth grade before anyone (besides me) realized that I couldn't see twenty feet in front of me. Our school had vision screenings every year, but somehow I had managed to fake good vision and pass the tests.

But then in the fifth grade, I got busted. It was my turn to go into the screening room, and I nervously took my seat in front of the testing machine. The nurse told me to look into the little black machine and tell her which direction the letter E's legs were pointing. Barely able to make out the black blob of an E, I strung together a guess: "Right, left, left, up, down, up, left, right." I looked up at her.

She squinted her eyes and studied my face for a moment. Then she said, "Could you repeat that?"

I panicked. I'd never been asked to repeat it. And I

hadn't memorized the guess I'd just made up. I was trapped. So, I peered into the machine again and made up another sequence of guesses. I glanced over at the nurse, who was leaning forward with a stern frown on her face.

"You have no idea which way they're facing, do you?" she asked.

"Not really," I confessed.

"Can you even see the E at all?" she asked.

"Sort of . . . no," I admitted.

"Then why didn't you just say so?" she demanded.

I didn't respond. I thought the answer was obvious. Glasses in the fifth grade were a social death sentence. I assumed she knew this, but apparently it had been a very long time since she had been ten years old.

So, she sent me home with a note for my mother that said I needed to visit the optometrist because I'd failed the vision test. The trip home that day was very slow.

My mother (who wears glasses) said it would all be just fine. It wouldn't hurt a bit, she said. But I wasn't worried about pain—I was worried about looking like Super Geek.

The next day, my mother dragged me to the eye doctor's office, where I flunked with flying colors. I picked out a set of frames and tried to believe my mother when she said they looked really good on me. The doctor said the glasses would be ready soon. But I wasn't ready, and I didn't think I ever would be.

When the glasses arrived, the eye doctor put them on my face and walked me out onto the sidewalk in front of his office. When I looked up from my shoes, I was born into a whole new world—a world filled with crisp images, bold colors and sharp detail everywhere I looked. Suddenly I noticed the beautiful outline of crimson leaves on trees. I could see the details of people's faces long before they were standing right in front of me. I could see my mother smiling, as she watched me see the world in a whole new way.

"Glasses aren't so bad, are they?" Mom asked.

Not bad at all, I thought to myself. On that first day, they were a miracle.

Then Monday morning came, and I had to face the kids in my classroom. And it happened, just like I feared it would. A mean kid pointed at me in the middle of math class and yelled, "Four eyes!" But at that same moment, looking through my new glasses, I could see all the way across the room that the kid who had said it had an awfully big nose.

Life has a way of balancing itself out sometimes.

Gwen Rockwood

My Most Embarrassing Moment

You grow up the day you have your first real laugh at yourself.

Ethel Barrymore

My most embarrassing moment happened when I was sitting at a table with my friends eating lunch. My chair was sticking out into the aisle and a guy tried to squeeze through without asking me to move. He got stuck for a minute but then he moved on. Everyone started laughing at me, but I had no idea why. One of my friends pointed to my head, and I reached up and felt something gooey. The guy had been eating a cheese stick and when he tried to squeeze by me it ended up all over my hair. I rushed to the bathroom and washed it off in the sink with hand soap. I didn't hear the end of it for days afterwards. It also put me off cheese for quite a while.

Denise Ramsden, thirteen

Once when I was with my first boyfriend, we decided to go to the movies. I didn't bring any money with me because I thought that he was paying for me. When he didn't buy my ticket, I casually asked him to lend me five dollars. He told me that he didn't bring any more money and he sounded annoyed. I ended up calling my mom and asking her to come and pick me up! We broke up the next week.

Marissa Hromek, thirteen

At school in science class, I was the only girl in a group of all boys working on a project. They started bugging me, trying to find out who I liked. It was really annoying and I finally screamed out, "I love Weston!!!!" Everyone in the whole class heard me! Luckily, my crush was sick at the time.

Ashley Treffert, twelve

Our new neighbors moved in during the summer, and they had a very cute son. Our families became really close and so when his grandparents invited him on a boat ride, one of his friends and my sister and I were invited too. It would be my first time out in a private boat, and it was going to be with my new crush! I got everything ready so when the day came I would be looking great in my black and green bikini. I knew he would notice me then! It was a little cold so I brought a sweatshirt along. I figured that when it got warmer I could take it off and impress him with my bikini. We were just about to leave for the lake, when I stood up and the back of my bikini broke and my top fell off! I had to borrow a suit from his mom, one that was a little old-fashioned. When we finally got to the lake to go tubing I was really embarrassed because the whole time we were there my crush and his friend were teasing me about it. It didn't take me long to find out you can't impress someone when you are wearing their mom's old swimsuit! Uh, well . . . I'll get him next time.

Whitney Allen, thirteen

I walked right into a flagpole while walking to the bus at school. I was saying good-bye to my friend and when I turned around, I hit it. Everyone was laughing at me so I started laughing, too. I guess now I should listen when someone says to watch where you're walking.

Alyssa Calilap, thirteen

We were in gym class and we had to see how many pull-ups we could do. It was my turn, and my best friend, and our usual crowd of guy-friends, were waiting in line to go after I was done. As I did my pull-ups, my pants got slightly loose. I'm sure if my friend hadn't pointed it out, no one would have noticed. But she said, "Hey! Nice pink, polka-dotted undies! Am I right?" I just kept my trap shut, although that didn't keep the guys from laughing. I was utterly embarrassed.

Anne Jennings, eleven

When we got in from recess we went to sit in a circle. I started to fool around by trying to do a backwards somersault when I heard a RIP!!! When I looked around I couldn't see anything wrong. Then my friend tapped me on the shoulder and told me there was a big hole in the front of my jeans and I lied to him and said that I knew. I got up and went to the office. The secretary had a sweater that she wrapped around my waist to cover the hole. I had to go through the whole day from lunch to art with an extra big hole in the middle of my jeans!

Bradley McDermid, ten

My embarrassing moment is when I was at a festival with my cousin. We played a game and when we were finished we had to put it back in a closet. As it turned out, the sound system that was broadcasting the music and announcements all through the festival was in the closet. The music was on a stereo, which was being picked up by a microphone. While we were in the closet we were talking about stuff we didn't want our parents to hear. When we came out, my mom and my cousin's dad were coming toward us, and guess what? They were laughing! They told us that everyone at the festival heard us over the speakers. I was so embarrassed!

Emily Belcik, ten

My friend and I were sending notes to each other. She was asking me if the boy she liked was showing any "signs" of liking her as well. Since I didn't want to hurt her feelings or anything I said yes. Just then our teacher announced a policy that she would read any notes that were being sent. Then my teacher picked up the note and read it to the whole class! When the teacher was finished, the guy she liked asked us what "signs" meant. My friend was too embarrassed to speak and I had to blurt out that she liked him. To get back at me, she told my secret crush that I liked him. We couldn't help but wish we never existed!

Briana Euell-Pilgram, eleven

In fourth grade I wore my pants inside out and backwards and did not realize it until music class—my last class of the day.

Katie Driver, eleven

I had just put on my soccer shoes before leaving the library to go to practice.

I stepped outside and suddenly realized that I'd forgotten one of my books, so I trotted back toward the study table.

As I approached the table, my soccer shoes slipped on the hardwood floor and I felt myself starting to fall. Desperate to regain my balance, I kicked my feet out in front of me and swung my arms in windmill circles but it didn't help. My momentum was still carrying me forward as I fell—HARD—hitting the floor about ten feet away from the table. If I'd been in other clothes it might have ended there, but my bottom was covered in very slippery nylon soccer shorts. When I hit the floor, I just kept on going. Realizing that there was nothing more I could do, I closed my eyes.

In the next instant, I heard chairs scraping and books thudding onto the floor . . . then dead silence. When I opened my eyes, I was underneath the table. I wasn't hurt, but as I slowly climbed out from under the table, my eyes fell on a boy who had been sitting at another table.

He stared wide-eyed at me, looking shocked at what he'd just witnessed. But he also looked like he was in pain from trying hard not to laugh.

I couldn't walk away unnoticed—couldn't pretend it hadn't happened. I did the only thing I could think to do. I faced him, took a wide bow, and sang "Taah, daah!"

He collapsed onto his books laughing so hard he couldn't catch his breath. I heard myself laughing too, and instead of dying from embarrassment, in that moment I learned not to take myself so seriously. Sometimes you just have to laugh it off and move on. If all else fails, just take a bow.

Quinn Thomas

$\overline{6}$
ON CHANGES

In a world filled with changes each and every day
I feel like I'm judged for what I do and say
I remember back to Barbies and play days in the park
When I didn't worry about other people's remarks.

But looking in the mirror I see to my surprise
A completely different person staring deep into my
 eyes
The carefree little child I saw at four and five
Has now become a preteen learning to survive.

Alexandria Robinson, twelve

Silence

You can't turn back the clock. But you can wind it up again.

Bonnie Prudden

It hits like a tornado hits. And, just like the changes in the atmosphere that signal that there is a tornado on the way, there are signs in a home that a divorce is in the air. There is yelling, crying and arguments, but the worst is the silence. During the silence, even if you try to tell yourself it's not true, you know in your heart that your parents are drifting apart. Then, just like a tornado . . . after it's over you have to step back and inspect the damage.

The damage that hurt the most was not leaving my friends, school or home. The worst damage was that my parents didn't love each other the way that they did when they were first married, had their four kids, bought a home or sent each kid to their first day of school. Now it was a different love, a love that had been forced way over the line . . . a tie of love that started thinning out at a slow pace but rapidly became more strained through the years of their tense relationship. The tie finally broke and they got a divorce.

The first few months after the divorce were hard. My relationship with my dad totally changed. Right after the divorce, the calls started . . . calls from my siblings and me to my dad. After his usual questions like, "How is school?" and "How are your friends?" came the worst question . . . "How is your mom?" There would be this terrible silence that made me run to my room after each call, to cry my heart out for hours.

My whole life had suddenly changed with one word. *Divorce*. It was hard to start over. It was hard on us all— my brother, my two sisters and me, but especially for my mom. She still loved Dad, not the same as before, of course, but you have to have some remainder of love for a man you spent almost twenty-three years of your life with.

My dad tried to come to see us every month, but he worked on the railroad, and vacations and time off for him were scarce. I can remember how we would get excited when he said he could come and see us, and be so disappointed when he would have to cancel if someone at his work got sick and he had to cover for them. I never told anyone . . . but I was a little glad when he had to cancel. I wouldn't have to deal with the awkward conversations . . . and the silence.

Then my mom met someone. His name is Shawn. At times I hated him when they first started dating. I had been secretly hoping that somehow my parents could get back together again, and things would be like they were before . . . when we were happy. Shawn became the reason why that would never happen . . . and I resented him for that.

It has taken a while, but now I see that Shawn is a good man. He was the one who took in a woman with four kids and never complained. At first, my dad hated Shawn and constantly reminded us kids that he still loved our mom. But now, after three years, my dad has released his grip and moved on just like my mom did. It's amazing, but my dad now works for my stepdad, so we get to see him more than we used to. He often eats supper with all of us. I think the silence has slowly turned into a new life for us all and we are finally happy again.

Elisabeth Copeland, thirteen

The Best Brother
in the Whole Wide World

A brother is a friend provided by nature.

Legouve Pere

In your life, a lot of people will come and go. Friends betray you, pets die and parents get divorced. But in my life, one person I've always remembered being there for me is my brother, Bear.

Bear was seven years old when I was born. That's a pretty big age gap, and anyone would think that we wouldn't be close. But we were. When I was five years old, my parents got a divorce and we both had to deal with a hard change. My mother remarried a sergeant in the Army, so we moved to Fort Bragg, North Carolina. Even at the age of six, I was very, very upset. I cried a lot, I had a hard time fitting in at my new school, and the quarrelling between my parents had discouraged me. But Bear made me feel safe and accepted.

During that summer, we would play together: trap insects, watch *Blues Clues* and do all sorts of crazy, mischievous stuff that normal brothers and sisters should do. Even though my brother was fourteen and I was only going on seven, we had the best time hanging out together. But, as time went by, things started to change.

Bear began to lose interest in playing with me—or spending time with the rest of the family, for that matter—and started to do normal "teenage" things . . . hang around girls, head-bang to rock music and tack posters of girls on his walls. Oh, yeah, and he spoke to me every once in awhile. But I missed the way we used to spend time together. I found myself missing him *a lot*— and we were living in the same house!

The trends changed, and so did he. He started to get into rap music and wanted so much to fit in. He laughed out loud at the thought of ever watching *Blues Clues* with me, and he was too busy socializing to even think about making me laugh the way he used to, or trapping insects, going on expeditions or bike rides. I felt lonely again.

I wasn't sure if things took a turn for the worse or the better when I received some news one day in July. I was coming home from my dad's house. My mom picked me up at our meeting place, and then she told me what had been going on since I'd been gone. What she said shocked me: Bear and his girlfriend, Elizabeth Anne, were going to get married.

All sorts of things raced through my mind. *Bear was only eighteen. He was my brother—brothers aren't supposed to get married! Did this mean that I would never see Bear again? Would he pull away from me permanently? Would he be too busy with his new family to even remember me?* While I was excited, I was also worried.

Bear, who was then working at a restaurant buffet down the street, had nowhere to turn for a career. He didn't want to go to college, so he joined the Army. Now it was my mother's turn to worry. Bear was gone, in Fort Knox, Kentucky, in basic training for almost three months until Christmas. I wrote him whenever I got the chance, and he wrote me back a couple of times. He was gone for another two months and then went to Alabama until April. Then more shocking news came: Bear was assigned to a military base in Hawaii!

In April, Bear and Elizabeth Anne got married. The wedding was very small, and I was the only bridesmaid. I wore a purple dress and almost cried when I watched Bear making his vows, giving himself away. When the wedding was over, I could not hold it in any longer. I broke down and bawled.

My brother acted shocked when he found me crying. He asked me why, and I just shook my head. I knew the reason—I would miss him *so much* but I could never tell him that. Even though I hadn't said a word, he understood. I threw my arms around him and hugged him very tight. He hugged back, and we stood there for a moment thinking about everything, until finally he broke away. He stood there looking at me and smiled. I was so proud of him at that moment, in his Army greens, smiling that same mischievous smile that he never outgrew. I looked at him and wondered for the final time if our relationship would ever suffer. *Would he neglect me again, this time for his new family? Would he forget about me? Would he ever begin to comprehend how much I would miss him?*

And then, as I hugged him one last time before he left for Hawaii, I rested my head on his shoulder and smiled. Because standing there with him, I knew the truth. A lot of people will come and go in my life, but no one else will ever be the best brother in the whole world to me . . . except Bear.

Katie Beauchamp, thirteen

[EDITORS' NOTE: *As* Chicken Soup for the Preteen Soul 2 *goes to press, the best brother in the world, Bear, is serving our country, stationed in Iraq.*]

Moving On

If we don't change, we don't grow. If we don't grow, we aren't really living.

Gail Sheehy

It was an early November morning when we said our final good-byes and pulled out of my grandparents' driveway. I was leaving my lifelong home in Wisconsin and heading to our new home in Arizona. Crying as I waved good-bye, I thought about all of the memories I was leaving behind. I already missed my friends and family and we hadn't even reached the main highway. They had been everything to me. I simply had no idea how I was going to survive without them. I knew this would probably be one of the most difficult journeys of my life.

For the next four days, we drove and drove and drove until, finally, we pulled into the driveway of our new home in Arizona. I was surprised to see that all of the houses in our neighborhood were the same and that there was barely any grass in the yards. When we got into the house, everyone chose their new bedroom. That part was pretty exciting.

Over the next few days we unpacked and moved in. About a week later, my brother, Nick, and I started school. When we got home and compared notes, we discovered that we both hated it there. Especially me. I had just started going to middle school in Wisconsin, and now I was going back to elementary school because there were no middle schools in my city. It was really awkward, and I felt like I didn't fit in. At first, my brother and I were totally depressed, but we pressed on and tried to adjust, and over time it got better.

I was too shy to ask anyone to come over to my house, so I just waited until someone invited me over to their house. Finally, one day, a girl in my class asked if I could come to her sleepover birthday party. I was so excited, I couldn't wait to finally go somewhere other than my house.

The night before the party, I went to bed early so I wouldn't be tired the next night. Well, around 1:00 A.M., I woke up to get a drink. When I opened my door, all of the lights in my house were on. I thought that was kind of weird, so I checked my clock again to see if I had slept into the afternoon. It definitely said 1:00 A.M., so I went to my parents' bedroom and found my mom packing clothes into a suitcase.

"Mom, what's going on?" I asked. She motioned for me to sit on her bed. Then she told me the worst news I had heard since we moved. My great-grandmother, who had leukemia, was in the hospital. My mom said that she didn't have much longer to live.

My family and I were always *very* close to my great-grandma, so in our minds, there was only one option for us. That same morning, my brother, Mom and I got on an airplane and flew back to Wisconsin. Sadly, we got there too late. Great-grandma had died that morning at 9:30. So, we stayed in Wisconsin and attended her funeral and visited our friends. I was really sad about the death of my great-grandma, but I was also happy that I was able to visit everyone that I had missed so much.

Well, after ten days, it was time for us to go back to Arizona. I was so sad on the plane ride home, I tried really hard to hold back tears. I missed my friends and family, but most of all, I missed my great-grandma. I never even got to say good-bye to her, and that hurt.

When we finally got back home, I became really depressed again. I cried almost every night. Every weekend, I'd talk to my friends on our cell phone. They were always talking about how much fun they were having and how they wished I was there with them. Every time I would even think about my friends, I'd get so sad that it felt like someone had ripped my heart out and stomped on it. I missed them all so badly.

Over the next few months, I realized that I couldn't have my old life back, no matter how badly I wanted things to be the way they had been. Realizing this, I gained a lot of courage, and I started to go up to people and talk to them, and I actually made a lot of new friends.

Now, almost a year later, I am a lot happier than I was when we first moved. I feel a lot better now, and I have a lot of friends. I still miss my friends and family, and I would much rather move back to Wisconsin than stay here, but I know we can't.

I learned a lot over the past year. I'm a lot less shy and a lot stronger now. I realized that when I moved, I wasn't leaving my memories behind; I would just treasure them now more than ever before.

Ellen Werle, twelve

My Problem

I wish they would only take me as I am.

Vincent Van Gogh

I'm an eleven-year-old, overweight boy. I have felt down in the dumps, felt bad about myself, felt left out and confused at one time or another over the past four years.

I've been overweight since I was three years old. My mom, dad, brother and sisters all worked at different times, and they didn't realize that when they came home and ate at different times, I would eat with each one of them. No one realized what it was doing to me until I was overweight.

When I started school, the kids made fun of me. They called me "fatso," and "fatty, fatty, four by four." This made me feel sad, mad and upset. Sometimes I wanted to hit them and tell them to leave me alone. Instead, I would walk away, and at times, I would go home and cry with my mom. I never let anyone know this because they would have just teased me for it instead of realizing how much I was hurting.

In sports, I was always picked last, making me feel like I couldn't do as well as the other kids. This, I believe, is part of the reason I don't enjoy sports very much.

When I was eight, my mom and I joined TOPS (Take Off Pounds Sensibly), a weight-loss support group. Since I've been in TOPS, I've learned to exercise and to count calories. While I was in TOPS, I became a Division winner for weight loss for my age group. I was proud to be on stage for this, especially knowing part of my TOPS group was there to support me. I've also learned how great it is to have my family support my efforts, as well. I try to give the same support either by talking to someone who has weight issues or by giving hugs to people who need them.

I now set small goals for myself, and one by one, I find that they are easier to achieve than really big ones. They all add up to a bigger change in my weight eventually. Seeing the success as I go also has helped me to believe in myself more than ever before.

Still, following new ways of healthy eating can be really tough. Sometimes I just want to eat everything in sight. It's hard when we go out to eat or go to functions where there is food. I know I can have some of whatever I want, I just need to watch how much I eat of it. Sometimes it doesn't seem fair being a kid and having to think about this!

I think because of what I've been though, I am more aware of how a person with disabilities feels. I try to help others and talk to them in a way that shows them respect. I never want to hurt anyone's feelings the way mine have been hurt.

My family and TOPS friends have taught me to treat people with respect. If I could say anything to people who make fun of others, it would be not to just look at the outside of a person. You should get to know them on the inside—get to know them for who and what they are.

Also remember, if you can't say something nice about someone, don't say anything at all. I might laugh at your joke about my weight, but inside . . . I might be crying.

Allen Smith, eleven

[EDITORS' NOTE: *For more information regarding weight issues, log on to* www.kidshealth.org *(key word search: "weight").*]

Waiting for Katie

Time is the wisest of all counselors.

Plutarch

My sister, Katie, has always been there for me, and I look up to her. She has been my hero. She has always been beautiful and kind to everyone and everything.

Two summers ago, I went off to camp knowing that my sister was sick. I knew something was wrong. She was too skinny. Two shrimp, three carrots and maybe an apple were her daily food intake. My mom, dad, brother and I told her that she needed more food to keep herself alive. She didn't listen to us, though, so I yelled and screamed at her out of love, not hatred. My parents did the same. My parents threatened to take away the number one thing that she loved: horseback riding.

When I came home from camp, sure enough, she was in the hospital. I went to visit her and give her the things that I had made for her at camp. That's when I noticed that something was really different about her. She wasn't nice to me anymore. She never opened up enough to try to help me understand what caused her to end up in the hospital. She never allowed me to help her by having honest, heart-to-heart talks.

My friends would always talk about how they went out shopping with their sisters, but that was out of the question for my sister and me. I felt ripped off by life. *Why did my sister have to get sick?* I'd think. *Doesn't she realize how much I love her and hate to see her so skinny and in the hospital?*

Sadly, I decided that she wasn't my hero anymore. She had ruined her body, and that wasn't anything I could look up to. I no longer envied her like I used to.

When she finally got out of the hospital, I thought that things would be better from then on, and that our relationship would bounce back. But boy, was *I* wrong. Every Thursday, I would tremble with fear knowing that she had clinic. I constantly wondered, *Will I see her when I get home from school, or will she be back in the hospital?* Then there was my mom who spent endless hours seeing that my sister got her every need met. It was hard to see her put so much love and energy out, only to have my sister continue to struggle. I wondered what our lives would be like if Katie wasn't anorexic. *Would there still be the horrible fights? Would my brother still have gone to boarding school?* I'd cry myself to sleep at night and worry about her so much that I couldn't think during my classes.

Then there was the fighting when I'd get home. It was unbearable. All I wanted to do was get away. Sometimes I would take long walks until my mom and sister were finished fighting. The anger bounced back and forth. When my sister would cry, I'd start with the tears, too. No matter what we've been through, we will always have a bond and a history, and I will love her—no matter what.

Eventually, I will adore my sister the way I used to. I

will look up to her and we will even go shopping together—but only when she gets better. It might take a long time to get there, but I will be here, waiting for her.

Erin Shirreff, twelve

[EDITORS' NOTE: *For more information about eating disorders, log on to* www.kidshealth.org *(key word search: "eating disorders").*]

©Reprinted with special permission of King Features Syndicate.

Bad Hair Day

As the Santa Ana winds blew in the fall, I started fifth grade at a new school in a new town. My parents had divorced a few months earlier. I was both excited and bewildered as I entered the classroom in my plaid jumper and crisp, white short-sleeved blouse tucked neatly inside. This would be my uniform for the year. My last school was public; this school was private and Catholic, complete with a nun standing at the blackboard. She was actually very nice, and I honestly felt she wanted me to fit in as she introduced me to the class.

"Class, I'd like you all to welcome Kerry." Quick whispers from a few kids buzzed in my ears while she was talking, and through the corner of my eye I noticed a couple of girls passing a note near the back of the class-room. Overall, the kids didn't look too mean.

The one saving grace about moving here was that we were living in the beach town where my sister and I had spent occasional weekends when Mom wanted to get away. Now that the divorce was final, we would be here permanently. So, no matter how bad school might turn out to be, I could look forward to playing in the ocean after school, on weekends and holidays.

By late November, I had done all right, made a few new friends and even found a love note on my desk from the cutest boy in class. The schoolwork was hard; I just managed to keep up. However, I excelled in volleyball. I met a girl, Janie, who laughed a lot and we became instant friends—best friends, eventually. We both loved volleyball, the beach and boys.

Christmas vacation was the best. I was so happy that Christmas vacation came a week earlier and lasted five days longer than at public school. I spent the entire two weeks with my older sister, Mary, at the beach, while our mom worked at her new job.

The one thing my sister was responsible for during that vacation was me. The one thing she forgot to remind me to do every day was to brush my hair. My hair was long, to the middle of my back, straight as a board, brown and streaked by the sun. By the end of vacation, a large rat's nest of matted hair had formed at the base of my neck. This thing was huge, I'm talkin' honkin', humongous.

When Mary discovered it, sheer panic set in. School would be starting back up the next morning, so she had to do something. She carefully picked at it with a comb, but soon realized that it would take about a year to undo the knot that way. So, she held the whole knot as tightly as she could and then yanked at it with a brush. No progress appeared to be made, so she tried hiding the knot by brushing some hair from the side of my head over it. My head was beginning to throb when I suggested we use peanut butter. "It takes gum out," I reminded her.

After that failed, she came up with one last, desperate idea—cut it.

At this point, I just wanted to get it out. My sister

searched the house for scissors; Mom was due home at any moment. "Ah ha!" she yelled, signaling her victory. She sat me down on a chair and said she would have to cut it pretty short because the knot was so honkin'. Then the cutting began. When she'd cut my hair halfway around my head I noticed she was using Mom's pinking shears, which have a zigzag pattern on the blades. At that very moment, the door flew open and Mom zoomed in on us. I'll never forget the look of horror in her eyes as she yelled, "What in God's name are you two doing?"

The last thing you want to do after your mother gets a divorce is upset her in any way. Too late. Now, not only was my hair a jagged mess, to make matters worse, my sister was grounded for a week. After my mother cried and brought out pictures of my long hair in braids, she had an idea. Early the next morning, she'd fix it. But overnight my hair went into total shock and was standing on end with static electricity. My mother stared at me.

"This will look so cute," she said. "Sort of like Betty Boop."

Oh great, I thought. *I'm ten—not four!*

First she had to even up the cut, which took it up to my ears. Then she greased the little bit of hair I had left to my head and plastered curls along my face, framing it . . . just like Betty Boop. Like I said, I didn't want to upset her, so I smiled at her when she dropped me at school that morning.

I had a sickening feeling as I walked into the classroom. The entire class stared; some kids dropped their jaws, others immediately gathered and whispered with friends. I took my seat with burning hot ears (my ears always burn when I get embarrassed). I lasted for three, maybe four seconds before leaping up and running out of the classroom and down the hall. I sat crying in the corner of the girls' bathroom, vowing never to leave.

Ten minutes or so passed before our teacher, Sister Ursula, showed up and sat in the corner with me. She held my hand and told me it didn't matter what my hair looked like, that true friends will like you for you, not your hair. She went on to say, "It's not what we look like on the outside that's important. It's what's on the inside that matters. When things like this happen to your hair, which *is* a little shocking," she added, "it becomes like a test to see who your real friends are."

That made sense to me and the "shocking" part also made me laugh, so I told her the whole story. We must have sat there on the cold concrete floor for forty-five minutes talking before I decided that I would leave the girls' bathroom.

When we returned to the classroom, Janie came by my desk and tried to say something comforting, but laughed and snorted instead. Other kids told me that my hair looked nice, which made me feel a little better, even though I found out later the principal had been there lecturing them about "putting themselves in my shoes." Later someone passed me a note that read, "Don't worry, it will grow back."

I think it was from the cutest boy in the class.

Kerry Germain

Get Over It and Go On

The ideal man bears the accidents of life with dignity and grace, making the best of circumstances.

Aristotle

I was a ten-year-old girl who loved to wrestle, build tree forts in the woods by my house and spend time with my friends—just like I had done on the night that my life changed. We were on our way home from my sister's birthday skating party, and my seven-year-old sister, Tiffany, and I were both exhausted after skating all night, so we were asleep in the back seat of the car.

I awoke to find myself in the hospital. At that moment, all of our lives were already changed. I just didn't fully realize to what extent things would be different. I soon learned that I had broken my back, which had damaged my spinal cord. I would spend the rest of my life in a wheelchair. My sister, who had two broken legs and a broken arm, would end up in foster care and become

separated from me. Mom had some broken bones, but that was mild compared with what would happen to her.
  Why?
Because she had been drinking and driving. The police figured that she fell asleep at the wheel and then crashed head-on into a tree while going about 75 miles per hour.

During the time that I was recovering in the hospital, my mom was convicted of drunk driving and child endangerment. They gave her a sentence of three years in prison and she lost her parental rights to us. This news hit me really hard. The courts decided to find my dad so that he could care for us girls, but that didn't go well. My dad was also on his way to prison after lots of problems with the law. He was sentenced to something like twenty-five years, so he wasn't able to do anything but give up his parental rights, as well.

So after the accident, my sister and I never went to live at home again. After five months of being in the hospital, I went to live in foster care with a nice couple who were already caring for my sister. Things were fine there, but one day, my sister and I were sent to live with a lady named Paula. Things were all right there for a little while, but then we were split up and my sister went to live with another family. At first, I wasn't that sad about it, maybe because I had so much to deal with after the accident, but I really began to miss my sister. I wonder about her all the time. I wish so much that we could grow up together, but the accident changed all that.

One day, Paula told me that she knew of a family that might want to adopt me. I said that I would meet them and see what they were like. So, I met the family—Sue and Chris and their two sons, Daniel and Josh, and I liked them a lot. I guess they liked me, because they adopted me.

I had to adjust to having two brothers, which was very different for me because I had never had a brother, let alone two. They act like typical boys and pester me sometimes, but overall, they're pretty nice.

My adopted mom, Sue, is a nurse, and she encouraged me to try physical therapy to see if I could learn to walk again. But after struggling with crutches and trying as hard as I could, it didn't work out. That's when I realized that I had a choice to make. I could put all my interests that involved physical activity aside and forget about them, or I could try doing what I could from a wheelchair.

After looking around for something that I'd like to be involved in, I found out about a wheelchair basketball team for nine- to eighteen-year-olds in our area. I tried out and I made the team! I'm proud to say that we have been number one in the nation for our age group for the past two years. We get to fly to tournaments in different states where we play against several teams over a weekend. That's the best part of all—traveling and seeing other places. I like meeting new people, too. Every summer now, I also go to two out-of-state basketball camps. The instructors are always really cool and usually teach us some pretty tricky maneuvers. Getting involved in something so much fun and so rewarding has shown me that things are possible, no matter what your situation is.

Just when my life began to level out and get better, my adoptive parents got a divorce, so now I live with my adoptive mom, two brothers and my biological sister. I sometimes wonder what things would have been like if my birth mom hadn't driven drunk and crashed that night. I can wonder all I want, but I guess it doesn't matter, 'cause I'll never know. I just know that life keeps changing, but we have to go on anyway—with or without some of the people that we love. Sometimes, we just don't have a choice. It's definitely not fair, but that's life. You can't let things get you down, because it gets you nowhere to sulk and feel sorry for yourself.

I know some people might get depressed if they had my life, but the way I see it, it's like, what's the point?

You just have to get over it and go on.

Christina Zucal, twelve

The Board

They won't last long, school days and childish things.
We're moving up, going our separate ways.
Enjoy your future, all the changes and shifts.
And remember these years were precious gifts.

Maria Lamblin

"We were the cutest babies in the world!" I smiled as I put up the picture of me riding a horse and pretending I could fly.

"I know, look at this one!" Rachel pointed to a picture of us at age five, dressed up in our mothers' clothing and wearing so much makeup that you could hardly see our skin. We both giggled and shook our heads. We couldn't believe that we would be graduating in a week.

As a way of celebrating our childhoods, we had been asked to bring in pictures of ourselves growing up. The board took up the space between the eighth-grade classroom and the bathrooms, and every square inch was now covered with pictures. As I looked from photo to photo, from kindergarteners to fourth-graders to sixth-graders, I began to look at my classmates around me.

First I looked at Rachel, and I remembered the first day of school. I was a scared little five-year-old, clinging to my mother for dear life. Then the unimaginable happened, she left me—she just set me down and *left* me! Having been abandoned by my mother in a room filled with books and crayons, I didn't know what else to do but cry. I was so busy crying that I didn't notice the twenty other kids around me that had been left to a similar fate. Then I felt a hand on my shoulder. Expecting to see the scary woman who would be in charge of us each morning, I turned around and saw Rachel. Her hair was darker than midnight, and her skin had a beautiful olive tone. But what was most beautiful about Rachel was her voice. It was the kind of voice that made you just want to listen for hours. It was the kind that was meant for the radio, the kind that captured people's attention. Even in kinder-garten, her voice captivated me, and the first words she spoke remain in my mind. "Why are you crying?"

"My mommy left me," I sobbed.

"What's your name?" she asked with confidence.

"Sarah," came my soggy reply.

"Well, Sarah, wanna play Chutes and Ladders?"

That got my attention. I loved board games. I started to play and after a few minutes I wasn't crying anymore, I was actually enjoying myself so much, that I cried when it was time to leave.

I looked back at the board and my eyes landed on a picture of TJ. TJ lives right next to me, and we have always been close. I was a bit of a tomboy until about fourth grade and I remember how much fun I had playing with the boys, and how it wouldn't have been allowed if it weren't for TJ.

"C'mon, she's a girl—she'll make you play Barbies or

somethin'," one of the boys on our block had said to TJ.

"Let's go, TJ," I said. I turned and started to walk away, tears welling up in my eyes, when I heard TJ answer the other boy.

"Nuh-uh, I wanna play with Sarah. She's more fun than you anyway. We're gonna play basketball."

After that day, people started to join our basketball games; first just a few boys brave enough to get beaten by a girl, but pretty soon we had the whole neighborhood on the court. And you know what? I was beating all of them.

"Sarah, Sarah! Earth to Sarah!" I snapped out of my daydream to see Rachel waving her hand in front of my face. "Why are you crying?" she asked, just as she had on that first day. I felt my face, and sure enough, there was a tear rolling down my cheek. Pretty soon, I was pouring out my heart and soul and my face was damp with tears. I was thinking about the million memories that I had collected over the past nine years, and how I was leaving. I was leaving this school. High school would be different. I was afraid that we weren't going to be as close. I couldn't imagine how that would feel, and I didn't even want to.

When I told Rachel this, she just smiled. "We are growing up. We may make new friends, but we will still have each other always."

She always knew what to say.

As I stood up to leave, I looked at the board once more and noticed how, in every picture, each of us were at different points of our lives, but we were always smiling. We were all okay, even through all the changes. We had grown up in those pictures, as we were growing up in real life.

I took one last sniffle and a deep breath.

I was finally ready for high school.

Sarah Kessler, thirteen

7

BUSTIN' DOWN WALLS

I did not struggle as invisible hands pulled me down.
I just waited for someone else to pull me out.
I wondered why no one did.
Finally, I realized others were reaching
They just couldn't reach far enough.
And no rope was long enough for me to grab.
So with all my strength, I started to climb the
* mountain.*
Because I began to realize that I was the only one
With a rope long enough to pull me out.

Jennifer Lynn Clay, fourteen

To a Different Drummer

*If a man does not keep pace with his compan-
ions, perhaps it is because he hears a different
drummer. Let him step to the music which he
hears, however measured or far away.*

Henry David Thoreau

"Come on—put up your hands and fight!"

I groaned. *Why was this happening to me?* My mother had
said, "No fighting," right before I left the house. After coming from London, England, to Kitchener, Canada, to live
with her, I was starting a new life. During recess, this kid
wanted to scrap with me, and now it looked like I
wouldn't even be able to get through my first day of
school and keep my promise to my mum.

"Naw," I replied.

"You're just chicken," he yelled. "Is that it? Are you
chicken?" The kid's red hair blazed in the winter sun and
his freckles seemed to jump out of his pale skin. At twelve,

I was tall for my age, but I was kind of skinny and lanky. He was taller than me, and with his heavy parka on, he looked heavier than me, too.

"No. I'm not chicken. My mother just told me to stay out of trouble."

"I don't care . . . I want to fight with you, anyway." He pushed me in my chest. Then he put up his hands. "Come on!"

So, I hit him. Down he went into the snow. Other kids on the playground started to circle around us. He got up. He put up his hands—and I hit him again. He went down for a second time. All the kids were yelling, "Fight! Fight!" This time, I kept my hands up just in case someone else in the circle of kids wanted a taste of me, too. I waited, and the kid got back up again.

He walked toward me, stuck out his hand and said, "Shake. I just wanted to see how tough you are. Wanna be friends?"

I heaved a sigh of relief and shook hands with him. I figured that I would need a friend. The snow, strange country, new school, the way that people spoke—different from my London street slang—and being the only black kid for miles around, all of this added up to being a weird new world for me.

I was born in London, England, and lived there with my mother until I was about eight years old. My mum wanted to find a better life for us, so she went to Chicago, in the United States. She left me with friends in London until she got settled enough to send for me. Mum ended up not staying in Chicago but moved to a small town in Canada because she had a friend there who helped her get a good job.

Meanwhile, back in England, I was getting into trouble. I had always felt like an outsider, different from the other kids. They didn't want to play with me. That made me mad, so I got into fights and ended up getting expelled for being a danger to the other kids at my school. The people I was staying with were upset with me and felt they couldn't manage me. So, after living with them for almost two years, they sent me to a home for kids—kind of a boarding school. I lived there for a year. I felt alone and bored, the food was gross, and I really missed my mother. Finally, she sent for me.

My mum met me at the airport in Toronto with a smile on her face, a warm hug and huge parka to put on. When we went outside the airport, there was snow all over the ground, the cars—everything! I didn't know what it was. I asked my mum, "What is this?" I touched the snow and was amazed by how cold and fluffy it was. It was different from anything I had ever seen before.

The weather was different, my school was different, the country was different, but some things were still the same—I was still getting into fights. Other kids picked on me about my accent, the color of my skin, my grades or whatever. I was different, still left out. It didn't matter; I hated getting picked on, and I let them know it—with my fists. All through grades seven and eight, I was sent to the principal's office so often that he and I became friends. Instead of punishing me, he would counsel me. He told me that I would be better off using the energy I had in more positive ways and encouraged me to play football and basketball after school. He also suggested that I check out boxing—maybe I could learn to use my fists in a constructive way instead of being on the destructive path I seemed to be headed for.

Even though I was an outsider and a loner, I liked going to school dances. At one of the dances, some of the guys wanted to fight a group of guys from another school. We agreed to meet them on neutral ground—the police boxing gym downtown. We showed up, but they didn't.

While we were hanging around waiting for them, one of the boxing trainers called out to me, "You, come over here."

I walked over to him and he asked me, "Do you want to go a few rounds with him?" He pointed to a guy getting into one of the rings. I was pretty full of myself and figured I could take him because he was small, so I said, "Sure, why not?"

I just couldn't hit the guy. He danced all around me while I tried to hit him. Then that little guy really connected with my nose. Not only did that make my eyes water, but it bruised my ego and made me realize that there was more to the sport of boxing than just swinging my fists. The coach put me into the ring with another fighter who was about my size, and I did pretty well. That was a moment of decision in my life. I remembered what my middle school principal had told me and everything clicked. The boxing ring was where I belonged.

All through high school, I played football, basketball and soccer, and I was on the track team. But from that day on, boxing was the sport that I liked the most. Because it's an individual sport, it's more challenging and exciting to me. I found that I enjoyed the thrill of one-on-one competition. I also liked the fact that it was up to me whether I won or lost—that I was the determining factor. I think I've always been a competitor, and winning would give me a glow of satisfaction and a good feeling about myself. There was always a bad feeling if I lost, and I didn't like that. I wanted to win—every time.

I started training with the man who got me into the ring that first time. He became my boxing coach, friend, mentor and a father figure for me to look up to. I learned that boxing is a sweet science where I could use my brain as well as my strength and size. I used my ability to focus under pressure. Under his training, I went from being a street fighter to a gold medal-winning Olympic champion.

Though I was basically an outsider, even as a little boy I wanted to be first in whatever I set my mind to. Once I went professional, I worked hard and got what I wanted. I have earned millions, but for me, it's not just about the money. I made my dreams come true. I did it my way. I stayed away from bad promoters and bad managers and upheld my integrity. Throughout my career, I have gained, regained and retained the WBC and IBF heavyweight belts, the most prestigious in the boxing world. I want my place in history, and I know I will have it.

A couple of years ago, I was given the title, Member of the Order of the British Empire, an honorary title bestowed by Queen Elizabeth II for distinguished achievement. I have come a long way from being a brawling London street kid to the man I am today—the man that my mum raised me to be.

Lennox Lewis
Undisputed WBC Heavyweight Champion of the World

Life Rolls On

In three words I can sum up everything I've learned about life. It goes on.

Robert Frost

I was about nine the first time I got on a board. Something inside of me connected to surfing unlike any other sport. I had played a bunch of different sports, like baseball, soccer and hockey, but surfing became my true life passion. I never regretted walking away from all other sports in the pursuit of surfing.

By the time I was eleven or twelve, I began to compete in surfing. Before long, I was rated number one in the Juniors level of the Pacific Surf Series. I was featured in surfing articles and magazines, and companies began sponsoring me.

I began traveling to surfing competitions to some of the most beautiful places in the world. Things were really looking up. My lifelong dream of becoming a professional surfer was finally on the verge of becoming a reality. Then came the day when my life changed forever.

I woke up like on any other day. I watched a little bit of a surf movie to pump myself up for my surf session. I was excited; the waves were going to be so good. I called my friends. When I pulled up to the beach at Zuma, the waves looked great. I put my wetsuit on and surfed for a while; then I caught this one perfect south swell peak. I stood up backside and pulled in the barrel. As I came out of the tube, the wave hit me in my back so fast that I didn't have time to put my hands up. I hit my head on a sandbar beneath the surface of the water. My whole body went numb and tingly, then I was floating face down—unable to move. When the next wave flipped me over, I yelled for help. At first nobody came to help me, then finally my best friend, Brad, came over to me. I told him, "You gotta keep my head out of the water or I'm gonna drown!"

With the help of another friend, Brett, Brad was able to get me out of the water and onto the beach. I *knew* I was paralyzed. As I lay on my back, my dreams of becoming a pro surfer, of having a wife and kids, and my hopes of being in a big surf movie flashed in front of my eyes. *What was going to happen to me? What kind of a life would I have if I was paralyzed forever? This can't happen to me!* Guess what? It did.

I was taken by helicopter to UCLA Medical Center where it was determined that I had suffered a severe spinal cord injury, just like Christopher Reeve. With the flip of a wave, I had become a quadriplegic with no sensation or movement below my mid-chest. In that split second, my surfing days as I had known them were over. With only limited use of my arms and hands, I spent most of my time in intensive care units and rehab hospitals instead of in the water surfing. My worst nightmare had come true, and I was forced to deal with it.

As bad as it was, and it was very bad sometimes, I

surprised myself by maintaining the will to live. I can't really say what made me go from not wanting to live if I couldn't surf—to embracing life without surfing—but by some miracle, it happened. Instead of being angry or afraid, I realized how fortunate I had been the first seventeen years of my life. I realized that I was still better off and more fortunate than some others. I had surfed the world—more than many could ever say.

That fall, I returned to school. I was elected Homecoming King, which was pretty cool, and ended up graduating on time. Shortly after my high school graduation, I enrolled at San Diego State University, stayed as busy as I was before the accident and graduated. I've got to say that I'm living my life to the fullest.

Every year, I speak to thousands of students in schools across the country. I really want kids to know that dreams can change and life can turn out different from what we sometimes expect. At the start of an assembly, I show a video of me surfing in competitions, rippin' on the waves and everything. They expect to see this high-profile surfer coming to speak to them, and then I come out in a wheelchair. They just don't anticipate that at all. I talk about the fact that my life has really just begun. I explain to them about the importance of family and friends. I tell them about how, since the accident, I've gone out on wave runners, gone waterskiing and inner tubing, played wheelchair tennis and ping pong, competed in a billiards tournament—playing pool with the best of them—and have even jumped out of an airplane skydiving!

I've traveled to places like Australia, France, Mexico, Spain, Italy and all over the United States. So many people have gotten behind me. Celebrities have helped me raise public awareness of the need to find a cure for spinal injuries, and I've also hung out with some very cool, great musicians.

But the highlight of my life since my injury came nearly four years after that fateful day. It took surfers like world champions Rob Machado, Kelly Slater and my brother Josh, and the guys from the Paskowitz Surfing Camp to figure out just how to get me back on a board again—and they did it.

I finally got back in the water that I had missed so much—on a surfboard. They rigged a board so that I could hold on to something and ride the waves. I ride lying down, more like a body boarder would, but hey, it's still surfing to me. It's different—but I'm in the water.

Some people kind of freak out, thinking about me out in the water surfing again, but I don't even think about the danger. I've got a lot of trust in my abilities and the people around me. I make my own path, my own decisions. I'm the last one who wants to get hurt. Still, if it weren't for the help of my buds, I might not have ever had the chance to get back out there. I don't know of another quadriplegic in the world who surfs.

I believe that someday I'll regain some use of my paralyzed limbs. It is no longer a question of if, but *when*. I'll be ready, when the time comes, to take advantage of the breakthroughs in modern medicine. I know I'll never achieve my dream of being the world's greatest surfer, but dreams are abundant. I still have so many that are just as worthy and exciting—so many dreams that I have yet to achieve. I know that I've got a lot of living left to do. Life rolls on, waves continue to roll on and I'm rollin' and surfing right along with it all.

Jesse Billauer

[EDITORS' NOTE: *To find out more about Jesse and his organization, Life Rolls On, log on to* www.liferollson.org.]

Kindness Is More Powerful

As the sun makes ice melt, kindness causes misunderstanding, mistrust, and hostility to evaporate.

Albert Schweitzer

"Is she coming?" my shaky voice cracked. I didn't dare look behind me. My sister, Kayleen, turned to see the front of the middle school where eager seventh- and eighth-graders were pushing their way to carpools or making their way down the sidewalk toward an evening of television and homework.

"No," she whispered, "but if we walk faster, maybe we'll miss her completely. I'll bet she's still waiting for you outside the gym door."

I walked faster with my head bent down because tears were stinging my eyes and my nose had started to run. My heart was beating furiously and I had a sick feeling in my stomach.

Who was "she"? you might be wondering. Her name

was Sabrina, and she was a bully. We were in gym class together, and I was less than athletic—more like pathetic! I didn't run very fast, and I was afraid of being hit by a ball, so I was a ducker not a catcher.

That day during gym class, we had played soccer. I not only embarrassed myself, I also made Sabrina mad—basically because she was on my team, and we didn't win. So, in the shower, she threatened me! "I'll meet you after class," she sneered, "and you will wish you and I had never met!"

I didn't need to wait until after class, I already wished we had never met!

As soon as class was over, I snuck out the teacher's entrance and ran to my locker where Kayleen was already waiting for me, so we could walk home together.

"What's up with you?" she asked, noticing the look of panic in my eyes. "Sabrina!" I choked. "We lost the soccer game in gym and it was my fault. She was on my team."

"Oh," Kayleen simply stated, but she patted my back in understanding. "Well," she said, "we'll walk down Seventeenth South instead of Harrison. It's out of the way enough that Sabrina won't have a clue."

Kayleen and I lived straight down the hill about a mile from Clayton Middle School. Sabrina lived somewhere in the middle. She had followed us most of the way chanting harassments since the first day of school. I couldn't figure out what I had ever done to her. She couldn't have had an idea of how bad I was at sports on the first day of school!

My mother said it was because I was quiet and kind and nonconfrontational that made me an easy target for bullies. I just felt like a loser! I was grateful for Kayleen, though. I always knew I could count on her. I think because she was my older sister, she felt like she needed to be my protector, and she was, always thinking of ways to avoid Sabrina or any of her sidekicks who enjoyed harassing me on a daily basis.

"Slow down!" Kayleen gasped. "You're practically running. We're far enough away now to be safe."

I looked up and Kayleen noticed my tears. "What about tomorrow?" I sobbed. "She'll just make it worse tomorrow!"

Kayleen stopped dead in her tracks, causing me to stop, as well. I turned to look at her. She stood there with her hands on her hips. "Well, then," she said in her favorite grown-up voice, "I guess you just might have to tell someone, then!"

"It will just make it worse," I mumbled.

The next day arrived in record time. As Kayleen and I made our way up the steep Harrison Avenue hill, I felt sick. "I still think you should tell somebody," Kayleen chirped every few minutes.

I never replied until she had said that at least ten times, and then I burst out, "Tell somebody *what*? That Sabrina is mean and scary and just creeps me out? She's never actually done anything! Am I supposed to just tell them I am a big, fat baby who can't handle seventh grade because she is in it, too? What am I supposed to say?" Kayleen didn't respond. We walked the rest of the way in silence.

In homeroom, Sabrina's best friend passed me a note that stated, "At lunch, you will pay for running away!" I didn't even look up, but I accidentally swallowed my gum and choked until Mr. McKonkie excused me to go and get a drink.

Walking down the hall, I felt a slight sense of relief and freedom. Still, the note had me scared, and I ducked into the girls' bathroom and just cried. When I calmed down enough, I washed my face so I could go back to class without it being totally obvious. As I made my way down the hallway, I had a sick feeling that I was being followed.

Suddenly, someone kicked me in the back of the leg, hard. I almost fell over. "You little chicken!" Sabrina's voice sneered. I didn't turn around, I just walked faster. *Why wasn't she in class?* I wondered in my panic. I turned to go into Mr. McKonkie's class, but Sabrina blocked me. I turned again and started running down the hall. I had no idea what she was going to do, but three months of constant harassment was weighing heavily on my mind, and I was really freaked out.

Sabrina was now chasing me. At last, she caught up with me enough to kick the back of my legs, trying to knock me down. In a panic, I swung around to the staircase that led to the science and math department. Sabrina was so close to me by then that my sudden shift in direction knocked her off balance and she toppled down the stairs. I stood there watching her fall.

At first, I felt a sudden independence and victory. I turned to walk away from her when I noticed she hadn't stood up yet. Instinct took over, and I suddenly wasn't afraid of her anymore. I practically jumped down the stairs and touched her shoulder. "Can I help?" I asked. When she looked up, I could tell she was in pain. "I can't walk," she moaned. I helped her into a standing position, put her arm around my shoulder and together we hobbled to the nurse's office.

Sabrina never harassed me after that. We never became friends, but from that moment at the foot of the stairs, I knew I had earned her respect. She still hated being on my team in gym class, but things were different. Her best friend would still start in on me sometimes, but Sabrina would shake her head and quietly say, "Leave her alone."

And she always would.

Janalea Jeppson

[EDITORS' NOTE: *For more information about how to deal with bullies, log on to* www.kidshealth.org *(key word search: "bullying").*]

Bully Girl

For a while now she's teased me
I've learned to ignore it
But some things she's said
Just stay in my head
The looks and the faces
Mean and unkind
Bugging me, bothering me
Scaring my mind

My life will get better
In the end she will see
Those things that she said
Brought the strength out in me
To stand up to her
Make her leave me alone
Then I'll finally shine
A light all my own.

Alex Estey, twelve

Anything Is Possible

When your heart is in your dream, no request is too extreme.

Jiminy Cricket

When I was a little kid, I would always come in last when my friends and I ran races. I was never fast at running. I also had a hard time playing basketball because I couldn't jump well. It's hard to jump when your ankles don't move. So, I was always picked last to be on a team. I used to get so frustrated and would be really upset about my "fake legs." But I made up for it all when I got my first pair of Rollerblades.

I was born with a condition that caused me to have to be fitted with prosthetic legs and feet. I got my first ones when I was eight months old. Also, my fingers on my left hand were joined together. I had to have surgery to separate them, and as a result, I now have only eight fingers. But for those of you who think that a person with no feet and only three fingers on one of his hands should be in "special ed" classes—well, you've got me way wrong.

At first it was pretty hard to learn to skate—I kept falling. But I liked the way I felt; while I was on skates, I felt like I was able to move just as fast as the other kids. So, I kept practicing—and I learned how to get up. Soon, I got better and faster. Then, when my friends were running races, I would put on a pair of Rollerblades and skate the race with them. Win or lose, I was able to keep up.

Since skating had become my favorite thing to do, I signed up for the local roller hockey team and then the ice hockey team. I began playing hockey year round.

When I first joined, I thought I would just skate up to the net and take a shot. But I soon found out it wasn't so easy. I didn't score one single goal that whole season.

So, I trained hard in the off-season and the next year I signed up again. When I got through with the tryout, I was actually put into an older age bracket. The problem was, the kids in the older group were *huge*, and I quickly became intimidated. They actually stole the puck from me during the first game, and I didn't know what to do. I remember thinking, *Aren't we on the same team?* It made me feel like quitting, and I didn't show up at the next game. But my parents and my younger brother encouraged me to get back in there and keep trying.

On the next game day, late in the game, we were losing four to five and I was playing right wing. Finally, a pass came to me and I took the shot. To me, everything went in slow motion. I saw the puck fly into the net just as the buzzer went off. My goal tied the game. When my team came skating over to me with excitement, I realized that I really could become good at this game. It would be the first of many goals.

Now, at thirteen years old, I have played in three all-star games for ice hockey and roller hockey, all on able-bodied teams, and I don't even know how many goals I've scored in my entire career. I play for the American Amputee Hockey Association as well. We play all over the country and we have even played in Canada and Russia. Recently, I got sponsored by Nexed, an inline-hockey skate company. I get free shirts, hats, skates—anything that has to do with inline hockey. And just think, all this stuff started with one little two-second goal—and an awesome prosthetist named Eric.

Eric makes my prosthetics and knows exactly what I want and need. He's always looking for ways to make them function better. Before this year, my prosthetic legs had no bendable ankles. I had to grow to a certain height—and this year Eric made them for me. Now I know what it's like to have my feet on the ground while my legs move around. These new prosthetics with ankles that bend are good for running, jumping, hiking, and golf, which I recently took up. However, the old style where the ankles don't bend, is great for hockey—and, as a matter of fact, creates an advantage for me over other kids, whose ankles can get strained or even broken during a game. Now, I can choose which prosthetic I want to wear, according to the sport I'm playing!

I can also decorate my legs any way I want. I bring Eric a T-shirt or patches and he laminates them right onto the legs. I used to have the Rangers and Yankee logos—once I even had the American flag. Now I have them with tie-dye and Green Day and Nirvana patches. Everyone thinks they're pretty cool.

I've had some pretty funny things happen, like the time that I joined an out-of-town roller hockey team. Most of the guys on the team and their parents didn't know that I wore prosthetics. (You can't tell with all my equipment on.) So, you can just imagine everyone's faces when one of my legs came flying off during the game, as I was trying to shoot a goal. My leg kept going toward the net almost scoring a goal! There was dead silence in the arena. I think everyone was in shock! The two coaches came to get me off the rink. One coach carried me, the other coach carried my leg.

When I got off the rink, everyone just started clapping and whistling—they were flipping out! I don't think anyone who was there will forget seeing that! My mom helped me get my leg back on and all we could do was laugh at what had just happened. When the game was over, people kept coming up to me and shaking my hand like I was the "most valuable player" or something.

I have never thought of myself as handicapped. I'm definitely differently-abled. I began skiing when I was only seven, and now I am a black diamond skier. I go to ski camp every year with my amputee friends and for the whole week we ski and hang out. Maybe some day I will train for the Paralympics, which is like the Olympics, only it's just for people who are physically challenged. Whatever I decide to do, I know I would have to train hard to be one of the best—just like any other pro.

As I get bigger, my prostheses get even better, and it gives me more courage to get out and try new stuff. One day, after I had run in a six-mile race, one of my friends asked me where I'd been all day. When I told him that I had just finished a six-mile race, he said, "I couldn't do that!"

Someday, I want to go to a good college and eventually play for a team in the National Hockey League. I also want to be on the All-Star Team. But more than anything, I want to beat Wayne Gretzky's record. My philosophy is, you just have to go for it. You'll never know until you try.

Hey, as they say, "Anything is possible!"

Danny Stein, thirteen

A Skater's Determination

*The man who can drive himself further once
the effort gets painful is the man who will win.*

Roger Bannister

It was just a simple request. I went to get Mat, "my
Mat," as I call him, his iced tea. I would never regret anything more than that.

My brother is a skateboarder through and through. He
always has been and always will be, and along with that
comes determination. Anytime he has fallen down, he
gets right back up and tries it again. If he has broken
something, he just keeps on skating. He has always been
such an inspiration to me, because he is so determined.
Sometimes that determination is good, but on this
particular day, it was a curse.

We were out in the front of my grandparents' house.
Mat was determined to "ollie" over a chair that he had
placed in the street. I was watching him try and try, over

and over again. Deep down, I was thinking, *If he really wants to jump over that chair so badly, why doesn't he just put down that board with wheels on it, and do it?* If you knew my brother, you would know that he wouldn't have stopped until he jumped on his skateboard over that chair many times.

I could see him sweating. As usual, it was a hot Texas day. I was worried that he would get heatstroke. Even though I was only about five, I had heard grown-ups talking about people dying of heatstroke, and I kind of understood what it was. I really didn't want my living, yet hardheaded, brother to get it.

So there I was, my chin cupped in my hands, sitting on the porch of my grandparents' house, worrying about my Mat and thinking of ways to keep him cool.

"Hey Brit, could you get me my tea?"

I snapped out of my thoughts and back to the heat of the day. I replied to his request with a nod and stood up to go get the iced tea. Even through my plastic pink sandals, I could feel the extreme heat of the concrete steps. It was burning my feet, so I quickly went inside the house.

I headed through the hallway toward Grandma's kitchen, on a mission. I was thinking of how sweet and delicious her iced tea is, so I didn't see Wetta, Grandma's Chihuahua. On my way, I tripped over her.

As I entered the kitchen, my nose was filled with the sweet smell of tea and cinnamon toast. It was in the early afternoon, but my grandma knew how much I loved her cinnamon toast, so she made it whenever I came over. As I was walking toward her, hoping to surprise her, she turned around. As she did, I heard the most bloodchilling sound I had ever heard in my short life. "What was that?" Grandma said. "Did you hear that? Did Matthew scream?"

"I dunno. I'll go see."

As I ran though the house toward the front door, I had one thing on my mind—HEATSTROKE. I wish I could say that was what happened. Instead, I saw something that will forever be burned into my mind.

My image of my Mat, my big brother, my protector was shattered. He lay, motionless on the pavement. I ran to him to see what was wrong. My grandma was far ahead of me, running as fast as she could. When she got there, she told me to go wait inside for her. People started to come out of their houses to see who screamed. Mat's friend, Jeffrey, was the first to call 911. When the paramedics got there, they took my brother to the hospital. I didn't get to see Mat for at least a month.

Finally, it was Easter, and I was going to get to see my brother. I couldn't have been happier. I had missed him so much. I made sure that my dress was straight and my shoes were buckled. I wanted to look my best for Mat. When we got to the hospital, I saw a giant bunny that was passing out candy to the patients. Mat gave me his candy.

After a few more weeks at the hospital, Mat came home. He wasn't supposed to get out of his wheelchair and walk around. The doctors said he wouldn't be able to walk after the accident.

But Mat did. He was determined to walk again. He would get up out of his wheelchair and try to walk around on his crutches. After awhile, he didn't even use his wheelchair. If he wanted to go somewhere, he would walk. Soon he didn't even need his crutches. He couldn't run yet, but he was really trying to become the guy he had been before the accident. He could play with me, and finally he went back to school. It didn't take long before Mat could run and play, like any other kid, but he knew what he wanted to do.

Mat was determined to skate again. He was so determined to get better at skating, that he turned his whole life around. He went from not being able to skate—or even walk for that matter—to being one of the best boardskaters that I know.

That changed my outlook on life. I now look at everything as a way to help me skate better and help me in other ways. I am always looking on the bright side. That is what I have learned from my brother—a skater's determination.

Brittany Nicole Henry, twelve

The Fall and Rise of a Star

I was sure everyone in my junior-high drama class saw the paper in my hands shaking when I stood up to audition for a lead role in the annual Christmas play. I was there, not by choice, but because the teacher wanted each of us to try out for a part.

As a "good" student, I did what I was asked, even if it was scary. I was small for my age, wore secondhand clothes and cried easily. At school, I was often the brunt of jokes and taunts and had no friends. I wanted desperately to shrink back into my seat and be invisible. But there I was, onstage. Reading was, at least, something I loved. So, I read.

Within moments, the fear was gone. I entered the beautiful world of make-believe. *So much better,* I thought, *than the real and cruel one.* I was reading the part for the main character, "Star." She was poor—like me. But unlike me, she had a positive outlook on life even though she was an orphan. I wasn't an orphan, but I felt like one. My dad had disappeared. My mom worked days, went to school at night and spent her weekends doing homework. I ached for more time with her. In the play, Star was a lonely child who longed for parents, a few kind words and a home. It was easy for me to feel that her words were also mine.

I finished reading and rushed back to my seat. The spell was broken. I was just me again, wanting to curl up and disappear. When the teacher read the cast list and called my name, I wasn't paying attention. No one ever chose me for anything.

"Patty," she repeated, "you are Star. Come and get your script."

This is impossible! How can it be? With a pounding heart and cold, moist palms, I felt nearly faint, but incredibly happy. I stumbled up to get the papers.

The cutest boy in class was playing the other lead. I didn't know him, but I wanted to. I was even hoping a little that some of his popularity might rub off on me. I was eager to learn my lines and wanted to do my best. So, I practiced every day—while walking to school, at lunchtime, before bedtime, even on weekends. At first, I was worried about forgetting parts of a long monologue that took place in one scene, but I managed to memorize it. I felt more confident after that.

Then we started to work on blocking, which is when the actors must touch, move and learn to use the props— in other words, really "act." The cute boy played a Scrooge-like character who refused to spend even a dime to put a candle in his window, so that the light would show passersby the slippery ice on the path below. On Christmas Eve, Star comes along, falls on the ice and sprains her ankle. The "Scrooge" finds himself helping her up, and in gratitude, she kisses him on the cheek.

One day, right before our drama class started, some of the kids were standing in front of the blackboard, snickering and looking at me. When they moved away, I saw a grotesque, cartoon like drawing of a girl with a huge behind and enormous, ugly lips. Above it were the words, "Falling Star."

I had been teased so often in the past that I had a sort of shield over my heart, which I tried to keep up in order to shut out the pain. But I wasn't very good at it, and this time, I was taken off guard. It really hurt. I was too embarrassed to even cry. Calmly, the teacher erased the picture. "Who did this?" she demanded. No one answered . . . of course.

We started to rehearse. I said my lines, but my heart wasn't in it. At the end of class, the teacher pulled me aside and told me not to pay any attention to the silliness. It probably wouldn't happen again. But she was wrong.

Every single day after that, a "Falling Star" picture, each one uglier and more embarrassing than the last, appeared on the board. Our teacher, who always had to rush from another class to ours, never caught the culprit. Each day it felt like I was entering a torture chamber. My dreams of being liked by my classmates were shattered. They all laughed at the pictures. I was sure that each and every one of them hated me as much as the person who drew the picture did.

In spite of that, at first, I refused to give up. I had worked too hard. Then I began to forget my lines, and I started to have nightmares about being onstage and unable to make a sound, while the audience laughed at me. Finally, I told the teacher to use my understudy for the part; I felt like I would be a terrible flop. She said, "No, you won't. You can do this. I know you can. I'll help you. If you want to, we'll use the auditorium, so you can feel comfortable there."

After that, we met several afternoons each week after school. She taught me to use my voice to show the emotions I was feeling and to fall without hurting myself. I had never worked so hard in my life at anything so terrifying . . . yet so much fun.

At last, it was the day before the show, time for the

dress rehearsal. I was excited, even confident. I really felt and looked like Star when I had on my stage makeup and the old-fashioned, long, soft-flannel green dress. With the full skirt, thick petticoats, knit hat and muff, the transformation was complete.

Everything went smoothly at the dress rehearsal until the scene where I slip on the ice and Scrooge helps me up. When I kissed him on the cheek, a loud, ugly noise sounded from behind the set, like someone farting, followed by loud laughter.

I ran to the stairs, dashed down the aisle into the empty auditorium, collapsed into a seat and started to cry.

"I can't do it. Get someone else!"

Suddenly, I felt gentle hands on my arms. I heard voices and a soft, warm hand took mine. I looked up through my tears to see concerned faces. Four girls, my classmates, had come after me.

"Please, don't drop out," they said. "You're really, really good! Don't pay any attention to that scum, Peter. He's an idiot!" So, *he* was my tormentor . . . the boy that everyone said was a bully. No one even liked him very much.

"You've got to go on," the girls said. "Our play will be a flop without you!"

One of them handed me a tissue. I wiped my eyes and blew my nose. "Okay," I said, giving them a shy smile. I went back onstage and finished the scene with no further interruptions.

The following day, two performances were scheduled for the whole school plus an evening show for families and friends. During the first show, everything went perfectly, and people even applauded in the middle of the play after my monologue! I was flying, dancing, filled with the greatest joy you could imagine.

During the second show, in the first act, part of the scenery fell down. The audience laughed, but I didn't care. I knew they weren't laughing at me. Applause was tremendous at the end of that performance—but the crowning event was the evening show when the parents attended, and my mom got to see me perform.

In the weeks that followed, kids at school came up to say, "You were good," even "great" or "terrific." Although frustrations and failures have come my way since then, along with them, I have also had great joy and success. At times I've felt discouraged, and I still do. But it helps to remember that I was once a fallen star who managed to rise and sparkle, through my own efforts, with the loving guidance of a great teacher and the help of a few unexpected friends.

Patty Zeitlin

Panic

What life means to us is determined, not so much by what life brings to us as by the attitude we bring to life; not so much by what happens to us as by our reaction to what happens.

Lewis L Dunnington

One October day, in eighth-grade English class, I sat taking notes while my teacher explained prepositional phrases for what felt like the eightieth time. Suddenly, my forehead and fingertips became numb, as if a crazed dentist had injected them with Novocain. I tried to concentrate on the teacher's lecture, but his words sounded garbled, like he was speaking through a long cardboard tube. My heart raced, and I couldn't breathe. I was either going to throw up or pass out.

It seemed like I was having a dream. *Was I really sitting in English class?* I turned my head to look at my classmates. They were moving slowly, like a film being viewed frame by frame. I touched the smooth Formica desk and squeezed my pen. I wasn't dreaming. *What was wrong with me?*

My friend touched my arm. "Are you okay?" she asked. "You're completely pale."

I raised my hand; it felt detached from my body. "Can I go to the nurse?" I asked. The voice came from my throat, but I didn't recognize its sound. Our teacher had told the last guy who asked for a pass to the nurse to wait until the bell. Before that could happen, he had hurled into his desk.

"Sure, go ahead," the teacher told me.

I rushed out of the room. The hallway's spotted floor seemed to slant under my feet. I rested my forehead against the cool turquoise tiles of the wall. *What was happening?*

The nurse had me lay down on her fake leather couch, and she popped a thermometer in my mouth. I prayed that I had a fever and could go home. After a few minutes, the nurse read my temperature. "No fever. Better go back to class," she told me.

"No, I can't," I nearly shouted. "Please, send me home," I begged.

The nurse frowned at my urgent tone. She paused a moment, then telephoned my mother.

Once I was home, I felt fine. I cuddled under my down comforter, read one of my favorite horror novels and then watched a soap opera on TV. My mother served me straw-berry Jell-O and sliced bananas for dinner. I was an only child, and my mom spoiled me. She gave me a hug. "You'll be up and around tomorrow," she assured me. At home, I was safe.

The next day, I convinced my parents that I was too weak to return to school, but I was really just afraid. "Okay, just one more day of rest," my mother told me, "but make sure you do the homework. You don't want to ruin your A average."

The following morning, my mother said, "Get up and get dressed, have a bit of breakfast and see how you feel." I knew this trick. She'd been using it on me since I was a kid. Once I had pulled on some clothes and had eaten, she'd say, "If you're healthy enough to be out of bed and keep cereal down, you're well enough to go to school." And, that's exactly what happened.

One afternoon a few days later, one of my classmates asked me to her house for dinner. Supper at her house was a foreign experience for me. She had a big family, and they all talked at the same time, fighting to be heard.

Suddenly, the hum of the kitchen lights became loud and drowned out their voices. Their faces looked too clear in the unnatural light. My cheeks began to go numb, and I felt like the floor was caving in under my feet. It was happening again. *Maybe one of the blood vessels in my brain is slowly leaking blood,* I thought. I had to get out. I had to find help. I mumbled, "Excuse me. I feel sick," and I bolted from the house.

I ran all the way home. I slammed the front door behind me and collapsed on the family-room sofa. "What in the world are you doing home so early?" my mother asked.

"I don't feel well, again," I told her. I felt tears well in my eyes. "What is wrong with me?"

My parents were concerned about me, but not as worried as I was about myself. They scheduled an appointment with my doctor. I explained the scary episodes to him. He ordered a test for diabetes. I had to swallow this super sweet, cola-flavored glucose drink, and I had blood taken from my arm. I went for stomach X rays, where I had to drink a chalky barium milkshake. Finally, he sent me for a full neurological exam.

When the test results were in, the doctor telephoned.

"I'm glad to say that you are perfectly healthy," the doctor told me. My parents thought that was great news, but I wasn't sure.

The next morning, I couldn't face going back to school and the frightening possibility of another episode. I lied and told my mother that my stomach hurt. "The doctor said you are healthy," she reminded me. "He didn't test me for the stomach flu," I insisted. That nonexistent stomach virus bought me two more days at home.

When the third morning arrived, I just couldn't drag myself to class. For two weeks, I refused to go. Each day, I cried, screamed and begged. At first, my parents tried to reason with me; then they threatened to punish me. My father yelled, and my mother dissolved into tears. Again, they turned to my doctor for help, and he suggested that I see a psychologist. *Oh, great, I am totally insane after all.*

I was queasy with nerves at my first appointment with the psychologist. He was an old guy, but he was funny. He told me about a time that he was giving a speech at the local high school. "My microphone wouldn't work, so the janitor hopped up on the stage to check out the equipment. After a bit of fiddling, the janitor shouted, 'There's a screw loose in the speaker!'" I giggled and the knot in my stomach disappeared.

He listened quietly as I told him about my problem. "Your racing heart, tingling hands and your need to escape sound like classic symptoms of a panic attack," he told me. "In a panic attack, your body reacts like someone just jumped out of the closet and scared you, but, really, no one is there. Many people suffer with panic disorder. With some work on your part, and courage, it is a condition that can be overcome."

I leaned back into the chair's overstuffed cushion. I felt so relieved to have a name for what was happening to me.

I was having panic attacks, and I wasn't the only one in the world, either.

The next few times I met with my therapist, he taught me relaxation exercises. He told me to close my eyes and picture a calm place. "I'm lying on the beach on a sunny July Fourth day," I told him. "Just leave before the fireworks," he joked. Then I had to imagine that my muscles were so relaxed and heavy that they were sinking into the warm sand. I was supposed to breathe deeply and slowly. We talked about how to use these techniques until a panic attack ended.

When I mastered these exercises, the psychologist took me to a 4 P.M. field trip to my school. I sat at my desk in the empty classroom and practiced my relaxation. We walked around the school until I felt comfortable.

"Tomorrow, you'll have to try a full classroom," he said.

My stomach tightened. "What if the teacher won't let me leave the class if I have to? What if the nurse won't let me go home?" I asked.

"We can take care of those fears," he assured me. My therapist made special arrangements with my teachers. They agreed that I could leave the room without asking for a pass, and the nurse would let me call home, no questions asked.

I was shaking the first morning when I entered homeroom, but my friends gathered around me and told me how great it was to have me there. "I've missed you guys," I told them. I was glad to be back.

It wasn't easy, though. The panic attacks were still the scariest things I'd ever experienced. Sometimes, I could stay in the classroom and relax through them. Other times, I slipped out the door and sat in the hall until they passed.

The popular kids made a warped game of trying to gross me out so I would leave the class. They would make disgusting vomiting noises or stare at me with their eye-lids turned inside out. I was so mad that I forced myself to stay in my seat. In a twisted way, their being mean actually helped me.

My real friends stood by me, though, and every day got a bit easier. Before my eighth-grade graduation, there was a school talent show. I played the piano in front of a full auditorium. When the judges handed me the first-place trophy, my parents and friends gave me a standing ova-tion. I felt so proud of myself, not because I'd won, but because I'd beaten the panic attacks. I couldn't wait for high school.

Marie-Therese Miller

Believing in My Strength

*What lies behind us and what lies ahead of us
are tiny matters compared to what lies within us.*

Oliver Wendell Holmes

I am different from a lot of other kids. I have cerebral palsy, which happened to me before I was born. I was born really early, and I had an injury to my brain; because of this I am not able to use some of the muscles in my body in a normal way. Kids like me who have CP may not be able to walk, talk, eat or play the same way as most other kids do.

One of my legs is shorter and smaller than my other leg. I don't have very much control over that leg and foot; for example, I can hardly bend my toes. When I try to move that foot, I get a tingly kind of pins-and-needles sensation, like it has fallen asleep. I have to wear a brace on my leg to keep it from curling up, and that makes it hard for me to balance. I bump into things a lot. You may think it is no big deal to have a weak leg and to come in last in all of the races you compete in . . . but it is. When you are growing up, you don't want to be the one who always lags behind.

Because I walk differently and wear a brace, kids call me "retard" and other names. People even imitate the way I run. You honestly don't know how cruel kids can be unless you experience it. I try to rise above it, but sometimes I just have to cry my feelings out. Sometimes I come home with my eyes red from crying. It's not fun to be made fun of over something that I can't control.

CP is not an illness or a disease. It isn't contagious. It will never go away. I will never grow out of it; I will have CP for my whole life. Over the years, I have learned to rise above the people who don't understand my situation. I have learned to look for my strong points and not be pulled down by my weaker ones. One of my strong points is singing, and I try to focus on that. I try especially hard at whatever I do. I think that is something that keeps me going every day.

If you have some kind of disability, I encourage you to start today to do something that makes you happy. You can do whatever you believe you can. Talk to someone who may struggle with the same thing that you do, because it may help you a lot.

I hope my story inspires you to take a better look at life and to let you know there are kids just like you who have a hard time, too. Just don't let your hard times take the place of your dreams, and keep reaching for the stars.

Kelsey Peters, ten

[EDITORS' NOTE: *For information on cerebral palsy go to* www.cdc.gov/ncbddd.]

8

FAMILY
TIES

A family's more special than diamonds or jewels
Or money or treasures galore
Its power, warmth and comfort
Is something that's not sold in stores
You share love with your family
They are people around you that care
And every day, from morning to night
Your family will always be there.

Jaimee Silber, eleven

Pushed by an Angel

Mom was running as fast as she could, knowing that her four-year-old daughter's life depended on it.

Melanie was going down the driveway, pushing along her doll buggy, completely unaware of the car that could have ended her life.

"Melanie! Stop right there!" Mom screamed as she watched the car come speeding up the road.

Melanie looked over at Mom and saw her running toward her. She must have thought her mom was playing a game, because she giggled and started running away. My dad, my two brothers and I were watching from the front deck, stunned.

As we all watched, my mom fell hard to the ground. Melanie looked back and saw Mom on the ground, unable to breathe. She started walking toward her, scared that Mom was hurt badly. The car passed our house. Two more steps toward the road and Melanie would have been hit.

My mom got up and picked up Melanie, holding her tight. When she finally caught her breath, she came up to the deck where we all were and said, "Who pushed me? Why did you push me?"

We looked at her with amazement and told her we hadn't moved. She kept saying that she had felt hands right on the middle of her back—and those hands shoved her HARD. At first, we all thought she was crazy. Now we believe that it was a guardian angel that pushed my mom to the ground. We realized that if my mom had kept running, Melanie would've kept running too, and she would have gone right out onto the road. The car would have ended her life. We now believe in guardian angels and believe that Melanie was very lucky that her guardian angel was looking out for her that afternoon.

I'm thankful that I have my little sister today. At times she is annoying, and I may call her names sometimes. But every time I get upset with her, I remember that day, and how Melanie was saved when my mom was pushed by an angel.

Erin Carthew, twelve

Three Days Old

Cherish your human connections: your relationships with friends and family.

Barbara Bush

The first time I held my little brother, Michael, he was only three days old. I was nine. It was the morning after he and my mom came home from the hospital. I woke up because I heard him crying from within my parents' bedroom. We lived in a pretty small apartment, and I could hear my parents awake and moving around in the kitchen. *So, why didn't they hear him crying?* I thought. I lay in bed waiting for someone to go to him. I decided that as soon as someone did, I would rush out of my bedroom to meet the baby. But Michael kept crying. Then I sensed an opportunity . . . should *I* go to him? Quickly, before anyone else could hear him, I crept toward my parents' room.

I had only seen him once before, at the hospital, when I looked through a big glass window into a nursery with a

lot of babies lying in tiny plastic cribs. When my dad
pointed to him and said, "Congratulations, new big sister,
that's your new baby brother!" I secretly felt terribly
disappointed. Michael was the *ugliest* baby in the whole
place! His face was all red and blotchy, his nose was
mashed down to one side, the top of his hairless, pointy
head seemed kind of orange, and compared to the other
newborns, he looked like a blimp! I imagined the kids in
the neighborhood teasing me for having such an ugly
brother. *Well,* I had thought to myself at the time, *I still love
him and at least he's mine. I've waited so, so long for him.*

Now that I was inside my parents' room, I was nervous
and excited as I did a fast tiptoe over to Michael. This was
our chance to be alone with one another. To really meet
for the first time. There in the crib, which used to be mine,
lay the most beautiful baby in the world. (In my opinion,
anyway.) Yes, it was the same baby from the hospital, all
right. But he looked much better! He was still practically
bald, but now there were little indications of reddish-
blond hair. His skin looked smooth and soft. He had these
big, blue eyes that so resembled marbles, I wondered if
they actually were. I just stared at him for a second. *Was
he real?*

Carefully, I picked him up. I made sure to place one
hand under his head for support. I held him close to me,
closer than I had ever held anyone before.

"Hi," I whispered, ". . . hi." I wondered if he could understand *hi.*

I was in love—love that I knew would never go away.
Not the mushy kind of love like girl-boy love. Not like the
way you love a friend. And not like loving a mother or
father, either. It was special. I had been waiting for years
to share it, because I had been an only child. I had always
been lonely, especially when it rained and I had to play at
home by myself. I felt empty when I watched my friends

get hugs from their little sisters and brothers when we all arrived home from school. My parents were fun, loving and kind. Yet, I sensed a blank space in our family. An extra picture frame with no photo. Something missing. I felt it. And it made me feel alone. Finally, after all these years of waiting, I didn't have to feel that way anymore. "How come you took so long to get here?" I breathed.

I was finally a sister. Better yet, I was Mikey's big sister. And he was my little brother. My *own* brother. He was so small—so dependent on me—yet, I needed him, too. I whispered more secrets to him. I told him I would love him no matter what. Good or bad, together or apart, I would always have love for him in my heart for the rest of my life. I wished with all my soul that he could understand me, even though I knew he couldn't—he was only three days old. Still, I wanted to tell him how lucky I felt. After nine years of growing up without him, I was old enough to realize something that most kids took for granted when their own brothers or sisters were born. Having a sibling in one's life is a gift straight from God.

I had friends, but my cousin had always told me, "Friends will come and go; family is forever." At the time, it seemed to be a weird thing to say. Holding Mikey now, I understood that special bond. Nothing could ever come between us. And, this very morning, I was given a chance to tell him that in private. I was smiling and sniffling all at the same time.

Mikey rested his little bald, orange head on my shoulder. He wasn't crying at all now. He closed his marbley eyes and fell fast asleep in my nine-year-old arms. Maybe, deep down, he had understood me after all.

Jill Helene Fettner

Cookin' in Brooke's Kitchen

Let us not be content to wait and see what will happen, but give us the determination to make the right things happen.

Peter Marshall

When I was six years old my five-year-old cousin, Juliana, got sick. My brother and I were in the family room watching television when my mom came in to tell us the bad news. I wasn't really sure what "cancer" meant, but I could tell it wasn't a good thing. My parents' faces were full of worry and tears, and that was enough to make me cry, too.

I asked, "Mom, what's the matter with Juliana? What *is* cancer?" My mom told us that Juliana had been diagnosed with ALL leukemia, a cancer of the blood and bone. My brother and I were so frightened, we really didn't even know what to think.

When we went to see Juliana in the hospital, she was lying in bed, and she had all these tubes and things hooked to her. It was confusing and scary.

As her treatments continued, Juliana seemed to be getting sicker and sicker. Every time I visited her, she looked different. The medication she took caused her to gain a lot of weight, and she lost all of her long, beautiful hair. I couldn't understand what the doctors were doing to her—it seemed like they were making her feel worse—not better.

Seeing my cousin in so much pain made me feel like my own heart was aching. Something needed to be done. I knew I wanted to help her get better faster, but at six years old, I wasn't sure how I could make a difference—I just knew I had to do something to help my cousin.

One night after we visited Juliana, all the way home I couldn't stop thinking about her. A hospital can be a very scary, cold place. I imagined how alone Juliana must have felt lying there during the night.

When we got home, I sat down at our kitchen table. I always liked writing stories and drawing pictures, and I started working at it like I had done so many other nights. But this night was different—I was thinking about Juliana. I thought, *What if I can sell my drawings? Then I can give the money to Juliana's doctors to help her get well faster and out of that hospital.*

When I told my parents, they thought it was a wonderful idea—but then we came up with an even better one. We would make a cookbook. I really liked cooking and baking plus writing and drawing—a cookbook had all these things combined.

The very next day, I asked all of our family and friends to send me their favorite recipes. To my surprise, everyone jumped at the chance to help. Mom helped to put everything together. Grandma typed recipes while I drew pictures that went into different sections of the cookbook.

My idea for a small cookbook quickly grew to over one hundred pages.

The local skating club paid for the first printing. We sold almost 300 books in our first week. I couldn't believe the response. I felt really good! I have never felt anything like it before.

Now the cookbook, which is called, *Cookin' in Brooke's Kitchen,* is in its fourth printing and, because of many requests, I am starting on a second cookbook. My wish to help my cousin has ended up helping lots of people. The money from the cookbook has all been donated to the Leukemia Research Fund of Canada. In fact, enough money has been raised to fund two research fellowships. I have been lucky enough to meet many leukemia survivors, and lots of them have shared their stories with me. Hearing their stories made me feel important and like I really have been able to make a difference.

Juliana recently turned eight and she is doing great! I often think back to the times we sat in the hospital making miles of paper chains to pass the time. We must have decorated most of her hospital wing! The coolest thing is that she says I am her best friend and favorite cousin.

Now that my cousin Juliana is healed, I am too. The heartache I felt was a part of the love I have for my family. I'm glad that not only was I able to help heal the pain within my own family, but also to help with what happens to other families, too. I guess life is all about mixing up the right ingredients—it takes equal parts of love and action to make the world a better place.

Brooke Harrison, nine
As told by Eryc Stevens

[EDITORS' NOTE: *To find out more about leukemia log on to* www.leukemia.ca *or* www.leukemia.org.]

Reprinted by permission of Leigh Rubin and Creators Syndicate, Inc.

Paybacks

Revenge is often like biting a dog because the dog bit you.

Austin O'Malley

I learned the danger of revenge and letting a "payback" escalate out of control the day I woke up with a long, curled black mustache on my upper lip. My sister had ever-so-carefully drawn it with a permanent marker as I slept!

It all began when I was eleven, the summer before I started seventh grade. My family had moved across state and since my boyfriend, David, and all of my childhood friends were in another town, I was miserable and dreading the start of a new school year. My sister, Rose, who is two years older, was bored and angry. And so, that summer we shared a room and a lot of pent-up frustration toward our parents and our situation. I guess feeling so powerless about an unwanted move made us feel a need to reclaim our power—any way that we could.

Our emotions led us to play crazy "practical jokes" on each other, which then spiraled into getting even, or paybacks, as we called it. It was my sister who really started it all.

I had met our neighbors, Randy and Britt, who were close to my age and a lot of fun. One night, when it was time to go in due to our curfew, I stayed out talking to my friends after Rose went in the house. When I finally went in, I quietly crept upstairs without turning on any lights. My sister had anticipated my every move and had piled chairs in the entry to our room. Of course, I came crashing into them and had to bite my lip to keep from yelling when I smacked my knees!

My surprise and anger turned into a plan to do a payback the next night. So at bedtime, I turned off the lights when my sister went to brush her teeth and took out a hidden bottle of airplane glue, which I poured onto the middle of her pillow. I had a vision of her waking up with the pillow all stuck to her head. But my plan was destroyed when she came in and smelled the glue.

"What is on my pillow?" she asked with wide eyes as she turned on the light.

"I don't know," I said innocently. Then I started to laugh so hard that I couldn't breathe.

"Mel Ann, you are so stupid!" she said with controlled anger in her voice. "So now if you don't want me to tell Mom and Dad that you ruined my pillowcase, you'll go make me a sandwich."

"Fine," I answered with resignation. I didn't feel like getting grounded, so I quietly went downstairs to the kitchen without waking my parents. But once I got there, more thoughts of revenge got the better of me, and I mischievously added hot sauce to Rose's sandwich. Rose got a hot mouthful in the first bite, so she yelled, "That's *it!* Now I'm telling on you!"

"No, no!" I begged her.

"Okay, then you eat it!" she demanded. So, I took a bite and instantly my mouth was on fire! I quickly and quietly went through the upstairs hallway to the bathroom for a glass of water.

When I returned, Rose said, "Okay, if you eat one more bite, we're even."

"All right, give it here," I said with a growing frustration about the mess I had created.

But this time when I took a bite, I gagged! I ran out of the room and back to the bathroom. Rose had put cold cream in the sandwich! That was it. I hit her really hard with a pillow and started chasing her around the room trying to whack her again. Finally, our yelling woke up our parents, who were not pleased about being awakened from a sound sleep late at night by ridiculous stunts—especially the night before the first day of school. We tried to explain, but in the end, my mom just sternly said, "I don't think this is funny. Now go to bed! And . . . you're both *grounded!*"

As she walked out of the room, Rose mumbled, "This is your fault! You got us grounded!"

"My fault? You started it with those stupid chairs!" I replied with anger.

Finally I went to bed and knew I'd think of an even better payback the next day. But little did I know what startling surprise the next morning would bring me. When I woke up, I went to the bathroom. As I walked by the mirror, I suddenly stopped to stare at my reflection. My sister had taken a black marker and drawn a long mustache on me that curled up onto my cheeks.

"Mom!" I yelled and ran to show my mother.

But my tired and grumpy mother was in no mood for

more pranks. So, she simply grounded my sister (again) and told me to "go to school." I was horrified! I scrubbed my face until only a little marker still showed, but then the hard rubbing made raised, red welts in place of the marker! I showed up at school looking totally ridiculous and realizing that paybacks never end; they only escalate into bigger messes.

Even if you think you've pulled off the greatest joke on someone, like your sister being glued to her pillow, you've only invited trouble to find you next—like a big, black mustache.

Mel Ann Coley

I Wish You Were Dead!

There is no man, however wise, who has not at some period of his youth said things, or lived in a way the consciousness of which is so unpleasant to him in later life that he would gladly, if he could, expunge it from his memory.

Marcel Proust

Even my locked bedroom door couldn't keep out the aroma of my mother's homemade spaghetti sauce. As I flipped through the pages of *Teen*, checking out the latest fashion trends, the celebrity scoop and my horoscope, my mouth began to water.

Just then, I heard my doorknob turn, and then a soft knock.

"Shannon, honey, can I come in?"

My mom hated it when I locked my door. What she didn't understand was that if I didn't, Brian would barge in and destroy my room. Ever since my brother grew armpit hair, he had turned into the biggest jerk in the world. He was either ignoring me or annoying me.

His latest torture was to walk into my room while I was in the middle of talking on the phone or writing in my journal. He wouldn't leave the first time I asked. Instead, he'd lie on the bed and tease me about whoever I was going out with at the time.

Then he would proceed to toss my stuffed animals around the room and move around my knick-knacks until I was screaming for him to leave. Last week, he got me so mad that I yelled after him, "I wish you were dead!"

Mom usually sided with him even though I was the youngest and I was used to getting my way. She was probably at my door right then to tell me that I needed to help him set the table or something lame like that.

Instead, she walked in and told me something that would change my life forever. Her eyes were swollen, and she covered her face. I told her to sit down, and I put my arm around her shoulder—not knowing what else to do.

"Mom, you're freaking me out. What is it?"

"Shannon, you know how your brother has been having joint pain and how we've been going to the doctor a lot lately?"

"Yeah, so?" I was really worried now. All along, I had thought his legs and arms were just worn out from tennis tryouts or that he was having another growth spurt.

"Shannon, your brother is sick. He has leukemia."

"What is that? Is that like a kind of cancer or something?" I scooted away from her and stood up to walk around in my room, which suddenly felt a lot smaller at that moment.

"Yes, honey, it is. Don't worry, though. Brian has the good kind."

"The good kind?" I stared at her in disbelief. "There is no *good* kind." All I had ever known about cancer was that when you get it, you lose your hair and die.

"Shannon, please sit down. I know you're upset. I'm upset too. The only people I've ever known with leukemia were two boys that I grew up with in Ohio who died from it. But treatments have changed so much. He's going to make it. I promise."

As we held each other, my mom's tears drenched my cheek and collar, and I could hear her muffled sobs. When she stood up, wiped her face and took a deep breath, I couldn't tell whether five or thirty minutes had passed. She flashed me a weak smile, told me that dinner would soon be ready and headed back downstairs.

I collapsed onto my bed, feeling paralyzed. I remembered the awful thing I had said to him, "I wish you were dead!" *Was this my fault? Had I actually played a hand in my brother's getting sick?* At that moment, I would have given anything to be able to take back those words that I had so passionately screamed at him. Then all kinds of images began to swirl around in my head like the flakes in a shaken snow globe.

There was Brian in his magician's cape finishing a trick with me, his "assistant," at his side. There was Brian interviewing me, in his most serious voice, for our taped news broadcast. There was Brian, laughing and smiling his big, buck-toothed grin as we watched *Saturday Night Live* together. There was Brian holding my hand, as we got off the plane to go visit our father in Texas.

In an instant, I knew exactly what I needed to do. I knew how bad I felt, so I couldn't imagine how bad Brian was feeling. I cleaned up my face so it didn't look as though I'd been crying. I grabbed a piece of poster board and my markers and headed downstairs.

When I entered the living room, he was sitting on the couch watching television. I placed all of my materials on

the floor and began working on a science project that was
due that week.

"Brian?"

"Yeah?"

"Can you help me with this stupid thing? I can't draw
an elephant, and I have to have an elephant on it to get a
good grade."

"I'll try."

As we sat on the living room floor, drawing and color-
ing without saying a word, I knew that something had
changed—something big. While he was concentrating on
the elephant's outline, I watched him.

All those fights. All those cross words. All those times
he made me mad. All the times he got to do something
that I didn't get to do. They just didn't matter anymore.
All that mattered was being next to him, right then, in
that moment.

Shannon Griffin

[EDITORS' NOTE: *Brian fully recovered and to this day is
cancer free. To help them both through the tough times, Brian and
Shannon relied upon the support of an organization that sends
kids with cancer to camp: Happy Days and Special Times, "The
Loving Answer for Children with Cancer." If you, or a sibling, are
dealing with cancer, try going to* www.cancersourcekids.com
for information about camps to attend.]

A Life's Moment

*Consider, when you are enraged at anyone,
what you would probably think if he should die
during the dispute.*

William Shenstone

One cold morning, I was getting ready for school. Our mom would be late if she didn't leave for work soon and she and my sister, Kameron, were fighting over something that had happened the night before. Mom left for work in a bad mood because of the fight they had, and my sister was really upset about what had just taken place. She came upstairs and told my brother, Shawn, and me to get our coats because it was time to leave.

Shawn and I hurried and got in Kam's car so we wouldn't be late for school. I asked my sister, "Are you okay? What happened between you and Mom this morning?" My sister looked at me with the glare that I often get from her when she is frustrated about something, and said, "I don't want to talk about it. We just have a disagreement over something and it's just confusing to me right now."

I looked at Shawn and he looked at me, and I could tell from the look that Shawn gave me that he was trying to tell me, "Don't ask about it—just keep quiet." Kam backed out of the driveway and we headed up the street. We were going pretty slowly, and Kam was watching out for other cars. Then she started to talk to me about what had happened with her and Mom.

"We had a fight, and it's nothing bad; but we both just really believe strongly in our own opinions. I really hate that, because we get into fights a lot because of it." As my sister was talking to me we had gotten to the end of our street.

Then, all of a sudden, a car that was coming from the opposite direction, going 90 miles an hour, rammed into ours. Our car spun out of control and hit the opposite curb. Kam and I were screaming. After our car finally stopped, we all got out of the car to look at the damage. I kept asking myself, *Is this real? Did this just really happen?*

My sister was in tears because she had just been in a car accident a month before and had to have back surgery. She called 911, and then she called our mom. Everything was a mess. It turns out that the guy who hit us was only eighteen and he had been racing some of his friends. Kam's car was in really bad shape, and she was in a lot of pain.

My sister talked on the phone to our mom for a long time, crying and telling her that she was sorry, that we could have all been killed and she wouldn't have been able to say good-bye. Kam could have died in that accident and it would have been so sad because she and our mom had fought right before it happened.

I could have lost Kam that day, and now I tell my family every day that I love them all. It just goes to show you that you never know when you could be gone. You need to appreciate the time you have with your loved ones. Life isn't promised to anyone, and it could be here one minute and gone the next.

Jordan Mitchell, thirteen

The Great Fish Story

Great things are only possible with outrageous requests.

Thea Alexander

One summer afternoon, my grandpa and I were out in his boat fishing, when I ran out of line on my fishing pole. Grandpa felt sorry for me, so he handed me his best, luckiest fishing pole to use.

On my second cast, the pole slipped out of my hands and went flying into the lake. I tried to grab it before it sank into the dark water, but I was too late. I jumped into the water after it, but it went down, down, down.

I climbed back into the boat feeling totally defeated. Then Grandpa came up with a plan to try to snag the line with our other two poles, by casting them down to grab the sunken line with one of the hooks. We tried about five times, but we had no luck. I felt so bad. It was Grandpa's favorite pole, and now it was lost forever.

Grandpa, not willing to give up yet, said, "Okay, Max, this will be our last time." Just then, my grandma, who had died two months earlier, popped into my mind. I thought, *Maybe Grandma can help.* So I prayed, *Grandma, please help Grandpa and me find his fishing pole,* over and over while I watched Grandpa hook his special silver lure onto the line.

When he was done fixing the lure into place, he threw it into the lake and dragged it around on the bottom. I kept praying to Grandma as I watched the line circle around the lake. When Grandpa reeled the line in, he had caught the sunken line in the middle! He pulled and pulled on one end of the line and then, out of the depths of the lake came his favorite fishing pole! I couldn't believe it! As he pulled, he noticed a tug and a strain on the line. It took some strength to bring it in. Suddenly, we heard a splash and there, on the end of the line was a beautiful fourteen-inch bass!

Grandpa and I laughed our heads off, while I thanked Grandma over and over in my head. I decided to tell Grandpa how I had been praying to Grandma as he searched for the pole. "Yep," he said, "I bet she did do this for us. That would be *just* like her."

When we told people what had happened, they said that it was "*the* fish story of all fish stories."

Two weeks after that incredible fishing trip, my grandpa died. I lost my amazing and wonderful grandma and grandpa within three months. It was so hard for my family to give them up.

Now I often ask both of them to help me with lots of different things. And you know what? After that amazing moment out on the lake, I know that they haven't really left me, and they *definitely* hear me.

Max Alexander, ten

Pap Pap's Hands

I remember how he used to pick me up
With his strong and gentle hands,
Hold me tight and cuddle me.
He was a person who fought for our country,
A father who loved his kids, the best husband a guy
  could be.
He was my savior, hero, a grandpa who meant
  everything to me.
As I sit here writing this, I hold tears inside.
I miss the man with strong hands to comfort me,
And tell me that everything was going to be okay.

Samantha Slaughter, twelve

I took his hands. They were old, worn out and shaky, but I held them anyway. He took a deep breath and sang "Down by the Old Mill Stream" to me. His voice was shaky, but to me, it was beautiful. I was amazed. After Mom had gone up to Pap Pap and hugged him, all of the grown-ups went into different rooms.

Later that day, I was lying on my bed at my Nana's house. As I was remembering Pap Pap's hands, I realized that his hands actually were not old or worn out, they were experienced. Experienced with love.

He had given love out to anyone who knew him. Especially his family. Oh, how much he loved his family. All of his children, grandchildren, great-grandchildren, any part of the family. His hands were shaky, though, because he was in pain. He had been suffering from many things over the years. I didn't care if his hands were shaky, as long as he loved me.

I thought he would be all right. Every time I visited my great-grandparents over that vacation, I held his hands, gave him a hug and said, "I love you." He got worse when I had hoped he'd be fine. He went into the hospital. I so badly wanted him to live.

But then I realized he was in too much pain. I know there are only two ways out of his misery: a miracle that will make all his pain go away . . . or he will go to heaven.

I know that he will have to go to heaven sometime. Maybe next week or next year. It is just hard to let someone go . . . a person who, while he held my hands, went through my soul and into my heart.

I hope Pap Pap knows I love him, because I really do. I know he loves me. I know God will do what's best for him.

Nicole Koah, eleven

Just the Two of Us

How rare and wonderful is that flash of a moment when we realize we have discovered a friend.

William E. Rothschild

Sometime, in your lifetime, you may be lucky enough to come across a person who knows exactly how you feel and is always there for you. Someone who loves you for who you are and doesn't judge you. Someone who believes in you and urges you to listen to your heart, no matter what anyone else thinks. This person helps you through your hardest days and assures you that tomorrow is always another day, a fresh beginning.

I didn't have anyone like this, until a stranger moved into my house, and became my sister.

When I was seven years old, my mom died, and my life changed forever. My dad became a widower and our family was left without a mother. Then, about two years ago, when I was twelve, my father remarried. My step-mother, Shelly, moved from New York to our small house in Missouri. She also brought along her daughter, an energetic and lively eleven-year-old named Ariele. With her beautiful blue eyes and winning smile, Ariele was always the center of attention. I never thought that I could bring myself to love her as a sister, because we didn't know each other at all.

It's amazing how opposite we are. I am a perfectionist and a neat freak. I say what I think people want to hear, and I hide what I'm really feeling. Ariele is so full of life, she lights up the room. She's extremely funny and cheerful, celebrating every moment of life. She always manages to crack my frown, figure out my problems and decode my weird moods. I hate to admit it, but even though I am one year older, she knows more about what really matters than I could ever hope to. There was one experience where I really found out how important it is to take each day as a blessing, and how to make the best of it.

Only a year and a half after Ariele came to live with us, my father accepted a new job as head of a private school. The benefits were great, but the only problem was that we would be forced to move across the country to Boston. I was going to have to leave all the people that I had grown to love and care about. I felt helpless. My life was a roller-coaster ride of mixed emotions, and I was stuck aboard, unable to make decisions or get off. But the one person who really helped me through my pain was my stepsister, Ariele. She had the best attitude from the start. She had just left her life in New York and moved when our parents got married. And although she had grown to love her new home, she realized that Boston was good for the family.

A few months later, after selling our home and packing up, we drove with our parents from St. Louis to New

Hampshire, where both of us would attend camp. We had to leave for the summer, knowing we wouldn't be back for a long time. But the ride across the country was one of the most memorable few days. We were on the road in a stuffed minivan, filled with luggage and food, but Ariele and I loved it.

Because the car ride was so long, our parents went out of their way to stop at places to show us some of the country. At Niagara Falls, after observing the magnificent display, we decided to get even closer to the edge and climb to the point where people get soaked by the freezing waters. As Ariele and I neared this breathtaking waterfall, and as I watched my sister laugh with joy and shriek from exhilaration, I saw everything in a new light. I hadn't been living each day fully with the excitement or joy that Ariele demonstrated to me.

With soaked jeans and high spirits, we climbed even higher, so that the foggy mist blinded us, and we huddled together to keep ourselves warm. Her shaking arms hugged me, and she told me that she loved me. Then she stood before the mighty waterfall, eyes closed, and arms spread out wide, to let the water soak her . . . giggling as dripping strands of hair tickled her face. She looked so beautiful. There was something so magical about that moment that it will always remain in my memory.

As I looked at her, I thought of how drastically my view changed when Ariele came into my life, and I remembered all the things she urged me to try. There were so many times she made me feel like a little kid, just having fun like the time in a park a few months ago. We went on a walk and passed by a large, sloppy puddle of mud created from the rain the day before. She started playing in it, covering her hands and legs with the mud, and urged me to do the same. I hesitated, because there were so many people around, but then I thought, *Who cares?* So, together, we slipped and slid in that mud and had the best time.

I thought of the many times we've been at the mall, and I've seen something I have really liked but didn't want to spend my money for it. Her mouth will turn up in a mischievous grin, and she will say, "You only live once!" Then I end up buying the shirt or CD that I wanted so badly. And during these moments, I can't help realizing how much I owe her for giving me another shot at life, another chance.

Before Ariele moved in, I was so scared of risking things and too shy to express myself as I wanted to. I was reluctant to step out of my preteen mind and enjoy those little pleasures. Even though she may not be aware of it, she has taught me that the person who risks nothing, will gain nothing. Pain and disappointment may be avoided, but one will simply never grow or learn. Without risks, one misses out on the incredible opportunities and experiences that make life worth living.

I owe everything to her. She is my better half and my best friend in the world.

So whenever we fight about our shared room, boys or simply how we've been acting toward each other, I remember all the times we've spent together and realize that no matter how hard and impossible it seems at times, we always find a way to work it out. And through all of our family ups and downs, we'll be in it and stay in it— together. Two sisters who bring out the very best in each other, every single day . . . and in every possible way.

Miriam Bard, fourteen

The Gift

One day a handsome black tomcat appeared at our back door. His coat had a white bib and four snowy paws, making him look like he was wearing a tuxedo. His tail was as crooked as a corkscrew.

My four-year-old brother Daniel and I had never had a pet. We both instantly fell in love with the gentle black and white cat. All that first afternoon, the three of us played together. When it got dark, we begged our parents to let our new friend come inside so we could feed him. Mom shook her head. "It might confuse him," she explained. "This cat looks too healthy to be a stray. He must have a home already."

But the next morning, the tuxedo cat was still there. He waited patiently by the front door like a butler at a mansion. "Yea!" said Daniel. "He wants to be our cat!"

It did seem like he was telling us something. He stuck around all day, playing with Daniel and me outside. When we went into the house, he jumped up on the barbecue and watched us through the window. The last thing I saw that night were his green eyes, staring in at me.

The next day, our parents warned us that we needed to try our best to find his owners. My mom helped me make a flyer that said "Found: black and white cat with crooked tail" with our phone number on it. I drew a picture of the cat on each one and we hung them around the neighborhood.

The second day, I named him Alley, as in "alley cat." The third day, our dad and mom let us put some food out for him. The fourth day, our parents broke down and we got to bring him inside.

Alley let me carry him like a baby, from room to room. Daniel built LEGO castles all around him. He followed us all around the house and at bedtime he jumped on each of our beds while we got tucked in, as if he was saying good night to us.

Alley was a dream pet.

Our family woke up from the dream about two weeks after we adopted him. That was the day a big, tattooed man appeared at our door holding one of our "Found Cat" flyers. Before anyone could say anything, Alley strolled over to the man and rubbed on his leg. It was obvious that they knew each other.

"My name's Mark Johnson," he announced, casually picking Alley up. "I see you've met my only roommate, Dewey. He kinda wanders when I'm out of town. Can I offer you good people a reward for watching him?"

"No," Dad said with a sigh. "It was a pleasure to have him as our guest." The rest of us were completely silent. At the door, Mr. Johnson turned back and faced us kids. That's when he must have seen the tears in my eyes. "Wow. I'm sorry," he said. "I didn't realize you kids had gotten so attached. Hey, I only live a few blocks away. If you two would ever like to visit old Dewey . . ."

"His name's not Dewey!" Daniel yelled at the top of his lungs. "It's Alley!" He ran sobbing to his room.

Mr. Johnson's eyes widened. The full meaning of his visit had sunk in at last. He slipped out awkwardly. Over his shoulder was slung Alley. Alley's unreadable green eyes looked back at me all the way down the walk.

For days, I found myself staring out of the window at the barbecue as if Alley might suddenly rematerialize there. Daniel went through spells of bursting into tears. Our parents tried to console us by keeping our family schedule full and entertaining. They even talked about going to the pound to pick out another pet.

Then one day, I heard Daniel yell, "He's back!" We all hurried into the family room. Sure enough, Alley was there by the door nuzzling Daniel, his crooked tail lashing Daniel's legs.

He had found his way home.

My heart was jumping with joy. Then Dad said, "Daniel. Sarah. He can't stay. He's not ours, remember?"

Daniel and I both looked at him like he was crazy. "But Dad . . ." Daniel began.

"Do we have to tell that Mr. Johnson guy?" I asked, looking into my dad's eyes.

Dad nodded his head. Even though I could tell it made him sad to do it, he looked up the name and left a message on Mr. Johnson's machine. "Your cat is here again," Dad said. "Would you please stop by and pick him up?"

I felt like this would be the last time we would ever see Alley. I figured Mr. Johnson would lock him up in his house. For the rest of the day we played with him; making cat fortresses out of cardboard boxes, dangling strings around corners, petting him and feeding him treats. Alley went along with it all, just like he expected that kind of treatment and wanted nothing less.

When Mr. Johnson arrived at 8:00, I had made a

decision. I waited in the hall behind Daniel and our dad, holding Alley in my arms. As soon as Dad opened the door, I said to Mr. Johnson, "I think he wants to live with us."

"Sarah . . ." Dad began.

But Mr. Johnson nodded at me, letting me know it was all right. Then he squatted down, so that he would be at the same level as Daniel and me.

"You know, Sarah, I think you're right. He seems to have made a decision. I think he must like kids," he said with a wink. He set down a small cardboard box. "I didn't come to take him. I just came by to bring you these." Inside was a bowl and several cans of cat food.

"You're letting us have him?" I asked, stunned. "Like a gift?"

"Well, kind of," he said with a shrug. A tattoo-scrawled arm darted out as he petted Alley. "Bye, Dewey. I'll miss you. But I have a feeling you'll be in good hands."

And, just like that, Mr. Johnson was gone. None of us ever saw him again.

From then on, the tuxedo cat was ours. In no time at all, he became a respected member of our family. He was a fierce hunter, yet he remained extremely gentle with us. Whatever room the family was in, Alley was there. Whenever Daniel and I were ready for bed, Alley popped in to say goodnight.

Sometimes I wonder what made our cat decide to stop being Dewey and want to become Alley. We will never really know, but it gave us all an example of what giving is all about. Because the truth of the matter was that Mr. Johnson hadn't given his pet away.

Alley had given himself to us.

Sarah Strickland
As told by Craig Strickland

$\overline{9}$

ON CHOICES

I don't wish I were in a different family
Or pick my friends by their popularity.
I don't change my looks so people will like me
Or make fun of people who are different.
I won't do drugs with you
Or lose my virginity at a young age.
This is how I choose to be.
Do you know why?
I know right from wrong, and choose to do right.
I choose to be me.

Nicole Koah, eleven

Hidden in Plain Sight

The real acid test of courage is to be just your honest self when everybody is trying to be like somebody else.

Andrew Jensen

It was a Thursday, and school was almost out. Our teacher was out of the classroom. Our homework sat on our desks. I fiddled with my pen while I listened to Joel and Bryan talk about a certain group of girls that we all knew.

"I like them," Bryan said, "but none of them would ever try drugs or even drink."

So what? Nobody does that stuff, I thought, but I didn't say it. Joel just nodded.

"Actually," Bryan continued, "Lisa wants to try them, so she's talking to me about it. Everyone thinks I'm the biggest druggie in the school." He paused. "Well, basically I am."

My pen fell out of my hand and bounced on the floor. I

stared at him, waiting for him to laugh, to smile—do anything—just to show that he was kidding. No one our age
did drugs. No one did drugs except for those huddled
people on the sidewalks who were so lost in their minds
that they didn't even know who or where they were anymore. Bryan's mouth stayed in a straight line, though. No
smile tugged at the corners.

"We're meeting at the park tonight," Bryan continued.
"I'm not gonna charge her anything this first time. I just
want her to like it. I'm bringing some friends, too. Joel,
Lance, you wanna come?"

"Sure," Joel said. My whole body locked up. What could
I say? What should I say?

Then, the door flung open and our teacher reentered
the room. We all turned to our homework and began
scribbling.

I turned and looked at Joel. *No,* I thought, *this isn't
happening.* I always knew that Joel wasn't the perfect child,
but who was? He certainly wasn't like Bryan, who
ditched school, stole and even did drugs. But Joel had
agreed to go to the park. I had known his family since I
was born. He was always smiling, cracking jokes, and we
hung out together almost every day. Yet he expected me
to go to the park with him.

Don't worry about it, I said to myself. *My parents won't let
me go to the park that late at night anyway.*

That night after I had finished dinner, I sat on the couch
watching TV. The doorbell rang. When I opened the door,
Joel was standing there. "What's up, Lance?" he asked.

"Not much," I said.

"So, are you coming to the park tonight?" he asked.

"I don't know," I said. "I have to ask my parents."

"No, you don't," he said, making a face as though he
had just eaten something rotten. "Ask if I can spend the
night and we'll just sneak out."

I frowned. "Why don't you just spend the night, and we don't sneak out? We'll have more fun here, anyway."

He groaned. "Well, I should have known that you wouldn't want to do anything slightly risky. I guess I'll find someone else." He turned and began walking away.

"No, no," I grabbed his arm. "I'll go."

He smiled.

It was ten-thirty. Lying in bed, I stared at the ceiling. In my mind, I kept thinking of ways to phrase the question, *Aren't you surprised that Bryan does drugs?* Or, *Do you think many kids are doing them?* Or even, *Do you do drugs, Joel?* I couldn't be sure now that I even knew my lifelong friend anymore. *Am I the only one who didn't know about Bryan's drug habit? Was I the only one who thinks that it matters?* I turned and stared at Joel. *Is there a side of him that I didn't even know about?* His sleeping bag ruffled as he crawled out.

"Let's go," he whispered. I opened the window, grimacing at the sound.

It was ten-fifty. We walked until we were about one hundred yards from the park. A heavy silence laced the air. I glanced at Joel. He was staring toward the dark playground.

"We don't have to go, Joel," I said.

"What's wrong with you?" he turned and faced me. "You worry about everything. We're not little kids anymore, Lance. It's time to realize that not everything adults tell us is true."

He turned and walked forward. I followed.

When we arrived at the playground, slides and swings were the only things there. I glanced at my watch. Ten fifty-seven. "Maybe they aren't coming after all," I said.

Joel groaned and kicked the sand into the air.

I stuffed my hands into my pockets and gazed out at the lights in town. I looked back at Joel. We had come to this very park so many years before. We had spent endless hours on the swings. He always boosted himself so high into the air. I wanted to be like him, to be able to swing that high, but I couldn't do it. He was the risk taker. I looked at him again. *I guess it's only fitting that he'll take the big risk tonight,* I thought. *It's just his nature.*

A laugh erupted through the silence. Joel and I turned. "It came from the creek," Joel said. We ran through the forest toward the water. We stopped when we got to the dense trees. I squinted to try to find footprints that led somewhere. Where was the brown, wooden picnic table that I had eaten lunch on so many times? Indented lines in the dirt caused by the legs of the table showed that it had been dragged deeper into the trees. I looked at Joel and saw that his eyes were focused on the tracks as well. "Come on," he whispered.

We followed the tracks until we reached a clearing surrounded by trees.

A white, powdery substance covered a mirror that lay on the picnic table. Jim, the kid I did a book report with in third grade, lay on the ground next to the picnic table. He trembled as if he were having a seizure. Beads of sweat lined his face. He squeezed a straw that he held in his hand. His eyes stared up into the sky. They looked as if a layer of Saran Wrap covered them. My eyes darted around. The people I grew up with were passing a pipe around in a circle. Robert, the first kid who talked to me in preschool, was taking shots of alcohol.

Bryan approached me. He squinted at me with his red eyes. A smell that made me want to gag surrounded him. "Come with me, Lance," he said. "We're taking some pipe hits."

I looked around me. *This is reality, isn't it?* I thought. *Everyone was doing it, and I never even knew about it. This is what I've been missing out on.*

I followed Bryan. The kids in the circle turned and

looked at me. I stared back. These were the kids I had played with since preschool.

Something tapped my shoulder. I turned and saw Joel.

"Where are you going?" he asked. I pointed at the circle. "Let's go," he whispered. I shook my head.

"You were right, Joel. Everybody we've ever known is here. This is just the way it is."

"No," he said. I turned and walked away. He grabbed the collar of my shirt and pulled.

"We're going," he said. The respect that I had always felt for him forced me to follow. When we got out of the trees to where the picnic bench used to be, we began talking again. "I didn't know it would be like that," Joel said.

"Everyone's doing it, Joel," I said. My voice cracked. "We're the only ones not doing it."

"Not everyone's doing it, Lance. I'm not. You're not. We both have our lives ahead of us."

I nodded as we walked away.

The streetlights glared down on us as we walked on those same sidewalks that we had passed over for so many years. I looked over at Joel. He stared down at the sidewalk, his hands in his pockets. I kept wondering why he had been the one who didn't try the drugs. After all, he was always the risk taker. He was always the one who pushed himself to his limits just like that time on the swing.

We reached my house. "I think I'm going to go home and sleep," he said. I nodded.

I pulled myself into my room through the window and collapsed onto my bed. *What had kept Joel from doing what I had almost done?* I wondered as I curled up in bed.

Finally, I made sense of it all. Joel took risks, and he had taken the biggest risk of all. He *hadn't* done what everybody else was doing. He had a sense of originality that drew all those who met him to admire him. He had what he wanted in life, and drugs would only set him back.

I looked over at a picture of Joel and me on my dresser. In the picture we were both kids, swinging on the swings, laughing our heads off. That's when I knew that we could get higher than any of those kids who were stumbling through the trees behind us, just by being ourselves.

Lance Johnson, fourteen

[EDITORS' NOTE: *For the straight scoop on drugs, log on to:* www.kidshealth.org *(key word search: "drugs").*]

Hot Potato/Cold Potato

Call it a clan, call it a network, call it a tribe, call it a family: Whatever you call it, whoever you are, you need one.

Jane Howard

"I hate you!" I yelled, as I ran up the stairs to my room. Throwing open my dresser drawers, I pulled out a clean T-shirt and jeans, threw them in my backpack and ran back down the steps. Mom and Dad stood there, looking like they were in shock.

"Where are you going?" Mom asked.

"Anywhere but here," I shouted as I ran out the door. They weren't fast enough to grab me, and I slipped away into the night. It was cold, but my hot temper warmed me, and I didn't feel it. Not at first, anyway.

I hit the streets with my thumb out. Hitchhiking wasn't safe, but I didn't care. It was the only way I knew, at fourteen years old, to get away from them. We'd moved three times in the last four years, so I was always the new kid in class, the one who didn't know what chapter we were working on or what project was due next week. I was always playing catch-up and trying to fit in.

Worse than trying to fit in at school was trying to make new friends wherever we moved. There were cliques of popular students who had known each other since grade school. Then there were the geeks and jocks who just didn't seem to interest me. I wasn't athletic and didn't excel at anything, really. Just an average high school kid looking for friends. Deep down inside, I knew my parents loved me, just like God loved me, but it wasn't enough.

I slept curled up on a park bench the first night I took off. It was hard as a rock, and I was surprised to find that I wasn't alone. With my arms wrapped tightly around me for warmth, I huddled on the bench closest to the street-light. Peeking through half-closed eyes, I could see other homeless people just like me, only they looked like they'd been there a long, long time. Some of them looked kind of scary, with dirty beards and baggy clothes. Some pushed grocery carts filled with their entire life's treasure. I didn't sleep much that night, and when the sun rose, I washed up in the park's restroom and hit the road.

By the end of the second day, I'd made my way to another city sixty-five miles away where I found a halfway house for runaways. I was tired, cold and hungry. By the time I got there, the kitchen was closed. All that was left on the table was a cold potato. I lifted it to my lips and bit into the wrinkled skin. It was crumbly and dry and stuck in my throat when I tried to swallow. That night I slept on a cot in a room with four other runaways. It wasn't a whole lot better than the park. The cot was hard and the blanket was scratchy, and those other kids looked like they'd been there a long, long time. I tossed and turned all night.

The next day, I changed into the only clean clothes I had and was shown how to use the washer and dryer to do my own laundry.

"The soap is over there," Carly told me. She was one of the other four runaways in my room. "Don't use too much, just half a scoop is all you need."

I wanted to ask her how long she'd been there, but she interrupted my thoughts.

"I've been here almost four months now," Carly said. "We have rules for what you can and can't do, so you better get used to it. You can't use the laundry before 8:00 in the morning and you can't watch TV after 10:00 at night. You have to be down at the kitchen table right at 12:00 and 5:00, or you don't eat, and you have to rotate chores every week. This is my week on kitchen duty. I help make lunches and dinners, and I clean up afterward. So, don't go makin' a big mess in there."

"When are you going home?" I asked her.

"I don't know and I don't care. My parents know I'm here but won't come by to even talk to me, and so what! You got something to say about that?"

Carly glared at me as she talked.

"No," I responded, but I felt sad for Carly. Her parents didn't even care! I was scared. Maybe my parents didn't care, either.

Three days later, my dad showed up at the front door of the halfway house. I don't know how he found out I was there, but part of me was glad he did, though I wouldn't admit it out loud. After gathering my few things, we drove home in silence. I could almost see the questions running through his head. *Why did she run away from home? What was so awful there that we couldn't talk about it?* I could see by the look on his face that he felt responsible for all my anger and sadness. I regretted shouting at my parents the night I ran away. It wasn't their fault that I felt this way.

I had a long time to think as we drove those many miles home, and I wondered why I hadn't seen all the things Dad had done for the family. He was trying to make a better life for us, moving us from one city to the next so he could get a better job. He was doing his best to put clothes on my back and shoes on my feet. It was up to me to make the best of a new school and to open up to new classmates. Hanging my head in the halls and not talking to anyone who even said "hi" wouldn't help me make friends. Maybe I could make more of an effort to reach out to others.

When we finally reached our house, Mom opened the front door as we walked up the stairs. I smelled a roast cooking and knew there'd be hot baked potatoes to go with it. As I stepped inside, she opened her arms wide and I fell into them. Dad was right behind me and put his arms around both of us. Ordinarily, I'd pull away, but this time I didn't.

They both released me a few moments later, and that's when I saw the tears in Mom's eyes. I lowered my head and blinked twice really fast, trying to hide my own tears. I made a promise to myself not to hurt them like that again. They were doing the best they could. It was up to me to meet them halfway.

I knew the changes I had to make wouldn't take place overnight, but as I looked at my parents and felt the warmth in my house, I realized there's no place like home.

B. J. Taylor

[EDITORS' NOTE: *If you or someone you know is considering running away from home, please log on to* www.covenant-house.org/nineline/kid.html *or call the NINELINE Hotline at 1-800-999-9999. It's free, it's confidential and it's 24/7!*]

Locks of Love

To find out what one is fitted to do, and to secure an opportunity to do it, is the key to happiness.

John Dewey

My cousin Patricia was more like my mother, my sister and my best friend all wrapped into one. When I was born, my mom and I lived with my Aunt Mary and my cousins Patricia and Elizabeth. Throughout my first year of life, Patricia, who was about nine years older than me, took care of me pretty often. After we moved on our own, Patricia would come and stay at our house a lot. We were a really close family, so we saw each other often.

When I was three, she found out that both she and her sister had colon cancer. Luckily, they were able to have it removed and ended up being fine.

A couple of years later, when I was about six, Patricia began having a lot of head pain. She told her mom, and they went to a doctor who said it might be cancer. He did some tests, and then a few days later the test results showed that she did have cancer. They weren't sure how advanced it was, but it got bad fast. She had to undergo radiation therapy, and within a few months, all of her long, pretty hair had fallen out—it was just gone. I felt so bad for her. I didn't know what to do for her that would help in any way.

By the time I was in fourth grade, she had been through about six brain surgeries. The doctors gave her steroids to help, but they only worked for a little bit.

Then, the following year when she was only nineteen and I was ten, she passed on as she lay in her bed holding her favorite teddy bear.

It hurt me so badly to know that such a good, warm-hearted, loving and caring person could be taken away from all our hearts like that. If I could do anything or take back what had happened, I would have.

About one-and-a-half years after Patricia passed away, I heard about an organization called Locks of Love that makes wigs for people who lose their hair due to cancer treatments. My aunt told me that Patricia had a wig that she often wore, that had been given to her from Locks of Love.

I really liked what they did for people like Patricia, so I decided that I would donate some of my hair to them. I took really good care of my hair for several months in order to be able to donate the minimum of one-and-a-half feet of hair. Then I made an appointment to have my hair cut off and I donated it to Locks of Love in memory of my cousin, Patricia Vanoni Petree.

Even though I couldn't think of anything that I could do for Patricia while she was sick, I am glad that I can help someone else who is suffering like she did. I'm also comforted by knowing that my cousin—who was like my

sister, mother and best friend all in one—would be proud
of me.

Amanda Macht, eleven

[EDITORS' NOTE: *For information about donating to Locks of
Love, check their Web site at* www.locksoflove.org *or call toll
free 1-888-896-1588.*]

Uncle Richie's Lesson

Bad habits are like a comfortable bed, easy to get into, but hard to get out of.

English Proverb

When I was younger, before I started school, I would be so excited when my mom would tell me that we were going to Grandma and Uncle Richie's house. My Uncle Richie was so much fun, and he always kept me busy. I always loved to see my grandma, too. My sister, Kelly, who is three years older than I am, was usually at school when my mom and I went to visit them. My younger brother, Kevin, hadn't been born yet. So, I feel very fortunate to have spent as much time with Uncle Richie and Grandma as I did.

Ever since I can remember, my uncle and my grandma had health problems and were in wheelchairs. They had also been smoking for a long time. When I was about four, my sister and I already knew that smoking was bad for you. We got this idea because my sister had seen a movie at school about smoking and told me all about it. Smoking cigarettes or cigars can cause many diseases that people can die from. It kills brain cells, damages body tissue and often eventually causes cancer. We didn't want our grandma having those bad things happen to her body, so we decided to help her quit. We actually begged our grandma to stop smoking. Begging does work sometimes, because after that, Grandma quit—or at least she didn't smoke when we were around, and we were there an awful lot. My sister and I feel that Grandma lived longer because she quit smoking. It will always be one of my greatest accomplishments in life, and I'll always look up to my grandma for having the strength to quit a very addictive habit.

Then we tried to convince our uncle to quit. I was always proud of Uncle Richie for everything he did, but I wasn't proud of the fact that he smoked. I was very proud of my mom, though, because she never started. My mom and my uncle spent a lot of time together as kids and did a lot of the same things. This was one of the few that they disagreed on. We tried and tried—you wouldn't *believe* how hard we tried to tell him it was bad, but he just told us he couldn't stop, that it was too hard for him.

Later on, when I was in about second grade, smoking all of those cigarettes caused Uncle Richie to develop heart problems. An artery in his leg was not circulating blood like it was supposed to. Part of this was because of smoking; part was because of not eating very healthy foods. His leg turned all purple and blue and was not a very pleasant thing to look at. As I said, he didn't exactly eat the healthiest, but smoking didn't help one bit. Then he started losing his memory. I would break out in tears every time I saw him because he couldn't even remember my name, his own niece!

Uncle Richie got so sick that he had to go to hospice, a place where they take care of people who are dying. Then one day, my mom told me that my Uncle Richie had passed away. I cried for so long that, in the end, I had no tears left to shed.

Even though my Uncle Richie left us so early, he taught me many things. He did teach me some funny things, like never to put my finger up my nose because it could get stuck, but he also taught me a more important thing. He taught me that if you make a choice to never start smoking, then you have a better shot at a future. He also taught me to live life to its fullest because you never know when it's going to end.

I believe strongly in not smoking, thanks to my Uncle Richie, who I will always love dearly. I hope that now his story can teach many others that the choice they make when someone asks them if they want to smoke can be a matter of life and death.

Michelle Collins, eleven

[EDITORS' NOTE: *For facts and more information about smoking, log on to* www.cdc.gov/tobacco/tips4youth.htm.]

Buckling Up

An ounce of prevention is worth a pound of cure.

Henry de Bracton

It was my seventh-grade year, and I had just started middle school. This was also the year that my brother, Chris, got his driver's license. So, every day after school, he would pick me up and we would go home together. Sometimes it was fun to goof off in the car, like hang out the window and yell at friends who had to walk home. One thing was for sure—I was never really concerned with wearing my seatbelt. No matter how many times my parents told me to wear my seatbelt in the car, I never thought it was necessary. I just knew that nothing would ever happen to *me*.

One day, Chris picked me up late because I had a choir audition after school. "How did the audition go?" he asked. "It was fun. I think I got the part!" I exclaimed excitedly as I got in the car.

As I settled into my seat, I had this distinct feeling that I should wear my seatbelt. At first I ignored it, but then I decided to put it on. *It won't kill me to wear it this once,* I thought to myself.

Not more than 20 seconds after I snapped the buckle, a car came barreling out from nowhere and sent us spinning down a hill.

"Ahhhhhhhh!" Chris screamed, as he was thrown forward. I also flew forward into my seatbelt. When we reached the bottom of the hill, I looked over to see if he was all right.

Miraculously, both of us were okay except for some bruising. We climbed out to inspect the damage and were shocked to find that the car was *totaled.*

The guy who hit us had been going sixty miles per hour in a thirty-five mile per hour zone.

Later on, I found out that if I hadn't been wearing my seatbelt, I would have been thrown through the front windshield and may not have survived.

I don't know what made me want to wear my seatbelt that day, but now I know just how true my thought, *It won't kill me to wear it just this once,* was. It saved my life.

I no longer go *anywhere* in a car without first buckling up.

Cassandra Scheidies

Angel

*Do not wait for extraordinary circumstances
to do good action; try to use ordinary situations.*

Jean Paul Richter

Two days before my birthday, I got an e-mail that
would first make me cry and then make me smile.

Patrick was a kid that I knew from 4-H. We became
friends when I taught him how to show horses and he
showed my horse in the Junior Division at the County
Horse Show. We weren't "close" friends, but he was a
pretty cool guy. I mean, how many guys like to show
horses and will let a *girl* teach them how to do it? Not very
many.

After the horse show and his leaving the club, we kind
of lost contact. He sent me a Christmas card with his e-
mail address in it, but I put off e-mailing him. I thought,
How much stuff would we be able to talk about anyway?

His e-mail address was in my address book, and when

I changed servers, my new address went to everyone on my list. A few days later I got a reply from Patrick. It was brief; he asked me how I was and told me that he had started riding lessons again. He also asked me how Theo, my horse, was and he gave me his e-mail address. He ended with:

Hope you have a nice day. Patrick.

I replied to his e-mail, just small talk, and my e-mail looked something like this:

Hi! Nice to hear from you. That's so cool you're taking lessons. I'm really sorry that I didn't e-mail you at all during the winter. School has been really busy for me this year. Theo is doing good. He still knocks my radio off the stall door when I have the music on too loud. You'll have to come out and visit sometime.

A few more lines ended my e-mail. When his came back, he had some questions for me.

That's cool. What kind of music do you listen to? I like country. Do you like hunting?

Turns out, country music is the only thing I will listen to! And hunting is one of my favorite pastimes. I had no idea we had so much in common. I thought, *This is cool, we actually like the same stuff!*

Those e-mails were the start of a two-month correspondence that covered a wide variety of subjects. Having a lot in common made it easy to just chat. And to tell you the truth, I enjoyed getting his e-mails.

Toward the end of June, I wrote him a reply to an e-mail I had received four days earlier from him. I felt bad about not getting back to him right away and my e-mail wasn't much more than a note, but what I got back from him took my breath away.

Patrick's e-mail was short. He started off by telling me

he was going to be on vacation for three weeks and other stuff like that. But the postscript is what got me. It read:

P.S. I really wanted to say thank you for talking to me through e-mail. I'm usually really shy and am afraid to tell people what my likes are and all, plus I really have been bored since school let out. E-mailing you, at least I can talk to someone. You like everything I like so far, and as long as I have lived I have never met anyone so much like me. I've been used to a lot of people picking on me, and I've been pretty down the past few years.

When I read that people picked on him, my thoughts were, *Why in the world are kids so mean? Don't they realize how they are making him feel?* It broke my heart to hear him say that he had been down the past few years. I actually started crying when I read how the other kids treated him. It was then that I understood that Patrick was a kid who had needed a friend. My taking the time to e-mail him had made him feel important, like someone really cared enough to talk to him instead of just picking on him.

I want to thank you again. You like just about everything I like—hunting, cars, country music, horses. To me you're like an angel.

Those last six words touched my heart. It made me feel so good I just can't explain it! No one had ever said anything that nice to me before, and to be called an "angel" just made my day! When I e-mailed him back, I sincerely thanked him for what he said and told him to hang on.

That day, I learned a lesson that would stay with me for the rest of my life. From now on, I will take the time to do the little things, like replying to an e-mail or card, even if it's just a line or two. You never know how you might help someone and become his or her "angel."

Jena Pallone, sixteen

Starring on the Six O'Clock News

It is wise to disclose what cannot be concealed.

Johann Friedrich Von Schiller

"Erin," my mom sighed, "why don't you ever finish what you start?"

I did have a restless nature, but the real truth was that I never quite felt that I fit in. My brother had graduated from high school the year before and was both athletically gifted and popular. He was a head taller than all the other guys and had a diamond smile. Everyone gravitated toward his down-to-earth quiet charm. His perfection was maddening. At fourteen, it was painfully obvious to me that I would never walk in his shoes, only his shadow.

I was plump and moody, and I felt dreadfully average. And, despite the messages teenagers get about self-confidence and individuality, despite the fact that he no longer attended my school, I was insanely jealous of my brother. I knew it was up to me to make my own mark in high school.

I worked hard at developing my own unique style. I built a collection of dark clothes and weird jean skirts made from old Levis I picked up from Goodwill. However, I knew that I could not complete my look unless I was properly pierced. I knew of no one of any status who didn't have at least double-pierced ears. My single-pierced ears were far too conservative for the look I was going for.

"Mom?" I asked one morning. "Could I get my ears double-pierced?"

"Absolutely not. You have enough holes in your head already," she said.

Of course, I wasn't at all surprised at her response. I was notorious for taking a mile when I got an inch, and she probably thought I would pierce every part of flesh exposed to daylight when she wasn't looking. So rather than take no for an answer, I decided to take the task into my own hands. With a gigantic sewing needle from the closet, an unbaked potato and some ice cubes out of the freezer, I went into the bathroom and began the task of transforming myself from an ordinary person to an absolute rebel. I nearly passed out when the needle popped partway through my left ear. I waited for the dizzy spell to pass before finishing the job and popping it the rest of the way through. My old gold posts seemed to get stuck and had to be twisted awkwardly through my ear but I managed. I drizzled hydrogen peroxide across my wound. In the grand tradition of not finishing what I started I made a decision. No way was I piercing the other. One ear was cool enough.

For the next six weeks I was grateful for the camouflage of my hair. I would leave home with the piercing carefully concealed beneath my curls and pull my hair up once I reached the bus stop. I was absolutely sure that everyone at school noticed my ears. It didn't take too long though, before the whole world noticed.

A week later, our football team won the state championship. We were a Class B school, little more than a bunch of farm kids who took time out from baling hay and milking cows to toss a football around, so it was a surprise to everyone that our underdog team had won. The school was on fire with anticipation! The local news channel got wind of our school's recent victory and showed up with news vans, cameras and well-dressed reporters to do a story on our team. They spotted me with my bouncy ponytail and uniquely pierced ears and decided to interview me. I was going to be a star!

I said stuff like, "Awesome!" "Powerful!" and "Really, really cool!" before the cameras left. My little brother Adam wanted to chat about the interview all the way home. Because I was now famous, I graciously answered his questions.

When we arrived home, Andy was there for a visit. My parents quickly gathered around the TV when my little brother announced that I was going to be on the six o'clock news. Dad scrambled for a VCR tape, and then . . . there I was in living color. The first thing I noticed was my new gold post in my left ear. It was like the North Star glinting in the light of the news camera. My brother Andy spotted it too. He looked at me and grinned knowingly.

"Um . . ." I said. "I have some homework to do."

"Wait," my mom said. "Sit down. Adam honey, will you rewind that again so we can all watch it once more?" He did, and my earring was now the size of a baseball glinting in the sunlight. I got up and bolted for the stairs. I only made it halfway up before I felt hands grasp my ankles and pull. Before I could catch my footing I was flat on my back staring up into my mother's face. I was busted.

"I don't believe it!" she said. "How long have you been hiding this?"

"A month or so," I admitted. Her eyes narrowed and I

knew I was in for it. But then suddenly the corners of her mouth creased and she laughed.

"You know I have to ground you for disobeying," she said through giggles and snorts. "Let me see the other one," she said.

"I couldn't finish it. The first one made me really dizzy," I confessed. This was too much for her, and she burst into peals of laughter. Before long, I was laughing too.

In that moment it didn't matter what anyone else thought of me. It didn't matter that I lost driving privileges for a week, or that I was being laughed at. What mattered was that deep down I knew that Mom understood and she liked me. She *liked* me despite my insecurities, my oddities and my restlessness and yes, even my rebelliousness. And somehow, getting that other ear pierced didn't matter to me anymore.

Erin K. Kilby

Most Popular

Nothing happens by itself . . . it all will come your way, once you understand that you have to make it come your way, by your own exertions.

Ben Stein

When I entered the sixth grade, I went from being someone—to being no one. After being a popular kid for three years in elementary school, I had a tough time adjusting to this. The kids in middle school were cruel. I had been at the top of the world in elementary school, and now, no one wanted me.

On the first day of school, a kid threw a rock at me and hit me in the back of the head. I couldn't do anything about it because he was much bigger than I was, and he would definitely beat me up.

As the days passed, I got teased more and more. I got angry and I tried to retaliate, but all that happened was that I got in trouble. Eventually, I got depressed. I couldn't believe all the competition.

Then one day, I decided that I had to motivate myself. No one else was going to do it for me. *I had always been the smart guy since second grade, right?* I thought.

I began to push myself. I started out by taking an after-school class to help me get my grades up. I also signed up for piano lessons, and then I joined the chess club and the math team. I went to a math competition and took home first in the district and went on to the competition for the counties! I couldn't believe it! After my victories, everyone adored me. At the end of the year, in our yearbook, they put me in as "Mister Smarty Pants"!

My mom always said, "If you don't protect yourself, no one will." This is just the same thing. If you don't push yourself, you'll just be a lazy bum! If I can do it, you can do it—so get up and put yourself in front of the class!

Nathan D. Phung, eleven

Lost and Found

The measure of a man's real character is what he would do if he knew he would never be found out.

Thomas B. Macaulay

It was my twelfth birthday, and what I really wanted most was a new bicycle. A blue low-rider with fat tires. But I knew that my family couldn't afford one. My parents said that I should be happy that I had a bicycle at all—if you can call that rickety old thing that I own a bike.

A new bike was just a dream, so I settled for a nightstand. I figured that at least I would have a safe place to keep my private stuff away from the reach of my pesky younger brothers. So, I asked my parents for a nightstand with lockable drawers. And that's what I got.

We went to the secondhand furniture store and found an old dark brown nightstand. It didn't look too cool, but at least it had drawers that I could keep locked. I decided that I would paint it and glue some stickers on it to make it look better.

After we took it home, I was getting ready to paint it. When I pulled the drawers out, I felt something stuck to the back of the lowest drawer. I reached in all the way to the back, and guess what I found? A Ziploc bag with some papers in it.

Cool! Maybe I've found somebody's secret stuff, I thought. When I opened the bag, I realized that the papers were some kind of official-looking documents. And, wrapped in the papers were a bunch of ten and twenty dollar bills! Talk about finding a treasure! And on my birthday!

"Is this some kind of joke?" I said aloud. Maybe my family was playing a trick on me. Maybe this was fake money. But it looked pretty real. Somebody had been stashing money in this bag and hiding it in the back of the locked drawer. I went ahead and read the papers, and it turned out to be a will. Some old lady was leaving her savings for her son and grandchildren.

All this was too weird. My mind was going crazy. *Was I the luckiest twelve-year-old ever? With this money I could buy the coolest bicycle. I could even buy bicycles for my brothers. Who knows? Maybe I even had enough here to get a car for my parents, so that they could trash that embarrassing old junker that we have for a car.*

"Finders keepers, losers weepers," I started singing as I began counting the money. When I reached a thousand dollars, I had to stop. My mother was knocking on my bedroom door. I quickly closed the drawer with the money in it.

"How is your painting job coming along? Do you want some help?"

"No . . . thanks, Mom, I haven't even started. I . . . I'll call you when it's ready."

"Is everything all right?" she asked.

No, everything was not right. Actually, my stomach was growling.

"I'm okay," I fibbed. "I'll let you know when it's ready."

When my mother left my room, I lay on my bed, and, staring at the ceiling, I started thinking about this past week. *First, I didn't make the basketball team. Then, I flunked the math test. Finally, my little brother destroyed my science project. (That's why I needed a nightstand with locked drawers.) And now, I found this money on my birthday—the only good news in a long time. A solution to my problems. Yet, I don't feel good about it. How come?*

I would have to make up lies to tell my family and friends. "Finders keepers . . ." the saying goes. But that money wasn't really meant for me, was it? The lady had been saving it for her family. She must have died and nobody knew about the money hidden in the nightstand. Her family donated it to the secondhand store, and now it was in my hands.

What a dilemma! I could keep it and get all kinds of stuff for me and my family. *It wouldn't be too bad for me to keep it, if I shared it . . . right?* I bargained with myself. *What about keeping some and returning the rest? After all, nobody knew how much money was there . . . and it was my birthday! Or I could give it all back. Tell the truth. No new bicycles. No car.*

"Somebody help me with this!" I pleaded. But I really didn't need someone else to give me the answer. I already knew right from wrong. That's why I flunked the math test even though I could have cheated. I decided not to flunk this test. It was a test of honor. My honor.

I called my parents and my brothers into my bedroom and showed them what I had found. They were wide-eyed—speechless! When they asked, "What should we do about this?" I already had the answer.

"Let's take it back to the store and find her family." As I said this, my stomach quieted down.

The store owners could not believe it when we told them the story.

"You mean to say you found over a thousand dollars in cash and you are here to return it?" they asked, almost at the same time.

Looking through their donation records, they found the family's telephone number. They phoned them right there and then, and within a few minutes, they all came over to the store: her son, his wife and their three children—a family pretty much like ours. The parents had tears in their eyes. The old lady's twelve-year-old grandson just kept looking at me as people were telling the story over and over.

You see, they were all still sad about her death. And the father had just lost his job. They had been praying for help, and it turned out that I brought in the answer to their prayers. My act of honesty not only helped them pay the rent, but strengthened their faith and gave them hope.

I had never felt better. No new bicycle could have made me feel as good about myself as I felt that day. I may have flunked the math test, but I passed a more important one—a lost and found test of my own character.

Antonio Angulo Jr., twelve
As told by Marisol Muñoz-Kiehne

10

ON DEATH & DYING

I cannot hear your laughter
I cannot see your smile.
I wish that we could talk again
If only for awhile.
I know you're watching over me
Seeing everything I do.
And though you'll always be with me
I will always be missing you.
You taught me that life is much too short
And at any time could end.
But know that no matter where you are
You will always be my friend.
And when it's time for me to go
You'll be there to show me the way
I wish that you could still be here
But I'll see you again someday.

Rachel Punches, seventeen

Don't Forget to Wait for Me

I never got enough time with you, you left
*   before I could.*
I saw you in the coffin, but I never understood.
You entered my heart and never left; you're
*   always on my mind.*
Daddy, I can't wait to see you again.
But, God will choose the time.

Brittany McCroy, twelve

I remember my dad so well: the way he laughed, the
way he smiled, the corny jokes he used to tell and that
goofy look he put on his face to cheer me up. When I was
growing up, my dad was in the Navy, first sailing, and
then later working in the office. I remember how his office
was covered in cards that I had made him.

After my father retired from the Navy, I got to know
him much better. We did more things together, we talked
more often and he'd always, always listen to everything I

had to say. I never guessed that those good times would come to such an abrupt end.

On April 21, my dad sat down with me and told me something that changed my life forever. He had terminal lung cancer. When he told me, I felt hot and cold all over at the same time. I couldn't move. I couldn't breathe. I couldn't make a sound. I just sat there, and we both began to cry.

Months went by with regular hospital visits, chemotherapy and radiation. My father looked better, but then started to get worse with each passing day. I watched him, that strong, amazing, fearless man that I once knew, become weak, sick and tired. As the weeks went on, he could no longer eat, and he was worse than ever before. My mother had planned to bring him home to visit, but as December came, he became too sick to come home.

December 11 came. My birthday. We brought a cake to his room and he tried to sing happy birthday for me, then he called me over to his bed and kissed my forehead. I tried to believe that everything would be all right. That everything would go back to normal.

Two days later, I spent the night with my dad. I sat by his bed and watched him sleep, and he looked so peaceful. It was really hard for me to see him the way he was though, with IVs in his hands, and tubes all over. I cried myself to sleep every night after that.

On the night of December 20, I spent the night at my mum's friend's house. I lay awake that night, thinking about the next morning and, for some reason, fearing it. Maybe I knew or maybe I had a sense that something was going to happen. The next morning, she took me to the hospital and my mum was there. I sat down on a chair in the lounge, and I overheard my mother talking to her friend.

"The nurses say that today is the day." I felt exactly like I had eight months ago, a surge of hot and cold filling my body. My grandparents were at the hospital too; my tiny grandmother was shaking, and my grandfather was talking to a nurse. I didn't cry, though. There were other patients in the room, and I didn't want to upset them.

I went to see my dad. He looked so sick, so thin, but I held back my tears. I didn't want him to see me crying. I walked over to his bed and I bent down and hugged him. He whispered into my ear, "I love you," and kissed my forehead. I hugged my dad, kissed his cheek and whispered, "I love you, too, Daddy."

I stayed with him in that room until the nurses told me that I should get something to eat. My two sisters, my brother and my sister's boyfriend were waiting for me, so that we could all go out to lunch together. We went across the road, and we were halfway through our lunch when my sister's cell phone rang. I dreaded this phone call. My sister, in tears, mumbled something to the caller and hung up. "It's time."

We quickly paid the check and ran across the street. There were cars coming, but we didn't care. We wanted to see our father. When we got there, my grandma was standing in the hall crying. She told us that he was gone. It was too late. My sister collapsed on the floor and couldn't get back up. I ran into my dad's room and saw his lifeless body, just lying there, motionless. My mum was beside him, holding his hand and crying. I didn't know what to do; I was so confused. I just started crying and ran up to him. I hugged him and said, "Daddy, come back, come back," but he didn't.

We had a service for him on December 27. My mum had put an announcement in the paper about his death, giving details about the service. There were so many people there. Most of them didn't talk; they just sat there and cried. My godfather and my aunt both gave speeches, and both burst into tears when they finished.

To this day, almost six months after my father's death, I think about all those people crying for one man, for my father. I think a lot about different things. I think about how he isn't suffering anymore and how he is up in heaven with his grandparents smiling down at me. I think about how he won't be there for my graduation, and how he won't be able to walk me down the aisle at my wedding, but I also think about how he'll always be here for me—not in body, but in spirit—and how he'll forever be in my heart.

If I could say one thing to him right now, and he would be able to hear it, it would be this . . . *Daddy, don't forget to wait for me.*

Heather McPherson, twelve

Dedicated to My Best Friend, Kenneth

Vanished . . . not forgotten.
Knowing that we can never again share, giggle,
  play.
The loss of all my dreams, future hopes and
  expectations makes me angry.
I'm also frightened because now I know that
  dying is not only for the very old. I've just
  realized that life is precious, and the only gift
  I can give my friend is to remember what we
  shared.

Lois Greene Stone

I was nine years old when my daddy ran out on us. I
felt lonely and all alone, like I didn't have anyone, until
one day in May.

My mom got a phone call from an old boyfriend of
hers. His name was Kenneth Ray and he lived in
Kentucky. My mom and Kenneth talked on the phone to
each other a lot over the next few months, and then

Kenneth decided to come to Michigan for a visit.

He looked like a giant the first time I saw him. He stood six feet, four inches tall and weighed about 350 pounds. At first, I didn't think that I would like him, but he turned out to be a very nice person. My mom said he was a big teddy bear. During his first visit, we spent a lot of time together, and I got to know him really well.

After that, we grew closer and closer. Kenneth would come to visit on holidays and for weeklong visits whenever he could. When he was at his house, he would call me every night to ask me about my day at school, tell me he missed me and that he would see me again real soon. He never failed to tell me good night and that he loved me, then remind me to say my prayers.

Kenneth and I became the best of friends. We talked about everything: my brothers, my sister, my nephews and my niece. Kenneth loved my whole family, but he loved me the most. He used to say that I was his boy and nobody could ever take me away from him.

One day in January, Kenneth came up for a visit and he brought my mom a surprise—a Chinese pug dog. Kenneth stayed with us for three days, and we played with the dog, wrestled, laughed and just had fun being together. Then came Friday morning, and Kenneth had to go. I got up early to see him off. He hugged me, and told me he loved me and I told him I loved him, too. As he pulled away, he leaned out of the car window and promised me he would call me as soon as he got home that night.

Kenneth lived about 500 miles from us, and it usually took him about eight hours to get home. This time, on the way, he stopped at a rest area somewhere in Ohio to stretch his legs. He went into the men's room and while he was in there, Kenneth had a heart attack. Someone found him about 30 minutes after it happened, but it was too late for Kenneth. He was gone.

My mom got a call about nine o'clock that night from someone letting her know that Kenneth had passed away. My mom just lost it. She kept crying and saying, "Please God, don't let him be gone! God—tell me this is a bad dream!"

But it wasn't just a bad dream. My best friend was gone, and I was all alone again. My mom kept telling me that God needed another angel, so he picked Kenneth to come to heaven to be with him. Nothing made me feel any better. I cried for days.

It's been very hard to get through this. My mom has helped a lot, and people at my school have helped, too. Mom says Kenneth can't come back to us, but some day we can go to see him.

Kenneth was like a best friend and a dad—he was everything to me. I'll always miss him. Until he came along, I had no man to look up to and want to be like; Kenneth played that part and made a big difference in my life. He'll live in my heart forever because he was my best friend in the whole world.

I love you, Kenneth.

Nicholas Hall, ten

Kristina

It was a dreary day, and my dad was driving me home to my mom's. I spent the weekends with my dad since my parents' divorce. I had grown accustomed to the fact that I would visit him separately, maybe because they divorced when I was so young.

Suddenly, my dad turned to me and said, "Ashley, your cousin Kristina has been diagnosed with cancer." The words threw daggers at my heart.

"What?" I gasped. I knew what cancer could do to a person because I remembered what had happened to my Granny. She died from it.

Shortly after my dad told me about Kristina, she started going to the hospital often. Sometimes when I went to visit her, I would have to wear a mask so that I wouldn't bring in any of my germs. Although she seemed uncomfortably pale and had tubes in her skin, everyone thought she would be fine, and it would soon be over. But "a few months" turned into two long years. During that time, her strength was an inspiration to me. When we played together, we would laugh and giggle, because we were both pretty young; she was only ten years old and I was only eight.

During the summer, it seemed that a miracle happened. For a few months, the cancer was still. Kristina was home, and it seemed that she was better, although she had a tube coming out of her chest that the doctors had used for her chemotherapy. Because of that, she wasn't allowed to go swimming, but she still wanted to go to the beach with me and our little cousins. She had to wear a hat at the beach because she was bald. Her beautiful, wavy brown hair had been lost. She would play with my long blonde hair and whisper, "You're so lucky to have hair like this." I didn't understand. Inside I felt lonely and confused, but Kristina seemed to be okay with what was going on, and she was really happy to be home with her family.

Kristina seemed to get better and she went back to school. She was through with her treatments, and her hair started to grow back. Then, early the next spring, she went back to the hospital for a checkup, and they found out that Kristina's cancer had spread. We were all slowly losing hope, though we continued to pray. I didn't get to visit her for a while, but then when I finally saw her again, the look of joy and laughter was gone from her eyes.

That whole summer, Kristina was in a wheelchair, and by August, she had grown thinner and thinner. I wasn't allowed to see her anymore because she was very tired all the time, and it was hard for her to breathe. Our whole family knew that she was dying. And she did, just like that. Even though we sort of expected it, it still hit everyone hard. Especially me. When I was told, I sat quietly collecting the pieces of shattered memories in my soul.

At the funeral, our family sat in the back. The room was so crowded with people who loved her. I just looked straight ahead. I wanted to mourn, but I couldn't. I would never accept her death, and I didn't know why.

Then Dad explained to me about the "Rainbow of Hope." It seems that when Kristina left us, her mom, my Aunt Kathy, had asked for one thing. She asked God for a sign that Kristina was safe with him. The very next evening a huge rainbow appeared in the sky, and my Aunt Kathy knew that she had her answer.

After the funeral, we tossed Kristina's ashes into the sea, near where we had scattered Granny's ashes. On the way home, a glittering star of all colors was shining in the sky. It was Kristina smiling down on us from heaven with peace, tenderness and love.

In Kristina's honor, Aunt Kathy and Uncle John joined an organization to help raise money for children with cancer and blood diseases. That year, my dad's whole family, and many friends, walked for Kristina in a fundraiser for the organization. We all walked proudly. Our group was called "Kristina's Krew." Every September we walk for Kristina—rain or shine.

The next year, Aunt Kathy designed a ribbon to bring awareness to people about childhood cancer. It has the rainbow on it that Kristina sent to us. Aunt Kathy went to our state government with her "Rainbow of Hope" pin, and New Jersey made it the official symbol for childhood cancer awareness in our state. The next year, Aunt Kathy started her own Web site called "Kristina's Rainbow of Hope."

I am at ease now with Kristina's death and have come to realize that everything happens for a reason. Because of Kristina, a lot of people will know more about the effects of childhood cancer and how they can help children in treatment. I know that would make Kristina happy.

Ashley Kopf, eleven

[EDITORS' NOTE: *Shortly after Kristina passed away, her mother, Kathy, noticed Kristina's* Chicken Soup for the Kid's Soul *book in her room. She sat down to look at the stories Kristina had been reading, and found that the book was opened to the story "Rebecca's Rainbow," a story about a young girl who, after her death, sends a rainbow to her mother. Kathy tells us that rainbows continue to touch her life in the most unexpected ways. For more information, visit Kathy's Web site at* www.kristinasrain bowsofhope.org.]

She Is Now My Sun

In the final analysis, the question of why bad things happen to good people transmutes itself into some very different questions, no longer asking why something happened, but asking how we will respond, what we intend to do now that it happened.

Rabbi Harold S. Kushner

To me, life is a gift no matter what shape or form.

One Thursday in April, I was awakened by the noise of my parents talking and making breakfast upstairs. My older brother and sister were upstairs running around trying to put their things together for school. I put on the new skirt I'd bought over the weekend while thinking about how I was going to make my day perfect. I ate breakfast with my family. Then my mom offered to walk me to school instead of my dad driving me. She said she wanted to walk for exercise, so I thought it would be fine.

My dad said that he wanted to take me—that he had a weird feeling. But my mom and I both agreed to walk.

As we were walking down the hill to my school, we were talking about how the body is like a chocolate-making machine—when you put the wrong ingredients in, like alcohol or drugs, the chocolate will come out wrong. Weird, how you remember certain stuff, like I did that conversation.

Holding hands, we crossed the crosswalk to get to my school, and that's when it happened.

A car came really fast, and my mom tried to push me out of the way, but I had already run to the sidewalk. When I turned around, I saw my mom flying through the air, her hands crossed and her eyes shut. For me, everything was in slow motion. Mom landed on her head, and it started to bleed. I screamed uncontrollably while some people called my dad and the police. Soon, I saw my dad come rushing down the street in his car with the most scared look on his face. He and I followed the ambulance to the hospital.

While we waited in the waiting room, I remember feeling like this can't be happening to me. I also felt that my mom's pain was happening because of me. If she hadn't walked me to school that day, none of this would have happened. When the nurse finally came to get us, I was scared of what I was going to see, but I ran and hugged my mother. I started to feel dizzy, so the nurse told me to sit down.

Later that day, we went to pick up my sister and then my brother. When we told my sister the horrible news, she started to scream and cry. When we told my brother, he just stayed silent. We all went to visit my mom at the hospital that night, and the next day at school, everyone made her cards.

A few days later, Mom was much better, it seemed.

They let her come home, and when I got home from school, I saw my mom up and about trying to clean the house. I was so shocked! I dropped all my stuff and ran to give her a huge hug. (Oh, how I wish I could do that now!)

A few months passed, and she became healthy again. My family and I cherished her much more then we had before. That summer we went to Disneyland. She was so excited that she would walk ahead of us like she was a little girl again. I loved those times.

Then on a dark day in October, she came down with this mysterious illness. She had a fever and pains in her face. Then she would need blankets because she was cold. Thinking that the pain in her face was because of her teeth, she had a root canal done. A few months later, her vision started to get blurry, and she couldn't taste her food very well. I got scared from not knowing what was happening to my mom. I just knew I wanted her back the way she had been before, when she was healthy

Soon, my mom started to lose her balance when she walked, but she still tried so hard to walk across the hall to kiss my sister and me good night. Then, finally, she couldn't even swallow or balance her head on her neck. She would stay in her bed all day in so much pain. I know she was scared. She tried so hard not to let us know, so we wouldn't get depressed!

Then in late March, I had a sleepover for my birthday with a few friends. The next morning, my mom left my house early in an ambulance to go to the hospital. I didn't realize that that was going to be her last day in our home. I wish I'd known that, so I could have spent more time with her. But I'd go visit her in the hospital about every day. When I would leave I'd say, "I love you, Mom. When you get home, I promise we'll go to Hawaii together."

The doctors took all these tests, biopsies and scans, but they couldn't find anything wrong with her. She had so many surgeries and biopsies and X rays, but they still couldn't find *anything*. Soon she lost her ability to speak, but before she did, she told us that she felt that her mysterious illness was a result of the head injury that she had from being hit by the car. We were so frustrated because we could get no medical proof of what was making her sick so that they could treat her.

Then one day, Mom just stopped breathing, and they decided to put a tube in her throat so a machine could help her breathe. A few months went by with her in constant pain because of the irritating tube in her throat.

Every night I would go to sleep thinking of how lonely she was in her hospital room, and I'd be scared of what tomorrow would bring. Sometimes, when I was visiting her, I would just stare into her eyes, and I'd get this amazing feeling of comfort. I'd feel like no one could hurt her or me.

Whenever we'd leave the hospital room, I'd get to see that half smile that took up all her energy, and I'd hold on to it like never before. In those eight months of her being in that hospital bed, all I thought about was her: at school, at home, at night, at the hospital. All I wanted was my mom back. Nothing in the world could heal my heart—she was the only one who could. She was the biggest thing that was in my life and I wanted to help her so badly!

She was my best friend.

She was my hero.

She was my one and only mom.

When I was a little girl, I remember hearing about my friend losing her mom, and I thought to myself, *Nothing like that could ever happen to me.* Now I look at the world so much differently!

After many visits filled with tears and sadness, the day came that the doctors began losing hope. Finally, my dad had to make the biggest decision of our lives. The doctors wanted to take out the tube to see if Mom could breathe without the machine's help. My dad thought of what she would have wanted and made the difficult decision to let nature take its course. So, he told the doctors to take it out. We all had hope in our hearts that she would learn how to breathe on her own and come back home.

The day the doctors took the machine off, we went to visit her. She was so much happier because she was finally a bit more comfortable after so many months of having that thing taped to her neck. Still, that visit was different. Deep inside, we all knew what was going to happen. This visit was full of tears from both her and us. When it was my turn to go to her, I held her hand and kissed it softly and caringly. I looked hard at her, for I knew that it might be the last time that I could. I looked at her cheeks because that is where I would always kiss her before I went to bed. I looked at her lips, and I remembered all the those times when I got hurt and only her soft loving kiss would make me better. Then I looked into her eyes and got that feeling of comfort. I put my arms around her, and she tried to do the same, but her body wouldn't let her. I kissed her once more and went to the corner of the room where I could think of all our times together.

Then the time came when we had to say good-bye. I didn't want to believe it, but I knew what was going to happen. As we said our last good-byes, I saw that smile— the smile that could bring out the sun no matter how cloudy it is. And that's exactly what it did for me. I will remember that smile for my lifetime, for my spirit's existence—for eternity.

As we left her hospital room, I turned around and saw her lying there looking so peaceful, her arms to her side and a fading smile on her face. I blew her one last kiss, then turned around.

That same night, clouds flew into my heart and a thunder-bolt burned a hole inside of me. She is now a part of the sun-set. She is now a streak in the rainbow. She is one with the ocean. She is now my sun that cleared away the clouds.

As much as I want to feel sorry for myself and not let my life move on and to always feel the pain she had to go through, I know that she would say to me, "Life is a gift, Amber, no matter what shape or form. Live it like it's your last day. Live it to the fullest, and take *nothing* for granted!"

Those words lead me every day. Those words are why I am still here. I want to cherish my gift of life for my mom. Every breath I breathe is for her. Every step I take is for her. Every smile I smile is for her. I dedicate my every day to her.

And now, no matter what happens, I will remember that smile of hers, and I will smile in honor of her, know-ing we both can take the clouds away and fill the world up with sunshine!

Amber Kury, eleven

Luann. *Reprinted by permission of United Feature Syndicate.*

The Baseball Spirit

Well, baseball was my whole life. Nothing's ever been as fun as baseball.

Mickey Mantle

It was summer, and my parents sent me to spend time with my grandpa for my thirteenth birthday. He had been diagnosed with cancer the Christmas before. I was in this strange rebellious stage, and I decided to bring my skateboard and skates and not spend much time with him. I knew some kids down the street, and I was going to hang out with them. I was a major baseball fan (I strongly favored the Cardinals), so when I was packing, I slipped my baseball glove in my backpack, too, thinking I could maybe play a little catch. I had planned everything.

Don't get me wrong, I wasn't trying to be mean or anything; I loved my grandparents, and it would be great to see my grandpa. I just wasn't planning on hanging out with him; but then, I never thought the spirit of baseball could bring two people together the way that it did that summer.

I was on the computer at my grandparent's house when Grandpa asked me if I wanted to play catch.

"Sure," I said, reluctantly.

We went outside to play catch, and at first I didn't think much of it, but with every throw, I realized that I was feeling more and more connected to him. I felt like I could have played catch with my grandpa forever. Later that night, he showed me his Mark McGwire first-baseman's mitt and his Mickey Mantle bat. I thought those were the coolest things in the world.

On August 13, we went to a St. Louis Cardinals' game at Busch Stadium. While I was watching *my* heroes, like Fernando Vina, Albert Pujols, Jim Edmonds and Mark McGwire, my grandpa was telling me all about *his* childhood heroes. Through that whole game, I felt even more connected to him.

Toward the end of my time in Illinois, I found Grandpa's book about Mark McGwire's historic 1998 season. He caught me looking at it so much that he decided I could keep it, and he signed it to me:

To: Caleb Mathewson
From: Maynard Mathewson "MATTY"
Remember the summer of 2001
Grandpa

I didn't think much of the autograph then, but later, I treasured it more than anything.

That night I had to get ready to go home, and we decided to go outside and play catch for what turned out to be one last time. My grandpa and I laughed and talked while I did my best imitation of the top Major League pitchers, not knowing how much I would treasure this moment later in life.

I came back to Illinois the next summer with my family to see him. My grandpa was confined to his bed and barely able to walk. The cancer had spread to every bone in his body.

The very last time I saw him was the last night I was there. I was in his room watching a Cardinals game on television with him. He struggled to sit up and said, "If anything happens to me, I want you to have my Mark McGwire first-baseman's mitt and my Mickey Mantle bat." It meant so much to me, I can't explain it. I could barely hold back my tears.

Two days later, his lungs filled up with fluid and on August 13, 2002, Maynard Mathewson died at 1:00 A.M., *exactly one year to the day* of attending that Cardinals game with me, which was still so fresh in my memory.

When I went to his funeral, on his casket there were two baseball caps. One was a Yankees cap and the other was the same St. Louis Cardinals cap that he wore to the Cardinals game that we attended together.

Because of my grandpa and the love for the game that we shared, I know that I'll always have the baseball spirit in me. The bat, the glove and the book that he gave me are always with me to remind me that my grandpa, Maynard Mathewson, and I will forever be connected by the spirit of baseball and the summer we spent together.

Caleb Mathewson, fourteen

"I think grandpas are just overgrown kids, Joey."

Forever in My Heart

The only cure for grief is action.

George Henry Lewis

When my brother Nathan was only five months old, he was diagnosed with an extremely rare kidney disease called Denys-Drash Syndrome. At about the age of one, my brother's kidneys weren't good anymore and he was going to need a new one. He went on home dialysis, and then my dad ended up giving my brother one of his kidneys. Children who have organ transplants need to take medicine to keep their bodies from rejecting the new organ, and this medicine also weakens their immune systems. So, Nathan had a lot of trouble fighting off infections after the organ transplant and was often sick.

When Nathan was two-and-a-half years old, he caught pneumonia and was in the hospital. Finally, he was able to come home, but, two nights later, he died. Even though I was devastated, I knew that our family could make it through and everything would all be okay if we just stuck together.

About six months after Nathan died, his third birthday came around, July 24. My birthday is a couple of days later, on July 29. Usually my family celebrated our birthdays together, but that year I really didn't feel like celebrating mine without him. So, we decided to go ahead and celebrate both of our birthdays and give the gifts that we would have given to Nathan to other kids.

That was Nathan's first toy drive. We gave all the toys to the children at the Cardinal Glennon Children's Hospital in St. Louis, where Nathan had stayed when he was in and out of the hospital. The following year, during the now-annual Nathan Weilbacher Toy Drive, I was able to donate $3,000 and over nine hundred new toys to the children at Cardinal Glennon. The toy drive that I started to honor my brother's memory gets bigger and better each year.

I once heard a saying that some lives go on forever in the hearts and the lives of the people they touch, and I know that this is true with my brother Nathan. I still miss him very much. I will always miss him. He touched my family and my life in so many ways. Recently, he sent me a healthy little brother that we named Nicholas Nathan. I know that my new little brother is a gift from Nathan, because I can see it every time I look into his eyes.

I want to thank Nathan for everything he has taught me and given to me, and I want him to know I love him. I realize that where he is now there is no more suffering and that he is at peace. Nathan, I will always remember you and I will always love you. You will forever be my little angel!

Lauren Ashley Weilbacher, thirteen

Guardian Angel

My dad's side of the family always meets on Christmas Eve to exchange gifts. My Uncle Terry and my Aunt Vikki and their kids, Colin, Maggie, Nolan, Ian and Jenal would come to celebrate Christmas at my dad's house. The December of 1995 was the last time I ever saw my cousin Colin.

I was staying with my dad for the weekend, about a week after Christmas. I was watching television in the bedroom, when he told me to come into the living room and asked me to sit down on the couch. Then he explained to me that my cousin Colin had died.

Colin had been at a friend's house and decided to go home. He called Jenal, his older sister, telling her that he was on his way. Colin never arrived, so on his way home from work Uncle Terry went looking for him and found Colin lying in the snow.

Uncle Terry called my Aunt Vikki, and they rushed Colin to the hospital. The doctors told them that Colin had had a stroke, and they put him on a life support machine. He would be able to live, but he would be a vegetable. My Uncle Terry held Colin in his arms while he and my Aunt Vikki made the hardest decision of their lives: to keep him on the machines or not. They felt Colin shouldn't live that way and decided to let him go. Colin Timothy O'Brien died on December 27, 1995, in Memorial Hospital. He was only eight years old.

I took it pretty hard. Colin and I were about the same age, and our birthdays were only three weeks apart. His viewing, when you go see the person in the casket, was about three or four days after his death. It was extremely sad. Everyone was crying. I still remember seeing him, lying there, so lifeless and peaceful. At his funeral, Father Cam, the priest at Corpus Christi where Colin went to school, said a few words and we all put flowers on top of his casket.

Afterwards, Uncle Terry and Aunt Vikki threw a huge memorial service for Colin at the Corpus Christi school gym. Uncle Terry said a few words, and I asked him if he missed Colin. His reply was, "Yes, I do. A lot." I remember thinking to myself, *so do I . . . a lot.*

After awhile, I couldn't take the fact that Colin was really gone. I couldn't seem to get it out of my mind. So, my mom and dad sent me to a place called hospice. It's a place where they help kids like me deal with the fact of death. I counseled with a lady named Michelle every Wednesday for about a month. We played with things like dolls and Play-Doh while I acted out how I felt about death and my other feelings. Michelle was very nice to me.

I also met with a group of other kids who had lost a family member or friend. We each made a book, which included a letter that we wrote to the loved one, a picture of us with our loved one and other things. The other kids were nice, and I made friends with one girl named Nicole, who had lost her grandma.

Later, I went to camp Evergreen, which was just like a regular camp, only we met in groups to talk about our loved ones, and death. Each camper has a counselor, or a "buddy," that they do almost everything with. My buddy was named Rebecca. On the first day, we all made a necklace with our name on the front and our buddy's name on the back.

I learned a lot from hospice. I understood that Colin was in a better place now and that he was happy. I still miss him every once in a while, and I get a little teary-eyed. But, life goes on. I turned thirteen this year, and I visited Colin's grave. I cried hard because he only got to live eight years of his life. He will never graduate from high school, get married or have kids.

I try to visit Colin's grave whenever I need to talk. I tell him what's going on with me, my friends, school, family, and even boyfriends. It makes me feel better. I believe that Colin is my guardian angel. Doesn't everyone need one?

Colleen O'Brien, thirteen

Dapples

When I first saw her, I knew we were perfect for each other.

And we were.

I had loved horses since I was six and having one changed my life. When I received her as a Christmas gift, I couldn't have been happier. Though she had been neglected and abused her whole life, over the next nine months, she gained trust with me. She soon followed me without my having to lead her, and we became the best of friends. I loved her.

Then, one day, I was riding her in the round pen when she suddenly bucked about four times. Birgit and Arnold, the people we boarded her with, thought that she was too high-strung for me. I cried as Birgit told me that there was a woman who was interested in buying her and would take care of her. The only words I could choke out were, "I don't want to sell her." The words they said after that were a blur because I was so upset I couldn't concentrate on what they were telling me. As I dismounted, I hugged her sweaty neck and cried. I'll never forget what Arnold told me next.

"She ain't goin' nowhere."

He said it to assure me they wouldn't sell her without my permission. Dapples nudged me apologetically. I left the round pen still crying. Over the next few weeks, she still bucked every time I rode her. However, I knew she wasn't trying to get me off intentionally, but she was bucking for some other reason I didn't know about. It made me sick inside that everyone was jumping to conclusions without considering what was going on with Dapples. My own mom even tried to talk me into selling her. I knew my mom was only concerned about my safety, and I also knew she didn't want to sell her any more than I did. My simple answer was always, "No." I would leave the room angry and upset all at once.

Then the unexpected happened. One morning at 5:00, I woke up to my mom talking on the phone to her work. All I can remember her saying is . . .

"Yes, I have a sick child." But I wasn't sick. *Who in my family was so sick that Mom would miss work for the day?*

Mom came into my room and gently shook me to wake me up. "I just got a call from Birgit," Mom said. "She said Dapples just doesn't seem like herself."

I panicked. Colic was the only thing I could think of. It was a horrible stomach sickness that can kill a horse within hours. There are lots of ways it can be caused, but not so many ways to make it go away. If the horse gets cramps, he wants to roll over on the ground to ease the pain. However, in the process, his intestines get twisted up, preventing his body from moving waste through correctly. This kills him if a vet cannot perform surgery and be successful in "untwisting" his gut. Also, if the horse eats dirt along with eating grass or hay, a stone will build up in his stomach and literally block his bowels.

When my sister, mom and I arrived at Birgit's house about an hour later, all I can remember is walking Dapples around in the arena for the next nine hours, trying to help move things through. We left that night exhausted and confused.

The next morning, my mom and I went out there, knowing that if there was no manure in her stall, we had to call the vet out for his last visit to her. I ran to her stall. I screamed as I saw the clean stall with Dapples lying in the corner. I picked up her head. She knew her time was near.

I didn't know what to do. How could I help her? She lay there in the wet dirt with her head in my lap. Her eyes were closed and her stomach was bloated. Two of her friends whinnied from other stalls close to hers. They knew her time was coming soon, too. My beautiful Arabian angel was suffering from colic, and no one could help her. When I looked into her eyes, the spunky Dapples I once knew was gone. All that was left was a helpless little mare, struggling to breathe. I stroked her beautiful face and as much as it killed me inside, I talked to her.

"Don't worry, Dap, you'll never be in a stall again. No more gates. No more saddle. You'll be a free Pegasus. Free to roam the skies. You'll forever live in peace. It'll be okay, Dapples. I'll be okay. I'll be fine. Just think about your wings. Think about your wings." I repeated myself many times. Not just for her, but for my own comfort. I must have told her I loved her a zillion times. I could hardly speak, because my throat felt as though it had closed in. I promised her that she would live in a big green pasture with no fences. I also told her that I would watch for a new star that night—a big, bright star.

While I told her this, she seemed to calm down a bit. I took her out in the arena and prayed for a miracle. She lay in the dirt, and I sat next to her, holding her head. About thirty minutes later the vet arrived, and it was time for

Dapples to stop suffering. The vet took the lead rope and said it would be best if I didn't see this. I kissed her on the mane. I could smell the wet dirt in her tangled hair. It was sprinkling outside. Perfect weather for the worst day. "I love you, Dapples," I said before running to the barn.

About two minutes later, I heard her crash to the ground. My mom and I covered her with a blue tarp and then cried together until a truck that hauls away dead animals arrived. I couldn't watch. I sat on a bench at the front of the house.

Soon I saw that horrible truck of death drive away with poor Dapples in the back. The man drove away as though she was worth nothing. I buried my face in my mom's arms and just cried my heart out.

I'll never forget that awful day. I remember telling my mom on the way there to turn off the radio. I didn't want to remember the song that played, because I knew I would hate it for the rest of my life. I still sit in my room and cry sometimes because I know I could have proven to everyone that just because she bucked didn't make her a criminal. It's just like people. Everyone has a chance to be as good as they want to be. It all depends on what goes on in their minds and hearts. I will never know how well Dapples would have done if she would have survived. I am forced to wonder the rest of my life.

She left me before I was ready, but in the short time I owned her, she showed me how strong friendship can be. It can survive anything, even if everyone else is against it.

She also taught me how to trust, to love and to have faith in others. I had faith in her when no one else did. And that is something I'll never regret, or forget.

Nicole Buckner, twelve

My Uncle Frank

If it weren't for memories, I'd probably still be crying. I have come to realize that sometimes, all you can hold on to are memories.

Brooke Raphalian, twelve

When my mom and dad bought their first house on Kendrick Loop, they moved right next door to Frank and Eleanor. Our house was a cute little three-bedroom rancher with a very big backyard and there was a fence between our yard and theirs.

That same year in May, I was born. When my mom and dad brought me home from the hospital, Frank and Eleanor were the first neighbors to hold me. He was over almost every day to see me and hold me. As I got older, he would come over and ask my mom if I could come over to his yard, so I could talk to him and keep him company while he worked in his garden. The best thing was that he had a big cherry tree in his backyard, and he would save one branch, one that I could reach, and let me pick all of the cherries and eat them. Before long, I began to call him Uncle Frank because he was just like family to me.

On special occasions like my birthdays and holidays, he would always remember me and come to the door with presents. On Halloween, he would save a big bag of candy for me. For Christmas, he would bring me a candy cane or a doll.

Uncle Frank was one of the kindest and most generous people I have ever met. He was always ready to help people out. I remember times when he drove people to the grocery store and helped them do their grocery shopping if they were sick or couldn't do it themselves.

Every summer, you would see Uncle Frank outside in his summer gardening outfit, which were his baggy shorts and sometimes no shirt. He wore a big straw hat with a wide, floppy brim, his gardening gloves, which were the kind of gloves women wear to wash dishes, and always his boots. In the winter, he wore his gardening overalls along with his boots and gardening gloves.

Uncle Frank's backyard was like the Garden of Eden. It was always perfectly groomed, with lots of flowering shrubs, blueberry bushes, grapevines, rose bushes, lilac bushes, and his grass was always very thick and green. He loved to garden, but he also loved to use his hands to build things. Uncle Frank built a gazebo so that his wife and daughter could sit outside in the backyard and have some shade. Then he built a smokehouse by hand with scrap lumber to smoke the fish that he caught on his fishing trips. And he made lots of bird feeders. He especially loved to feed the birds.

But Uncle Frank was happiest when he was working on something special in his woodworking shop. His shop was full of power tools and everything was always very neat and organized. Everywhere you looked, you would see jars of nuts, bolts and screws and tidy rows of screw-drivers, hammers, saws and all sorts of other tools. His shop was *always* clean and tidy.

Uncle Frank just loved our old dog, Kodiak. He was a big malamute and husky cross with blue eyes. Uncle Frank loved him so much that he cut a big round hole in the fence so that Kodiak could stick his head through the hole and see him while he was gardening. Kodiak was too heavy, so he was on diet dog food that he really hated. Although he never ate his dinner, he was gaining weight! One day, we found out why. Feeling sorry for Kodiak, Uncle Frank and Eleanor had been feeding him things like Black Forest ham, cheese, salami and anything else they had that they thought Kodiak would like.

One day, Uncle Frank had smoked some salmon and put it out to cool in his backyard. Someone had left our back gate open, and when Uncle Frank came out after lunch he discovered that all of his smoked salmon was gone. Then he found Kodiak lying on his back in the shade, picking and eating grapes off of his grape vines! Kodiak would spend all day with Uncle Frank, keeping him company. Even after we told them that Kodiak was on a strict diet, every once in a while, Eleanor or Uncle Frank would sneak him a special treat.

When we moved into a bigger house that was across the street and five houses down, Uncle Frank was very sad to see us go. But almost every day, he would stop in to see us or wave to us as he rode his bike to the mailbox. In the summer, he would stop by to see if I wanted to come over for a cold drink and a visit in his gazebo or to pick cherries. He loved to talk about how he met and fell in love with his wife, and he loved to talk about his four children and all of his grandchildren.

Once or twice, he took my friend Jeffrey and me to Dairy Queen for some ice cream. He also took many videos of Jeffrey and me as we grew up. He loved and knew every kid on our block, but I know I was special to him.

One Tuesday in November, I was walking home from school with my friends when I saw a fire truck come screaming down our street with the lights and sirens on. My dad and his fellow firefighters were on the truck. The truck stopped in front of Uncle Frank's house. Eleanor was in their front yard waving frantically. My dad ran inside with his medical bag in his hand. Peter, the fire chief arrived next, followed by Rescue 11 and an ambulance. By this time, I knew that something terrible had happened to Uncle Frank. I saw Uncle Frank being carried outside on a backboard; he was wearing his gardening overalls. They lifted him over the fence in front of his house, placed him on a stretcher and rushed him into the ambulance and off to the hospital. Then I saw my dad come out; he was kind of crying. He told me that Uncle Frank had suffered a massive heart attack and that he had tried to save him with CPR, but he didn't think he would make it. He put me in his truck and some of the firemen that I know came over to talk to me. My dad took me home and snuggled with me for a while, and then he had to go back to work at the fire hall.

It was a very sad day for me, one I will never forget. I still find it hard to believe that Uncle Frank is gone, and every time we walk or drive by his house, I expect to see him out in his front yard in his overalls and sun hat, watering his garden and waving to us. I loved him very much and I will never, ever forget him. I know he is up in heaven with Kodiak, eating smoked salmon and grapes and looking down on me.

MacKenzie Exner, thirteen

Ramon

I didn't know about the feelings you felt
You should have told me, I could of helped
I didn't know, and now I just cry
Suicide is a horrible thing—you were too young
*   to die.*

Tori Lowes, twelve

It was an average April day when the phone rang. I rushed to answer it.

"Hello," I answered

"Hi, Emma, it's Kim. Is your mom home?"

Kim is my mom's friend, and she sounded like something was urgent.

"She's out of town but should be back this evening," I replied, wondering what had happened.

"Well, is your dad home?" she asked quickly.

My dad was in the shower, so I told her that he couldn't

talk at the moment. She told me to tell him to call her as soon as possible. I hung up the phone thinking, *What could be that important? Had something really gone wrong? Had something happened to her son, Bain, who had been in my class since kindergarten?*

I sat down to read, but I was shaken.

A while later, I was reading and had forgotten to tell my dad about the phone call, even though he had been out of the shower for quite some time. The sky was dimming, and it was getting to be dinnertime. I was jolted from my story by the ring of the phone. I hopped up to get it.

It was Kim again. I handed the phone to my dad, who had come into the kitchen to see if it was for him. I went back to my chair to read, but of course I wasn't really reading, but rather pretending to read while I listened intently to their conversation.

My dad's voice became serious and solemn, and as I listened, it seemed to become more so. I heard things like, "I'm so sorry," and "He was a great kid."

My stomach became queasy. *What did my dad mean by, "He was a great kid"? Who was he talking about?* I felt nervous and scared.

I heard my dad say a quiet, "Good-bye," and a click. The floorboards creaked as my dad headed across the kitchen toward me. I braced myself for whatever news I was about to hear. Dad came to stand next to me and was silent for a moment before he spoke. He seemed very nervous and things felt awkward.

"Emma," he began. I stared up at him, dreading the news, yet wanting to hear it.

"Ramon's dead," he said quietly.

My stomach lurched. I shook. *Had I heard wrong? This couldn't be right, but my dad wouldn't joke about such things.*

Ramon had been in my class since grade one, and had become an important part of my school. He had come from Germany, not knowing a word of English, but he learned the language rapidly since reading had become a passion of his. He had loved the outdoors, excelled in soccer and had been quite a gentleman. He had been my teammate and classmate. At one point, I had even had a crush on him. And now he was gone.

I thought back to that day at school when he and Shane had been playing roughly. Ramon hit his head, but he had seemed all right afterwards, though not in the best mood.

"He hit his head pretty hard at school today when he and Shane were fooling around," I told my dad, wondering if the accident had been more than it seemed. I tried hard not to cry.

"That wasn't quite the reason for his death," my dad said. "It seems that he hanged himself."

That made it even more horrible. *How could someone who was so full of life just take it away? So what if he had been suspended? That was no reason for him to do this. He had been a very emotional guy; when he was happy the world was heaven, but when he was mad, the world was . . . well, you know.*

"Oh," I responded, not knowing what else to say.

"I'm really sorry," my dad told me—truly meaning it.

At that moment, I really wished my mom were there. I love my dad dearly, but my mom was so much more comforting. I stood up and wrapped my arms around my father, and he returned the embrace warmly.

A few minutes later, my mom came through the door calling to us happily and talking about her trip. My dad and I didn't say much until she had gotten up the stairs. We then told her what happened. Tears rolled down her cheeks as my dad told her the horrible news. I held her close and cried.

The next morning, my teacher told us to come to school with our parents, and that it would be a half-day in which we would grieve together. That day we shared stories and experiences that included the happy Ramon. I saw people cry who had never cried in front of me before. That day brought my class together in a way nothing ever had.

Weeks later our class went to Ramon's house to plant a garden in his honor. We planted cloves (his favorite) and wild plants. His mom watched with tears in her eyes, touched by what we had done in his memory.

I have learned so much from this, but most of all, to be kind to people, for even if it seems what you are doing and saying is harmless, it may not be so harmless to the person you're aiming it at. Be kind and think before you act—you may save a life out of your kindness.

I hope that Ramon has found peace and happiness where he is now, which he was unable to find here. And, although I may not pass to Ramon in soccer anymore, I'll always remember his big smile.

Emma Fraser, twelve

[EDITORS' NOTE: *If you, or someone you know, is thinking about suicide, call 1-800-suicide or log on to* www.save.org.].

11

ALL ABOUT ATTITUDE

One hundred years from now, it won't matter how
*   you did on a test*
Or how popular you were.
No one will care about how many hits you got in
*   a baseball game.*
It won't matter if you miss a day of school
Or what you got for your eleventh birthday.
Your highest score on a computer game won't be
*   remembered*
Or if your family had a swimming pool.
No one will care who came in first in that one
*   race.*
It won't matter if your handwriting was messy
Or if all your artwork wasn't the best.
But, if you made life a little better
*   for just one other person*
That's what will be remembered.
That's what will matter.

Sydney Miller, twelve

Adult Teeth

As a young girl, two of my wishes were to have glasses and to have braces, items that I associated with the magical preteen world of growing up. I got the glasses in second grade, and quickly realized that I had been wrong—I did not want to wear glasses, after all.

Still though, I clung to the romantic vision of braces, the metal and plastic that would transform me into someone older and infinitely more appealing.

As my adult teeth started to grow in, I was horrified to realize that my neat little rows of baby teeth were being replaced by a mouthful of mismatched, overlapping grown-up teeth.

In sixth grade, at last, I got my braces. And again, I found that the reality was far different than I'd imagined. I didn't like the way that the braces looked on me, but far worse was the way they felt.

The first night after I got my braces on was the worst. My teeth felt as if a world-class bodybuilder was yanking them apart. Hard. My mother made hamburgers for dinner, and I was starving, but I could only eat slowly, miserably, with a minimum of chewing and a maximum of pain.

Two excruciatingly long years later, after months and months of those agonizing torture sessions called "getting your braces tightened," I was finally, *finally,* scheduled to have my braces removed. I was also, my orthodontist mentioned in an offhand way, going to need gum surgery.

My mother immediately made an appointment with an oral surgeon whose office was in a nearby city, an hour away from our small town.

I sat in the passenger seat of the car, staring out the window as we drove.

"You'll be fine," she assured me.

"How do you know? You'll be out in the waiting room reading *Cosmo*," I muttered sourly.

As she had predicted, I did survive the procedure.

Afterward, since we were in the city already, my mother decided to do a little shopping. I should mention that she is not a cruel woman, and that this was toilet-paper-in-bulk kind of shopping, not just felt-like-another-new-dress shopping. Also, neither one of us realized at first that my mouth had been numbed to the point where I could no longer swallow.

I followed her into a large retail store with my jaw drooping and my own drool hanging from my mouth. I had never realized how many times a day I swallowed automatically, without ever giving it a thought.

Distracted by the immediate problems at hand—trying to avoid slobbering on the floor, periodically sopping up the spit with a handkerchief—it took me a few minutes to notice what was going on around us. As we walked, everyone we passed was staring at us. Their expressions ranged from curiosity to pity to revulsion. They didn't know what was wrong with me, but whatever it was, they weren't sticking around long enough to see whether it might be catching. No one knew that I had just undergone gum surgery.

Mom and I finished our errands and drove home. The anesthetic wore off, and I went back to involuntary swallowing. With my gums healed and my braces removed, I used my now smooth, even teeth to eat whole hamburgers and grin like a Cheshire cat at every person I saw.

When I was alone, though, I spent a lot of time thinking about how people had looked at me when I was in the store that day, when they had thought that perhaps I was a mentally or developmentally disabled teen. I was fourteen years old and, I had never in my life been looked at that way. I also thought about how my mom (who could have walked ahead and pretended that she didn't know me) stood by my side talking to me as she always did, and ignoring the stares.

This experience didn't drastically change me or my life. What it did do, though, was to alter my perception of the world just a little. It changed the way I thought about appearances, making them seem a little less important. It also gave new weight to the clichés my mom had been repeating ever since I was little: "Don't judge a book by its cover," "Everyone has feelings," and "You have to walk a mile in someone else's shoes."

I knew that I had only walked a few steps in someone else's shoes, but I was newly determined to treat other people—regardless of their appearance—with more compassion and respect.

And that, I realized, was something truly grown-up.

Leah Browning

Staying True to Myself

This above all; to thine own self be true.

William Shakespeare

I don't know why I believed them after all the teasing and bullying they had put me through.

When the bell rang for our lunch period, once again, the four of them tricked me. "Oh, y'all, we're just gonna go out and play," they said as two of them grabbed my hands.

It was cold outside and there was a lot of snow on the ground. They led me far away from where all the other kids were playing and then, before I knew it, they pushed me down and began hitting me. They said all kinds of mean things to me, like I was the teacher's pet and that I thought I was better than them. Then they dug my head into the snow until I thought I was about to suffocate.

"Stop it. I can't breathe! *I can't breathe!*" I pleaded. That kind of scared them, and they finally got off me, pulled me up out of the slush and helped me into the nurse's office. Scratched, bruised and cold, I listened to them tell the nurse, "We was just playin' and all of a sudden she say she can't breathe." I couldn't wait for those girls to get out of the nurse's office, so that I could tell the truth.

After that, my mother came up to the school and had meetings with everybody she could, but nothing changed. The girls continued to bully me every chance they got.

As a fourth-grader growing up in a small town in Illinois, I didn't have the best of everything, like designer clothes, but Mom made sure my clothes were clean. I was light skinned with long hair, and it could be that those girls thought that I was stuck up because of it. But I was just a kid who enjoyed doing my schoolwork and getting good grades. I always tried to make friends with everybody. As far as I knew, I never did anything wrong to any of those four girls.

After that day on the playground, I was scared every single day. Being at school was a living nightmare. Even after school I was terrified that once I left the classroom to go to my grandmother's car, the girls would jump me. So, I had to have a security officer escort me out every day. My mother had to take me to the doctor's office all the time because there would be something wrong with my stomach, but they could never figure out what it was. Finally, in the fifth grade, I switched elementary schools. School is supposed to be where you learn and make friends—it shouldn't be about having your grades suffer because you gotta watch your back instead of pay attention and do the work.

For the next two years, my school life was wonderful. I made good grades and good friends. Then in seventh grade, I had to face the bully girls again. We hadn't seen each other in several years, so I was thinking that maybe they had grown up some. You know, I actually almost befriended them because I was so scared that if I didn't, they would mess with me again. But I asked myself, *Do I change or stay myself and succeed?* I chose to stay true to myself.

As the year went on, the girls would get into fights all the time and mess with other girls. At one point, some friends of mine that I had grown up with got into it with them. It was one group of girls against the other group of girls. The bully girls were pressuring me to fight on their side. I figured that if I didn't, I would probably become their target of abuse again.

I knew it was about to be blood, sweat and tears in the hallway, and I felt trapped. Then, just as the fight was about to go down, I heard one of the girls say, "Don't mess with her." I was like, *Thank you, 'cause I didn't do anything.* I strongly believe that this was God's protection for me.

I quickly ran into a nearby classroom, and I told the teacher what was about to happen. But before anyone could stop them, the fight began. Girls were screaming, punching, pulling hair and just going crazy. Thankfully, the teachers and principal stopped them before anyone got seriously hurt.

From then on, I knew that God really was looking out for me. I was able to trust him with my life and move forward with less fear of the bully girls. Amazingly, they finally lost interest in me and picked on other girls instead. When high school came, we were zoned to go to different schools. Finally, I had the peace of knowing that I never had to deal with them again.

As I matured and was able to look at those girls' situations, I realized that most of them did not have the love and support of a stable family. I had both parents at home and a very close family. Plus, I was raised in church, and there is something different about people who really are committed to having a Christian life. I had a strong knowledge that I was unique and that the people who really mattered to me loved me. Those girls could never persuade me that being part of a gang could offer me more than that truth. But since they didn't have a strong family or spiritual life, I guess being part of that girl gang gave them a sense of belonging and some security.

My small town hasn't changed much. Over the years, when I go home, I sometimes hear about what has become of the girls who bullied me. One was always back and forth into juvenile hall. I'm not sure what became of her in the long run. All I know is, I wouldn't trade places with any of them.

I'm just so thankful that I stayed on track with my studies and stayed true to expressing my talents and interests. It has taken me to the most amazing places: best-selling records, Grammys, a leading role on Broadway. . . .

From here, my destiny is in God's hands, just as it always has been.

Michelle Williams
Destiny's Child

[EDITORS' NOTE: *For more information about how to deal with bullies, log on to* www.kidshealth.org. *(key word search: "bullying").*]

No, Really . . .
Barney Ate My Report Card!

It is easy to dodge our responsibilities, but we cannot dodge the consequences of dodging our responsibilities.

Sir Josiah Stamp

As a preteen, I felt hopelessly ordinary. When I had to go to a new school where I didn't know anyone, I decided that I was going to make a lot of friends quickly and be really popular. I decided that the only way I could be popular was to make myself interesting, intriguing and therefore, worth knowing. So . . . I decided to tell fibs to get people to like me.

Most of the fibs I told were what my grandmother called "white lies," which are lies you tell people that "won't hurt them." I made up tall tales about celebrities I knew, how rich my family was and exotic places I had visited. I figured that since these lies didn't hurt anyone, that made them only "white lies."

My strategy began to work, and I suddenly became very popular. All my new friends thought I was cool. Of course, none of the stuff I told them was true and eventually, I started to feel a little guilty about it. My newfound popularity was also causing my grades to suffer terribly because being very social was my main focus. I simply didn't have time for homework.

The day our third semester report cards came out, my heart dropped into my stomach. My grade point average went from a 92 percent to a 79 percent. And . . . I had actually flunked English! How crazy was that?

I visualized what kind of torturous punishment my parents would have in store for me because of my bad grades. I figured it would be something like losing my phone privileges, or being grounded until the following semester.

Before I went home that day, my new best friend invited me to her birthday sleepover party. Everyone who was anyone in the school was going to be there. There was no doubt in my mind that my parents wouldn't allow me to go after they saw my report card. There was only one thing for me to do. I would hide my report card until after the party was over.

Weeks went by and my parents asked me every day where my report card was. I kept telling them that I hadn't gotten it yet. They had no reason *not* to believe me, as I had never lied to them before.

The party came and went and I decided that I was ready to face the music about my report card. There was just one little problem. I forgot where I had put it!

One morning at breakfast, Mom finally threatened to call the school. I panicked. I needed more time to try and find where I'd hidden it. If she called the school, she'd find out that I'd gotten the report card almost a month before. Somehow, I talked her out of it.

When I came home from school that day, I glanced at my dog Barney, who was lying on the floor. I noticed a little piece of blue paper sticking out of her mouth and I froze in my tracks. There was my dog, sitting in the middle of the kitchen floor, chewing on *my report card*! My mind reeled. Then, I remembered. I had hidden it in the downstairs closet on the shelf below the dog food. I thought that no one would find it there. Okay—no one with two legs, anyway. With perfect timing, my mom walked into the room, and asked the million dollar question:

"What's Barney chewing on?"

I felt like I was wearing cement shoes as my mother walked over to the dog and pulled the report card out of her mouth. Unfortunately for me, the paper apparently wasn't too appetizing to a dog's taste buds. All of my substandard grades were still as clear as day. So was the date on the top of the report card, which was dated four weeks before.

Needless to say, for lying to them (more so than for the bad grades) my parents grounded me from the phone *and* from going anywhere with my friends until the end of the school year. That really screwed up my social life. Plus, I had bragged to my friends about how cool my parents were because they *never* grounded me.

When my friends called, not only did they find out that the "no grounding" policy was not exactly accurate, but through conversations with my parents, they found out that I had been lying about almost everything else, as well.

It took a long time for me to get my friends' trust back, and even longer for me to regain my parents' belief in me. But I learned the most valuable lesson in my life—there is no such thing as a white lie. Every lie, no matter how small it may seem, is still a lie. Eventually, it will end up biting you in the rear.

Jenn Dlugos

There Is Always
Someone Less Fortunate

Self-denial is painful for a moment, but very agreeable in the end.

Jane Taylor

It's 8:00 A.M., and Mum just called me to get up. I'm lying in bed daydreaming about what I want to do today. I want to stay home and listen to my CDs. I want to work on my tan and then swim in the pool when I get hot. I want to play basketball with my friends and just hang out. I want to watch television and go on my PC and chat with my friends online.

It's 8:30 A.M. now, and Mum is shouting at me to get up. So, I get up, put my swimsuit on and take my CD Walkman outside and lie in the sun for a little bit.

Then my mum comes out telling me that I need to get dressed into some nice clothes that are not going to be too hot for me to walk around in. I ask why do I need to do that—I'm staying home, working on my tan and just chilling for the day. But Mum wants me to go out with her. She tells me a lot about this place called Give Kids the World. It's a special place for families to spend a vacation when a child has a life-threatening illness. She sometimes goes and meets families at the airport and escorts them to the village. There are several jobs she does there, including serving ice cream and gift giving. I expect this is a very boring job to do, but Mum says I will enjoy it.

So, I get dressed in suitable clothes, get in the car and Mum drives to this place. I think it looks really childlike and silly. There is a warehouse at the back of the village that we go into to do our work. I have to put food into boxes. I don't know why, but I do it anyway. Then I have to put some gifts on the back of a golf cart. Mum tells me we are going to deliver a toy to every child in the village. Mum and I then start off on the rounds. We go to the first villa but no one is home, so we leave the gifts for the children to find when they get back.

We pull up to the next house, and I knock on the door and shout, "Gift giving," and a woman answers the door. She tells me I can come in, so I go in. Sitting in the middle of the living room is a young boy in a wheelchair. I give him the gifts I have for him, and his face lights up with joy. I walk out and think to myself, *That must be a real pain, not being able to jump around or play basketball.*

At another villa a bit later on, I knock on the door, again shouting "Gift giving," and another person answers the door. I go in this villa, and lying on a chair is a little girl with tubes in her nose and one coming from her tummy. Her brother is feeding her through a tube. The food is a milky liquid and looks disgusting. I did the same as before—gave them their gifts and walked out. I suddenly thought that it must really be uncomfortable lying there not being able to feed yourself or to be able to eat anything you want, especially sweets and chocolate.

I get to the third house, and I do the same process again. As I come in with the gifts, it seems a little strange that the child doesn't notice me. Her mum says that she is deaf and only partially sighted, so I need to go and stand in front of her, so she can see the gift. When I do that, she gets very excited and makes a sign with her hands. Her mum tells me this is the sign for thank you. I ask her mum how you say good-bye in sign language. She shows me and I sign to the little girl, and she signs back as I leave the house.

Once back in the cart, I ask my mum what is wrong with these kids. Mum tells me that they all have life-threatening illnesses and that they might not live to see tomorrow. That is shocking to me. Suddenly, I realize that I should be more thankful that I don't have these ill-nesses—that I am not in the same position as these kids. I no longer want to be at home working on my tan, listening to my CDs, playing basketball or swimming in the pool. I would much rather be doing this, seeing things that not a lot of people really get to see, maybe making a difference in these kids' lives.

My first visit to Give Kids the World was over six months ago, and I now go on a regular basis. I have even taken one of my friends along as well. I do miss spending the time at home and hanging out with my friends, but I wouldn't want to miss the opportunity to make a differ-ence to these kids who are much worse off than I am.

Amy Mallinder-Morgan, twelve

[EDITORS' NOTE: *For information about Give Kids the World, go to* www.gktw.org.]

Thirteen Candles

When my thirteenth birthday came around, I didn't announce the occasion to anyone and made no plans.

"What do you want to do for your birthday?" my mother asked me.

"Nothing," I said.

"Do you want to invite any friends over?"

"What friends?"

My expectations for this birthday were set low. That way, whatever happened, I would be pleasantly surprised that anyone bothered to even take notice.

At school, as predicted, nobody mentioned my birthday except for some old friends whom I'd known since kindergarten. The fact that they actually remembered my birthday didn't earn them any points. I mean, what kind of creepy girls would want to be friends with me? And who would be dumb enough to remember my birthday? I had zits and braces and frizzy hair.

At home, the evening went about the same as any other evening, except that there was cake for dessert and a few presents for me to open. My two younger sisters got me some dumb stuff—stationery sets and candy and hand-drawn cards. There was one big box from my mother. The card read "Love from Mom and Dad," but I knew my dad had nothing to do with it. My dad *never* shopped. In fact, he was hardly ever home. Like most nights, he was still working at the hospital, doing some sort of surgery or something like that.

I reached over for the big metallic-gold Nordstrom box, and when I shook it, I knew there were clothes inside. *Thank you, God,* I thought to myself. *Maybe this birthday won't be so bad, after all.* Being in middle school had made me incredibly insecure about my wardrobe, so I hoped that this package would contain something magical to make me fit in. I opened the box and pulled out a pair of tangerine cropped pants and a matching cotton tangerine striped shirt. *Tangerine!* It was hideous. I'd never owned anything tangerine in my life and wasn't about to start now. I smiled weakly.

"Wow, Mom!" I faked a happy grin. "Thank you so much!"

My mother was onto me right away. "You don't like it," she growled.

"No, I do," I lied. "I really like the outfit."

But I hated it. I'd never received a gift so ugly or so unflattering. Besides, my mother should have known that I couldn't wear tangerine!

She was getting angrier. "You don't like it, I'll take it back," she fumed.

Wallowing further into my low self-esteem black hole, I replied, "Fine, take it back. I don't deserve any presents anyway."

This made her even angrier. "You ungrateful child. Don't you know how much I do for you? I shopped for this present. I cooked you dinner. I have tried to make this evening special, and this is the kind of thanks I get?"

I stared at my mother silently, waiting for her full fury to hit me like a hurricane. My sisters knew the drill by heart now, so they got up from the table and quietly snuck up to their rooms to hide. She continued to yell— about how I ruined her day and how I never thank her for anything or appreciate what she does, and how I never help out around the house, and how bad traffic was this evening on the bridge, and how all I do is take, take, take.

"So . . . take . . . the . . . present . . . back," I said, now with tears streaming down my cheeks, barely getting the words out between my gurgling hiccups and sniffing wet snot back up into my head. My mother always knew exactly how to make me truly miserable.

After she was done yelling, my mother cut half of the birthday cake, about five or six slices, put it on a plate and made her usual Alka-Seltzer evening cocktail. Then she announced to no one in particular, "I'm going to my room and I don't want to be disturbed!"

I carefully refolded the tangerine pants and top, wrapped them back up in tissue paper and placed them inside the metallic-gold Nordstrom box. "There," I announced to nobody. "A perfectly ruined birthday. Just as I expected."

The next morning, the gold box with the tangerine clothes carefully wrapped inside was still sitting on the kitchen table. As I poured myself a bowl of cereal, it occurred to me how ridiculous the box looked, and how even more ridiculous I had acted the night before. I replayed the series of miserable events over in my head. The misery was all mine—I had set myself up for a disappointing birthday because I didn't feel I deserved anything more than that. So, what did I get? Disappointment, *duh!*

I unwrapped the box and pulled out the tangerine clothes. *I could wear these pants with my black top*, I thought. *And*

I could wear the shirt with jeans. Nobody said I had to wear a completely tangerine outfit. After thinking it through, I realized that the gift was completely salvageable, and I was much happier about the whole thing.

My mom came downstairs to the kitchen. She was still in her nightgown and her face was slightly puffy. She looked at me, then at the clothes and the cereal on the kitchen table. "I'm sorry about yesterday, honey," she said, groggily.

"I'm sorry too, Mom," I said.

"Can we start over with the birthday?" We said it in unison, then we laughed.

Allison Ellis

Disabilities

What really matters is what you do with what you have.

Shirley Lord

Step by step, Rebekah pulled herself along the sidewalk with her walker on a cold but sunny day. She looked back at me and, laughing, said, "You can't catch me!" She turned around and started to run, fast but stumbling, her walker wheels bumping over little rocks on the pavement. I jumped up and started jogging toward my little sister, and thought about how far she has come since her birth three-and-a-half years ago.

Rebekah was born with spina bifida, a condition in which a baby is born with a hole in its back, and the spinal cord hangs out of it. Right away, she went to the Neonatal Intensive Care Unit where very sick babies are sent. She had surgery to close her spine when she was only twenty-two hours old. I wanted to visit my baby sister, but children weren't allowed in the NICU because doctors were afraid that they would bring in germs.

Rebekah was eight days old before she was well enough to come home. She looked like a pretzel, because her legs were bent the wrong way, so that they touched her chest. Her feet were both clubbed, so they were turned in toward one another. I was only five, and I didn't know what to think about my new little sister. She was home for only four days before she had to go back to the hospital. Her head was swelling badly and she had to have brain surgery to put in a shunt, which is a tube that drains extra fluid away from the brain.

By the time she was three, Rebekah had already gone through nine operations. She has had bladder surgery, four operations on her feet, and hip surgery too. Recovering from her surgeries was a long and painful process. She usually had to wear casts for six to twelve weeks. After foot surgery, she had to wear braces to keep her feet from going back to the way they had been.

When she was about a year old, she started having physical therapy to make her legs and body stronger. The muscles below her knees don't work because nerves in her spinal cord were damaged. Because of this, the muscles in her thighs have to do all the work. Rebekah was about a year-and-a-half old when she started to walk. She got a walker to help her keep her balance when she walked. Each time she had surgery, she had to learn how to walk all over again, which is very hard to do.

Her attitude is remarkable after all she's been through. Rebekah is determined to not let her disabilities get in the way of the things she wants to do. She does not understand that she is handicapped, so she does the same things as everyone else. She might have to do them differently, but she still does them. She walks, she runs, she jumps, she dances, she kicks balls, and she loves to play outside like most kids do. She has to work harder for everything she does, but she doesn't complain.

For Rebekah, standing and walking is like you or me carrying someone our own size on our back all the time. She has a wheelchair, but she likes to walk the best. She walks well with her crutches and walker, but she's trying to walk without help. She has taught herself to take five steps without help, and she's still working on it.

I've learned a lot about disabilities since my little sister was born. I used to think it was scary to have a handicapped person in my family. Now I don't think it's scary at all. Rebekah is the same as everyone else. She has taught me a lot of things, but the most important thing I've learned is that if you keep a positive attitude and work hard, you can overcome just about anything that life hands you.

Heather Bradley, eight

The Helpful Stranger

All of us, at certain moments of our lives, need to take advice and to receive help from other people.

Alexis Carrel

With Christmas vacation coming up, I was hoping that we would get a lot of snow, so I could go tobogganing with my friends. I had also asked for a snowboard for Christmas, so I was really hoping for snow to try it out.

On Christmas morning, not only did I awaken to find that it was snowing outside, but I also found an awesome new snowboard under the tree. I begged my mom and dad to take me to the toboggan hill, so I could try out my new snowboard. They agreed, so off we went through snow so thick that we could barely see where we were going.

I got on my board for the first time and made it only a quarter of the way down the hill when I fell off. I became very discouraged and didn't think that I was any good. I made an instant decision that I didn't want to do it any more.

A few days after Christmas, my friend Zachary came over with his snowboard to go to the hill near my house with me. Zachary was very good at snowboarding, and since I could barely do it at all, that made me feel even worse. I wondered if maybe my new board wasn't the right size for me, so I tried riding Zachary's board. I still wasn't able to get very far. Finally I just gave up and said, "I can't do it."

But while I struggled with my new board, Zachary was making run after run down the hill and having a great time. He asked me if we could go to our favorite hill a little farther away to do some more runs, and not wanting to spoil his fun, I reluctantly said I would go.

While out on the new hill, I still struggled to stay up. I had fallen a few times when a teenager that I had never met before noticed that I was getting frustrated. He called over to me to give me some advice about how to snowboard. I don't talk to strangers as a rule, but my mom was with me so I felt safe. So, I listened to what he had to say, and then I tried again. I was able to go farther down the hill than I had before. He watched as I made one more run, and then he came over to give me more pointers, like where to place my feet and what to do with my hands. He also told me that I should lean a little bit forward once I got up. I tried what he told me to do, and I was able to go all the way down the hill without falling! It seemed so much easier with the instructions that he gave me. He continued to help me a number of times and gave me lots of encouragement.

I find it hard sometimes to listen to other people when they are telling me what to do, but this guy was very helpful and nice about the way he instructed me.

He could have chosen to make a few more runs for the day, instead of taking time to help me—a kid he didn't even know.

As younger preteens, sometimes when we think of teenagers, we think about those that are "trouble makers," or some who intimidate us. But this teenager was not like that at all. He made me feel comfortable around him and was really helpful and kind to me.

I'm a much better snowboarder now, thanks to a very helpful and considerate teenage stranger.

Alex Judge, ten

Foxtrot. ©2003 Bill Amend. Reprinted with permission of UNIVERSAL PRESS SYNDICATE.
All rights reserved.

12

ECLECTIC WISDOM

Wise is the determined job-seeker
Who knocks on every door
And the rags-to-riches millionaire
Who shares his wealth with the poor.
Wise is the legendary movie star
Who takes time to pose with a fan
Or the stranded plane pilot
Who writes his name in the sand.
Wise is the designated driver
Who refuses to touch a drop
And wise is the class clown
Who knows when to stop.

Lauren M. Maffeo, fourteen

Covered

One important key to success is self-confidence.
An important key to self-confidence is preparation.

Arthur Ashe

The day began like most days; I was running behind. After wolfing down breakfast, I ran out the door and down the street to my friend Teresa's house, only to find she wasn't going to school that day.

I knew if I went back for Mom, I would be late for school, so I ignored her warnings about the dangers of being at the bus stop alone. If I'd had a clue as to what was in store for me, I would have chosen to be late.

As it was, the bus itself was late, so I sat on the grass under a tree and opened a book. I got so into what I was reading, that I didn't pay much attention to the men in the pickup as they passed by, or when they stopped up the road and backed up. They caught my attention when they spoke to me, but I didn't understand what they said. I stood up and asked, "Pardon me?"

The truck held two men who were in their mid-twenties. The driver had dark hair and a tattoo on the arm he had hanging out the window; the other man had long blond hair.

I knew not to speak to strangers, but I asked again, "Pardon me? I didn't understand what you said."

The driver asked, "Have you seen a black lab running loose? He disappeared out of our yard last night, and I can't find him anywhere."

While he was talking, something in the back of my mind told me I shouldn't be having this conversation at all. Finally, a bell went off in my mind and I remembered Mom and Dad having Mr. Jay come into our karate class and act out this very same scenario with all the younger students.

It was like déjà vu. The man in the truck uttered the very same words Mr. Jay had used during our self-defense class, "How about coming over here so I can show you his picture. That way you can let me know if you see him. Maybe you will see him while you're on the bus, or something."

Under the tree, I was well away from the road, but I still began to back up.

"Come on, it will only take a minute to look. What if it was your dog, wouldn't you want somebody to help you find him?"

My emphatic "No! You look for your own dog" wasn't the answer he was looking for, and when the driver first opened his door, I was shocked. No one in class had ever said someone would actually get out of their vehicle and come after me. They did always have a saying in class though, "He who runs away, lives to fight another day."

I ran.

When I looked back, the blond guy had slid over to the

steering wheel and was driving on the road parallel to me while the other guy was gaining ground behind me. It was then that I really started to get scared.

I tried to pray, but all that would run through my head was, *Oh God! Oh God! Please don't let him get me!*

When the man latched onto the neck of my T-shirt and pulled me backward, I couldn't scream, claw, bite, punch or kick, because I froze.

It was only when he let go of my shirt and grabbed my wrist that I was once again able to move. We had covered wrist grabs many times, and thankfully, lessons that had been repeatedly practiced became instinctual.

I stepped back and executed the twisting yank against his thumb that also caused my upper body to twist away from him. When I realized it had worked, I almost froze again, but instead, I finished the technique they had taught me.

Using the torque of my twisted body, I swung back around at the man and landed a back fist to his face. Between the torque, the adrenaline and my height, I made a solid connection that made his nose bleed. I allowed my body to continue on past with the back fist and gave the strongest spinning back kick I could to the man's knees.

With blood running down his face and hopping on one leg, the guy began to curse me, but I didn't wait around to hear much. I ran across the field, crawled through the fence of a horse farm, ran past the horses and on to the closest house. Luckily, I knew the people who lived there. From there, I called the police and then my mom.

When Mom heard what had happened, she began to cry and shake. It wasn't until we got to the sheriff's office and I told them my story that I began to cry, too.

Two weeks later, the paper reported the abduction of a twelve-year-old girl not far from our home who was taken by two men in a truck that matched the description I had given the deputy. I often wonder if some martial arts training could have helped to save her.

Later on I heard Mom and Dad discussing what had happened. I heard my mom say to him, "All those years of karate really helped her defend herself when she really needed it. But, knowing what happened to that other girl, I think Victoria had a little extra help that day. I believe that God covered her back, too."

Victoria Perry, twelve
As told by Tenna Perry

Pyramid Surprise

People seldom refuse help, if one offers it in the right way.

A. C. Benson

Nellie and I have been best friends for as long as I can remember. We were born only a few days apart, so every year we plan a combined birthday party. The year we were in seventh grade, we were especially excited. Our moms said we could finally invite boys. Our theme, we decided, was "Discover the Pyramids."

Nellie was writing out the invitation list when my mom came up and peered over her shoulder.

"What about inviting John?" Mom asked.

John had been in our class for only a few months, but he was already getting better grades in math and science than anyone else in class. He was a loner, though, and hadn't made very many friends.

I wrinkled my nose. "Mom, he wears the same pants to school every day. How could he even afford a costume?"

Mom frowned. "The same pants?"

"Yes. Brown corduroy ones." I felt a twinge of guilt. My family didn't have a lot of money either, but my mom was a whiz at bargain shopping. I never had to wear the same thing twice in one week.

"Hmm," said Mom. Her office phone rang, and off she went.

After school the next day, as Nellie and I were cutting paper for party decorations, Mom waltzed up and handed me an envelope.

"What's that?" I asked.

"Nellie's mom and I thought it would be nice for you two to give this to John," Mom said as she headed back to her office.

I opened the envelope delicately and gasped. Inside was a gift certificate for our favorite department store.

"Wow," said Nellie. We both knew how many cute clothes that would buy.

I stared at the certificate in awe. "So, are we going to just hand it to him?"

"How embarrassing would *that* be," Nellie scoffed.

She was right. John would be totally humiliated if we gave him money for clothes. "What if we slipped it into his desk when no one is looking?"

"He'd probably give it to the teacher, and then we'd have to say it was for him in front of the whole class." Nellie rolled her eyes. *"Triple embarrassing.* We have to think of something else."

"Hmm. What if we ask our teacher . . ."

"Wait a second. *Stop everything.* I have an idea." Nellie snatched the envelope and started hopping up and down.

"What? What?"

Still bouncing, she sang, "I'm not going to tell you!" I pestered, I wheedled, I glowered. But Nellie wouldn't budge.

For days I watched Nellie and John carefully. No new pants.

Maybe he's saving them for the party, I thought. *Or worse, maybe Nellie was going to give them to him there!* For just one tiny second, I wondered if she might have confiscated the gift certificate and used it herself.

She wouldn't do that, I told myself. But I watched in vain for new pants to appear.

On the day of our party, kids arrived dressed in white sheets, black wigs and snake bracelets. John arrived in a dingy sheet, with—no surprise—the brown corduroy pants underneath.

Nobody seemed to care, though. We danced, ate Mediterranean snacks, and divided everyone into teams for a mummy wrap contest and a hieroglyphic scavenger hunt.

"And now for the grand prize game," Nellie announced. *Grand prize?* My mouth dropped. This was not in the plan.

"Get your pencils ready! The grand prize game is the following riddle: Osiris and Isis were building pyramids. Osiris' bricks were 4 feet cubed, and he worked at the rate of 8 bricks per hour. Isis' bricks were 3 feet cubed, and she worked at the rate of 12 bricks per hour. They both started with a base 60 feet square. If their pyramids had to be 60 feet high, who finished first?"

A math game. *Of course!* Nellie winked at me. Neither one of us was surprised when John came up with the answer way before anyone else and walked off with the envelope.

Everyone ooohed and aaahed when our moms brought out an enormous chocolate pyramid cake. I noticed John took particular delight in slicing off the very top.

The next week, he wore a new pair of pants every day, and even a couple of new shirts. The whole time he had a big grin on his face.

And so did we. I have never been more proud to be Nellie's best friend.

Holly Cupala

Initiation

Do not do what you would undo if caught.

Leah Arendt

"I'll bet you won't do it," Tiffany whispered.

"Shut up and leave me alone," I said.

"Wimp!" Tiffany said. "I do it all the time. We all had to do it. You won't get caught. You're just chicken!"

"I am not!" I said hotly. "I just need a minute to figure out which one I want."

"Hurry up! Just stick it in your pocket. She's not looking. Do it now!" Tiffany ordered as she walked out of the store.

I stood in front of a nail polish display in a costume jewelry shop at the mall, nervous as I could be. Sweat popped out on my forehead. I felt my underarms getting sticky. I checked once more to see if the girl at the register was looking at me. Confident that she wasn't, I quickly jammed a bottle of the nail polish into the pocket of my jeans and walked out of the store.

I hurried to the food court where my friends were waiting. Still sweating profusely, I held my head up high and smiled. "I got it!" I exclaimed proudly.

"I don't believe you. Let me see it," Tiffany demanded.

Tiffany was the unofficial leader. You did what she said, or else. I was the new girl, so I had to be initiated. My job was to steal two different things from the same store, two separate times. Up to this point in my life, I had never stolen anything. I lived with my grandparents and I knew that they would be disappointed in me if I ever got caught stealing.

"Ha!" I said, pulling the polish out of my pocket. All the girls nodded approvingly when they saw the polish.

"Give it to me, now!" Tiffany commanded. "And go back in there and get something else."

"I don't want to go back in there right now," I said. "Can't we eat lunch first?"

"I guess. Honestly, DeAnna, you are such a baby," Tiffany said as she headed for Arby's.

She's so mean to me. Why do I even want to hang out with them, anyway? I thought to myself. It only took me a minute to remember why. Tiffany was the baddest girl at school. Nobody messed with her or the girls who hung out with her. If they did, she took care of it after school.

We ate, and then she announced that it was time for round two. We all headed back to the store. They left me by the entrance and made their way toward a different store.

"There are some earrings down there that I want and Jen is going to get them for me. By the way, we're leaving in ten minutes. You'd better hurry or we'll leave without you," Tiffany said.

I took a deep breath and walked back into the store. I felt a little less guilty, because Tiffany now had the nail polish and my pockets were free. *Tiffany wouldn't know if I just bought something instead of stealing, would she?* I made up my mind. I wanted more than anything to be accepted. If I were one of Tiffany's friends then nobody would pick on me—nobody would call me names. Nobody except Tiffany.

I kept thinking about my grandparents and how proud of me they were. I knew how hard they worked to teach me right from wrong. They just didn't know what it was like at school. I was in the seventh grade, and I had no friends. Tiffany wasn't really my friend. I knew that. The more I thought about it, she wasn't really *anybody's* friend.

I decided right then and there that she wasn't worth it. I wasn't going to let her use me like she did Jen and Katie. I picked out a key chain and stepped up to the register to pay for it. I saw the nail polish display and I started to sweat again. "Are you alright?" the girl asked me.

"Yeah, I'm fine. I'm just a little tired," I lied, grabbing a bottle of white nail polish. I put it with the key chain on the counter and paid for them. It was one way that I thought I could help to make it right.

I went to the store where they had gone but Tiffany, Jen and Katie weren't there. After looking throughout the mall for about half an hour, I concluded that they had left me. It was kind of weird, but I felt relieved that I didn't have to deal with them anymore. I realized that I'd probably get it when I got to school on Monday, but I just didn't care. Who I wanted to be was more important than being so-called friends with them. It would be worth what they would put me through just to be free of them.

I used the pay phone to call my grandmother and asked her to pick me up. As I sat outside the mall waiting, I clutched the bag containing the polish and the key chain that I had bought and thought about the decision that I had made. Then I smiled, because I knew it was the right one.

DeAnna Doherty

My Dad, the Superhero

When I was only seven my family took a road trip to San Francisco. My father was driving our family car along the highway during an intense rainstorm. The rain was drenching the entire road and each drop of rain felt as if it were going to break the windshield. As soon as the windshield wipers would sweep the water off, a fresh blast of water would already be there, making it very difficult to see.

I wasn't scared. The downpour mesmerized me. My brother, who is three years older than me, was asserting his power over me in the backseat. He was inflicting me with some sort of older brother torture that is apparently essential for all older siblings to do to the younger ones. Every time I tried to block his hits, he would outwit me by hitting me someplace else. And each time I tried to grab his arm, his other hand would strike like a venomous snake. My only defense was to complain to Mom.

I complained to her in detail about the injustice going on in the backseat, but it was relatively ineffective. My father, who was driving, knew that the only way to get us to stop fighting was to distract us. So he said, "Spencer, do you know that I have learned magic?"

I was stunned at first, and both my brother and I stopped immediately. "What?" I asked for clarification.

My father replied, "Do you want me to show you some magic?"

I got excited. It was every child's dream to have a superhero father. Even my brother was curious about what Dad was saying.

"I have the ability to stop the rain from falling. It's only for short periods of time, so you have to pay close attention," he instructed.

I was speechless. This seemed to be an incredible feat, even for a superhero. All I could do was stare at him through the rearview mirror in suspense.

"Are you ready?" he asked.

"Yes!" we both answered.

"Okay. Let me summon my powers." There was a short pause. "Okay. First, I have to say the magic words, 'Abra Cadabra.' Here we go . . . *Abra Cadabra!*"

And just like THAT, for one split second, the rain stopped! The great drops ceased to fall from the heavens. It was a miracle! I was shocked. My dad really was a superhero. How could I not have known? For years, his powers had eluded me. He must have hidden his gadgets and weapons in the garage. I bet his old Ford was just a cover so that the villains wouldn't know who he *really* was.

"Wow!" I said to my brother, who seemed to be just as amazed as I was.

"Wow . . ." was all he could say, too.

Then our car drove under another overpass.

Spencer Westcott

Grandma's Pearls

When the heart grieves over what it has lost,
the spirit rejoices over what it has left.

Sufi Epigram

Two weeks after Grandpa died, Grandma came to live with us. Every day, she sat in a rocker in the living room, staring out the window and fingering a small red pouch that she kept with her always. I would try to joke with her and make her laugh like she used to, but she would just nod sadly and continue rocking.

One day, I noticed Grandma looking out the window. I stood up, stretched my cramped legs and walked over to her. "What are you watching, Grandma?" I asked.

Grandma's head jerked, like she was waking up from a nap. "Nothing, really. Just looking into the past."

I didn't really know what to say. Grandma stared at me, seeming to really see me for the first time in the weeks since she'd moved in. I pointed to her lap. "Why do you keep that red bag with you?"

Grandma's skinny, bent fingers moved lovingly along the bright velvet. "Everything I ever learned is in this bag," she said.

I pulled up a stool and sat by her knees. "What do you mean?"

"I'll show you." Grandma gently pulled the worn ribbons that held the bag closed, then reached in and removed a strand of large, silvery-white pearls.

"It's beautiful!" I said. Leaning closer, I realized the huge pearls were strung on a slender length of leather.

"Your great-great-grandmother gave this to my mother, who gave it to me." Her eyes glistened. "I remember it like it was yesterday. She gave me this piece of leather, with one pearl strung on it. She called it a pearl of wisdom. She gave it to me because I ignored the stories everyone was telling about a man who had moved into town with his two daughters. I made friends with the girls, even though I lost my old friends for awhile. And she gave me this one when I didn't ask Jim Redmond to the Sadie Hawkins dance, even though I was terribly in love with him, because my best friend Penny wanted to ask him.

"She gave me another pearl each time she felt I'd done something special, learned some kind of lesson, or had done something she felt was wise."

"So, every pearl is a pearl of wisdom," I whispered, running my hand over the cool spheres.

"That's right," she said, slipping the pearls back into their bag. She pulled the ribbons tightly and smiled at me. "Your grandfather gave me the last one, on our fiftieth wedding anniversary, because he said marrying him was the wisest thing I'd ever done." We both laughed.

Grandmother died that fall. After the funeral, my mother gave me a round jewelry box of polished dark wood, with cut glass set in the top. "Your grandmother wanted you to have this."

I lifted the lid. Inside the box rested the red velvet pouch with a note written in my grandmother's crooked scrawl. "I should have given these to your mother a long time ago, but I always felt like I still had things to learn. I hope you'll keep these pearls safe, and continue the tradition with your own child."

Angry and sad, I stuffed the box with its contents into the very back of my dresser's bottom drawer. *All the wisdom in the world didn't keep you from dying,* I thought.

Three years later, I was fourteen. The last thing I wanted was to start high school with glasses so thick you couldn't see my eyes. I wanted contacts, but my parents couldn't afford them.

I mowed every lawn in the neighborhood that summer. I pulled weeds, painted garage doors and washed cars. Two weeks before school started, I picked up the contacts I had been able to order with the money I had earned.

I took the hated glasses and stuffed them in the very back of my bottom dresser drawer, and there was the box. I took it out and opened the lid. Smiling, I untied the leather and let all but one of the pearls fall into the pouch. "I'm not going to continue the tradition with my own child," I whispered, "I'll continue with me."

I had worked hard for something I wanted instead of expecting someone else to hand it to me. I added one more pearl, retied the ends and put the box on my dresser, where it should have been all along.

In those few moments, I felt I had learned something important. In my memories, and in those pearls, my grandmother and her wisdom lived on.

Catherine Adams

Preteen Wisdom

What I've Learned So Far . . .

Straight-A students aren't always the smartest people.
Give your estranged friends a second chance. Everybody changes.
Never let a baby walk down the stairs by herself.

Lauren Maffeo, fourteen

Summer love is only one summer.

Jon Tracey, eleven

Don't cook marshmallows in the microwave.
If you make a mistake, don't feel bad; consider it a lesson.

Emma Paradis, twelve

by Robert Berardi

Never stuff your bra; I mean I have never done it before, but you can really tell when someone has something in there.

Rachelle K. Carpenter, twelve

Never laugh when you're under water.

Melanie Nickolson, ten

Mom is allowed to date anyone she wants and have a social life—she doesn't have to date who I want her to date; whatever makes *her* happy.

Jordan Rakes, twelve

When you have bad grades, show the good grades to your mom first.

Zainab Mahmood, twelve

When you want something, you have to go after it. Waiting won't make your dreams come true.

Ailene Evangelista, thirteen

It's impossible to sneeze with both eyes open.

Alexander Siu, twelve

Talking back to your mom doesn't get you anywhere, except in more trouble.

Alexandra Mendoza, eleven

Try new things. Some things may look gross (like Mom's leftover surprise) but could turn out real great.

Don't run away from your problems; they'll just come back to haunt you.

When you're in pain, don't just sit around and do nothing; get up and do something you love to make it better.

Don't let one little mistake get you down, learn from it and prepare for your next obstacle.

Don't hide your flaws; show them, learn from them and move on.

Emily Kent, eleven

Don't try to cut your hair on your own.

Hayley Hunter, twelve

The world does not revolve around me.

Sara Mangos, eleven

If you punch a person who punched you, then you are just as bad as they are. You've sunk down to their level.

Don't feed your cat cheese! It gives them gas.

Alec Don, eleven

Attitude is a little thing but makes a big difference.

Always let your dog out when it needs to go to the toilet.

When you're shopping, always remember which changing room your mom is in.

Nikollas Van Den Broek, eleven

Never touch a smoking TV.

If your parents promise you money, write it down.

Never ask your sister for a favor; you never know what you'll have to do in return.

Louise East, twelve

You must adjust to life, life cannot adjust to you.

Everything with a good side has a bad side, and everything with a bad side has a good side.

Just because a thousand people say it's so doesn't make it so.

Love will always find a way. Just have patience.

Annie Gao, thirteen

There are a lot of people in the world who are going through the same things as you: maybe it's getting braces, a first boyfriend or girlfriend, or puberty. So, I think about that, and I'm not as scared or confused.

Emily Craft, eleven

You Know You're Growing Up When . . .

People stop saying that you're too young to understand.

You outgrow the "girls" clothes section and move on to the "juniors."

Jenna Druce, twelve

You realize you've been sleeping without a nightlight and decide it's actually okay, after all.

Nicole Paquette, eleven

"I know all kids go through it, but just when is he *not* 'going to be going through a stage' when he's embarrassed to be seen with his parents?"

By permission of Leigh Rubin and Creators Syndicate, Inc.

You're not too "cool" to give your mom or dad a hug in public.

Emily Craft, eleven

You discover hair in different places.

Jon Tracey, eleven

You start putting money in your purse and not in your pocket.

Alexandra Mendoza, eleven

The phone bill goes up.
You take responsibility for your actions.

Emma Paradis, twelve

You can go through sitting in health class without bursting out in laughter when they mention a funny body part.
Kissing on TV doesn't make you feel sick to your stomach.

Ailene Evangelista, thirteen

Your sister says you stopped being annoying.

Hamizatul Nisa, thirteen

World problems mean something to you.

Sara Hess, twelve

You are willing to give up something you really want to make somebody else happy.

Ambreen Hooda, eleven

Afterword

I am a bud that has not yet bloomed
I am a sleeping princess that has never been kissed
I am not a child, and not an adult
I am a caterpillar in a chrysalis
I am a potted plant that has not been transplanted
I am not dumb, nor am I a genius
I am a book that has not been published
I am in the middle
I am in-between
I am not big, nor am I small
I am, I am, a preteen

Jessica Sagers, eleven

IT'S A TATTOO --- I LIKE HAPPY ENDINGS.

Frank & Ernest. *Reprinted by permission of Newspaper Enterprise Association, Inc.*

More Chicken Soup?

Many of the stories and poems you have read in this book were submitted by readers like you who had read earlier *Chicken Soup for the Soul* books. We invite you to contribute a story to a future volume.

Your true, nonfiction story may be up to twelve hundred words.

To obtain a copy of our submission guidelines and a listing of upcoming *Chicken Soup* books, please check our Website.

Please send your submissions to:

Chicken Soup for the Soul
P.O. Box 30880, Santa Barbara, CA 93130
fax: 805-563-2945
Website: *www.chickensoupforthesoul.com*

Supporting Preteens

In the spirit of supporting preteens everywhere, donations from a portion of the profits from *Chicken Soup for the Preteen Soul 2* will be contributed to the following nonprofit organizations.

Always Dream Foundation, founded by ice skating legend Kristi Yamaguchi in 1996, was established with one purpose in mind: to support organizations that have a positive influence on children. The foundation strives to find innovative ways to provide funding for a diverse range of programs designed to inspire and embrace the hopes and dreams of children and adolescents.

The motto "Always Dream" has served as Kristi's personal inspiration for many years. It is her constant reminder to dream big, never lose sight of her goals, and strive to become a better person.

Kristi Yamaguchi's Always Dream Foundation
1212 Preservation Parkway
Oakland, CA 94612
jim@alwaysdream.org
www.alwaysdream.org

Through recreational, educational and developmental programs, the **Life Rolls On Foundation** raises money to fund research for the treatment and cure of paralysis caused by spinal cord injuries (SCI).

The foundation supports the Christopher Reeve Paralysis Foundation, as well as other charities. Its mission is to spread the word and to instill in the lives of our nation's injured that life with SCI does indeed "Roll On."

Life Rolls On Foundation
Attention: Josh Billauer
7770 Regents Road, Suite 113-199
San Diego, CA 92122
contact@*liferollson.org*
www.liferollson.org

The United Nations Children's Fund (UNICEF), with more than 7,000 people working in 158 countries, is helping to build a world where the rights of every child are realized. UNICEF works worldwide to overcome poverty, violence, disease and discrimination.

The main goals of UNICEF are to give infants a good start in life, promote girls' education and to see that all children are immunized against common childhood diseases and are well nourished.

UNICEF also strives to prevent the spread of HIV/AIDS among young people and to relieve suffering during natural disasters or war. UNICEF believes that no child should be exposed to violence, abuse or exploitation. They also encourage young people to speak out and participate in the decisions that affect their lives.

UNICEF House
3 United Nations Plaza
New York, New York 10017
www.unicef.org

Who Is Jack Canfield?

Jack Canfield is one of America's leading experts in the development of human potential and personal effectiveness. He is both a dynamic, entertaining speaker and a highly sought-after trainer. Jack has a wonderful ability to inform and inspire audiences toward increased levels of self-esteem and peak performance.

He is the author and narrator of several bestselling audio- and videocassette programs, including *Self-Esteem and Peak Performance, How to Build High Self-Esteem, Self-Esteem in the Classroom* and *Chicken Soup for the Soul—Live*. He is regularly seen on television shows such as *Good Morning America, 20/20* and *NBC Nightly News*. Jack has coauthored numerous books, including the *Chicken Soup for the Soul* series, *Dare to Win* and *The Aladdin Factor* (all with Mark Victor Hansen), *100 Ways to Build Self-Concept in the Classroom* (with Harold C. Wells), *Heart at Work* (with Jacqueline Miller) and *The Power of Focus* (with Les Hewitt and Mark Victor Hansen).

Jack is a regularly featured speaker for professional associations, school districts, government agencies, churches, hospitals, sales organizations and corporations. His clients have included the American Dental Association, the American Management Association, AT&T, Campbell's Soup, Clairol, Domino's Pizza, GE, ITT, Hartford Insurance, Johnson & Johnson, the Million Dollar Roundtable, NCR, New England Telephone, Re/Max, Scott Paper, TRW and Virgin Records. Jack has taught on the faculty of Income Builders International, a school for entrepreneurs.

Jack conducts an annual seven-day Training of Trainers program in the areas of self-esteem and peak performance. It attracts entrepreneurs, educators, counselors, parenting trainers, corporate trainers, professional speakers, ministers and others interested in developing their speaking and seminar-leading skills.

For further information about Jack's books, tapes and training programs, or to schedule him for a presentation, please contact:

Self-Esteem Seminars
P.O. Box 30880
Santa Barbara, CA 93130
phone: 805-563-2935 • fax: 805-563-2945
Website: *www.jackcanfield.com*

Who Is Mark Victor Hansen?

In the area of human potential, no one is better known and more respected than Mark Victor Hansen. For more than thirty years, Mark has focused solely on helping people from all walks of life reshape their personal vision of what's possible. His powerful messages of possibility, opportunity and action have helped create startling and powerful change in thousands of organizations and millions of individuals worldwide.

He is a sought-after keynote speaker, bestselling author and marketing maven. Mark's credentials include a lifetime of entrepreneurial success, in addition to an extensive academic background. He is a prolific writer with many bestselling books such as *The One Minute Millionaire, The Power of Focus, The Aladdin Factor* and *Dare to Win,* in addition to the *Chicken Soup for the Soul* series. Mark has also made a profound influence through his extensive library of audio programs, video programs and enriching articles in the areas of big thinking, sales achievement, wealth building, publishing success, and personal and professional development.

Mark is the founder of MEGA Book Marketing University and Building Your MEGA Speaking Empire. Both are annual conferences where Mark coaches and teaches new and aspiring authors, speakers and experts on building lucrative publishing and speaking careers.

His energy and exuberance travel still further through mediums such as television *(Oprah, CNN* and *The Today Show),* print *(Time, U.S. News & World Report, USA Today, New York Times* and *Entrepreneur)* and countless radio and newspaper interviews as he assures our planet's people that *"You can easily create the life you deserve."*

As a passionate philanthropist and humanitarian, he's been the recipient of numerous awards that honor his entrepreneurial spirit, philanthropic heart and business acumen, including the prestigious Horatio Alger Award for his extraordinary life achievements, which stand as a powerful example that the free enterprise system still offers opportunity to all.

Mark Victor Hansen is an enthusiastic crusader of what's possible and is driven to make the world a better place.

Mark Victor Hansen & Associates, Inc.
P.O. Box 7665 • Newport Beach, CA 92658
phone: 949-764-2640 • fax: 949-722-6912
FREE resources online at: *www.markvictorhansen.com*

Who Is Patty Hansen?

Patty Hansen, with her partner Irene, authored *Chicken Soup for the Kid's Soul, Chicken Soup for the Preteen Soul* and *Chicken Soup for the Soul Christmas Treasury for Kids,* books that kids ages nine through thirteen love to read and use as guides for everyday life. Patty is also the contributor of some of the most loved stories in the *Chicken Soup for the Soul* series; coauthor of *Condensed Chicken Soup for the Soul* from Health Communications, Inc.; and *Out of the Blue: Delight Comes into Our Lives* from HarperCollins.

Because of her love for preteens, Patty created a Website, *www.Preteenplanet.com,* to give preteens a fun and safe cyberspace experience where they can also become empowered to make their world a better place.

Prior to her career as an author, Patty worked for United Airlines as a flight attendant for thirteen years. During that time, she received two commendations for bravery. She received the first one when (as the only flight attendant on board) she prepared forty-four passengers for a successful planned emergency landing. The second was for single-handedly extinguishing a fire onboard a mid-Pacific flight, thus averting an emergency situation and saving hundreds of lives.

After "hanging up her wings," Patty became the chief financial officer for M.V. Hansen and Associates, Inc., in Newport Beach, California. Currently, as President of Legal and Licensing for *Chicken Soup for the Soul Enterprises, Inc.,* she has helped to create an entire line of Chicken Soup for the Soul products and licenses.

In 1998, Mom's House, Inc., a nonprofit organization that provides free childcare for school-age mothers, nominated Patty as Celebrity Mother of the Year. Each year since, the Patty Hansen Scholarship is funded by a $10,000 grant and is awarded by Mom's House to deserving single mothers who wish to attend college.

Patty shares her home with her two daughters Elisabeth and Melanie; her mother, Shirley; housekeeper and friend, Eva; three rabbits, one peahen, one guinea hen, three horses, four dogs, eight cats, five birds, thirty-four fish, nine pigeons, twenty-seven chickens (yes, they all have names), a haven for hummingbirds and a butterfly farm.

If you would like to contact Patty:

Patty Hansen
P.O. Box 10879
Costa Mesa, CA 92627
phone: 949-645-5240 • fax: 949-645-3203
e-mail: *patty@preteenplanet.com* • *www.Preteenplanet.com*

Who Is Irene Dunlap?

Irene Dunlap, coauthor of *Chicken Soup for the Kid's Soul, Chicken Soup for the Preteen Soul* and *Chicken Soup for the Soul Christmas Treasury for Kids,* began her writing career in elementary school. It was then that she first discovered her love for creating poetry, a passion she believes to have inherited from her paternal grandmother. She expressed her love for words through writing fictional short stories, lyrics, as a participant in speech competitions and eventually as a vocalist.

During her college years, Irene traveled around the world as a student of the Semester at Sea program, aboard a ship that served as a classroom, as well as home base, for over five hundred college students. After earning a bachelor of arts degree in communications, she became the media director of Irvine Meadows Amphitheatre in Irvine, California. She went on to co-own an advertising and public relations agency that specialized in entertainment and health-care clients.

Irene released her first book in a series titled, *TRUE—Real Stories About God Showing Up in the Lives of Teens,* in February 2004, in order to encourage teens and young adults in their faith. While creating difference-making books, which she sees as a blessing, Irene continues to support her two teens with their interests in music, theatre and sports activities. She also carries on a successful singing career, performing various styles ranging from jump swing and jazz to contemporary Christian in clubs, at church and at special events.

Irene lives in Newport Beach, California, with her husband, Kent; daughter, Marleigh; son, Weston; and Australian shepherd, Gracie. In her spare time, Irene enjoys horseback riding, painting, gardening and cooking. If you are wondering how she does it all, she will refer you to her favorite Bible passage for her answer—Ephesians 3:20.

If you would like to contact Irene, write to her at:

Irene Dunlap
P.O. Box 10879
Costa Mesa, CA 92627
phone: 949-645-5240
fax: 949-645-3203
e-mail: *irene@lifewriters.com*
www.LifeWriters.com

Contributors

Andrea Adair is a mom to three girls, a children's librarian assistant and a freelance writer. She has been published in *Horizons, The Toastmaster* and *Signatures* and is currently writing a mystery.

Catherine Adams received a bachelor of science in medical technology from Texas Christian University and works as a clinical laboratory scientist. She's recently been published in multiple genres and enjoys reading, writing and spending time with her family. Send e-mails to *rachbo03@yahoo.com.*

Max Alexander is now fourteen. Even though they passed away four years ago, at times it is still hard for Max to deal with the death of his grandparents; but he enjoys remembering the good times.

Scott Allen was twelve when he wrote "The Big Slip." He is currently attending classes at the University of Michigan working toward an engineering degree. He enjoys golfing, running, playing piano and spending time with friends. Please e-mail him at *allensc@umich.edu.*

Bill Amend started drawing cartoons for fun when he was nine years old, including frogs and dinosaurs, which may partly explain the iguana in his strip. He earned a Bachelor degree in physics from Amherst College and apart from taking a basic drawing class his senior year, never really studied art. His syndicated *Foxtrot* comic began running in newspapers in 1988. He lives with his wife and his two young children.

Laura Andrade has over ten years experience as a teacher and administrator. With a doctorate in educational leadership and B.S. in biology, it's clear that she is passionate about education. Laura shares her California home with her husband, two cats, two dogs and two horses. Contact her at *mandrade29@cox.net.*

Antonio Angelo Jr. lives with his family and attends high school in northern California. He also holds jobs in an office and in construction. He is interested in pursuing a career in the military service.

Tom Armstrong was the staff cartoonist of the campus newspaper at his university. After getting his degree in fine arts, Armstrong worked as a freelance illustrator and did work for several magazines and advertising agencies. In 1979, he teamed up with fellow artist Tom Batiuk to create talk show host John Darling. Armstrong left the comic in 1985 to concentrate on the highly successful *Marvin*, a comic he created in 1982.

Miriam Bard is a first-year student at Sarah Lawrence College where she majors in English literature. She volunteers teaching English as a second language at a local public school and enjoys traveling, art history, creative writing and camping. She plans to be a travel journalist. E-mail her at *mbard@slc.edu.*

Robert Berardi was born in New York and educated at University of the Arts, Philadelphia. Robert writes and draws *No Rodeo*, a comic strip about a Latina preteen named Desiree. *No Rodeo* can be seen on *www.PreteenPlanet.com,* and will soon be syndicated to daily and Sunday newspapers.

Katie Beauchamp is an eighth-grader who serves as a Beta Club officer, chief editor of her school's literary magazine, is captain of the Affirmative Team in Debate Club; and is in her fifth year of studying the viola. She has won awards with the Young Authors Competition and Future Problem Solving program at state and national levels.

Jesse Billauer was born in Pacific Palisades, California. At the age of nine, he found his true passion in life—surfing. He began traveling the world surfing in competitions when he was twelve years old and was named one of the top 100 up-and-coming surfers in the world by *Surfer Magazine.* After suffering a spinal cord injury from surfing, Jesse was left quadriplegic, but continues to surf and travel, and has become a motivational speaker. He has helped raise money and awareness to find a cure for paralysis through his nonprofit foundation, Life Rolls On. Jesse continues to inspire people with his message to "live life to the fullest and never give up on your hopes and dreams."

Jim Borgman, a Pulitzer Prize winner, is among the most respected cartoonists in America. On the basis of his tenure as staff artist and editorial cartoonist for the *Kenyon Collegian* at Kenyon College in Gambier, Ohio, *The Cincinnati Enquirer* hired him in 1976 to begin work immediately following his graduation. He created *Zits*, his first comic strip, in collaboration with cartoonist Jerry Scott. It debuted in July 1997 in more than 200 newspapers. King Features now distributes *Zits* to 900 newspapers.

Heather Bradley lives with her mother and two sisters in Southern California where she is currently in seventh grade. Heather enjoys writing, reading, horseback riding, camping and just hanging out with her friends.

Kirk Brandt, Eagle Scout and youngest of six, acquired passionate drive from his dad and compassion for service from his mom. He was raised with a lot of love and wants to share it. He is also a vegan raw foodist. Kirk's message to his father is, "Dad, I love and miss you."

Leah Browning is a freelance writer whose published work includes stories, essays, articles and poetry. She is currently writing her second novel. When not working, Leah enjoys reading, spending time with her family, or practicing piano. (She is a late beginner.) A native of New Mexico, Leah lives in Minnesota.

Nicole Buckner is twelve years old and attends middle school. She enjoys reading, writing stories, poetry and horseback riding. Her story "Dapples" tells about the loss of her beloved horse. This tragic event, and her love for horses, has inspired her to become a veterinarian one day.

Chiara Cabiglio has always had a passion for writing. At thirteen, she has already written over forty songs and hopes to become a famous singer and songwriter. She loves to snowboard, sing, shop, play basketball, and travel (especially to Italy since she's of Italian descent).

Stephanie Caffall, age thirteen, was inspired to write "Friends at First Sight" because of her friendship with Jesse, whom she still considers a true friend. She'd like to thank Jesse for being able to count on him. Thanks, Jesse! Love, Steffie. By the way, Jesse, now fourteen, would still rather escort a spider outside than kill it. He is currently working on his Eagle rank in Boy Scouts.

Danny Cannizzaro is a nineteen-year-old currently attending Brown University and studying illustration at Rhode Island School for Design. He plans to major in visual art, while also studying biology and chemistry in hopes of going to medical school upon graduation. He would like to thank his preteen little sister and brother, Diana and Joey, for their inspiration in designing the cover to this book.

Hector D. Cantú created his first newspaper cartoon at the young age of twelve and went on to study journalism at the University of Texas at Austin. His writing has appeared in *The Los Angeles Times Magazine* and *The Hollywood Reporter*. Today Hector is an assistant features editor at *The Dallas Morning News*. He also writes a nationally distributed business column for Knight Ridder/Tribune News Service. Hector lives in Dallas with his wife, Linda, and three kids: Maya, Sofia and Max.

Mel Caro received her bachelor of science in finance from New York University and works in New York as an equity trader. She began writing as a hobby and is now in the process of working on several short stories on a variety of topics. Mel is a certified personal trainer and enjoys running, yoga and painting.

Erin Carthew is an eighth-grade student who has had an extreme interest in writing and artwork for several years, and hopes to make it her career. Erin has two brothers and one sister. Her hobbies include crafts, playing the drums and mentoring younger children.

Carlos Castellanos was always interested in creating art and while in college, he began his freelance career as an illustrator and never looked back. He keeps himself busy doing work for magazines, book publishers, ad agencies and corporate clients in Florida and nationally. Carlos lives in West Palm Beach, Florida with his wife, Maria; sons Chase and Alec; dogs Indy and Sai Hung; and a cat named Lagger.

Jennifer Lynn Clay is a straight-A student at her middle school. She has been published over eighteen times in both national and international magazines. She was a member of the seventh grade Power of the Pen team that won the state title in 2003 and hopes her school's team repeats as state champions this year.

Tiffany Clifton graduated from the Academy of Career Sciences in 2003. She works as a secretary at a manufacturing company and hopes to pursue a career in writing. She enjoys reading, writing and spending time with her family and fiancé, Timmy Oliver. Contact her at *peachy_172002@yahoo.com.*

Mel Ann McLarty Coley received her bachelor of science in education from the University of North Texas in 1976. A loving mother to two pre-teens, she taught developmental writing at Richland College and was teaching writing courses for elementary school students at the time of her passing on November 29, 2003. She will be missed.

Michelle Collins is fourteen years old and lives in Illinois with her mom, dad, sister and brother. She likes to talk online, hang out with friends, swim and just have a good time. She would like to say "hi" to all her family and friends.

Heather Comeau just finished her first screenplay and is currently working on her first novel. She can be contacted at *comeauhez@hotmail.com.*

Elisabeth Copeland is a freshman in high school in Tennessee. She hopes to move back to Alabama where she was born. She likes acting and making people laugh. Elisabeth wrote her story about her experience when her parents got divorced.

Mallorie Cuevas attends high school and enjoys playing basketball, swimming, reading and hanging out with her friends. She plans to go to college.

Holly Cupala paints, writes and lives with her husband and new baby in Seattle, Washington. She loves traveling to exotic places and imagining the stories of the people she meets. Her advice to budding writers is to write down your ideas and read everything! See her Website at *www.hollycupala.com.*

Michele Davis is in her first year at the University of Western Ontario in London, Ontario. She enjoys writing and dancing in her spare time. She gets her inspiration from her friends and family.

Jenn Dlugos is a comedy writer and stand-up comedian in the New England area. She has a book coming out in 2004 entitled *Public Health Disturbance.*

DeAnna Doherty has a bachelor of science in psychology. She is a stay-at-home mom with a two-year-old daughter, Ayden and a six-month-old son, Conner. She enjoys writing children's stories and reading.

Allison Ellis is a youth media specialist and editor and writer for teen fashion Website, *www.BPnordstrom.com.* Prior to that she was the vice president of *www.FoxKids.com/FoxFamilychannel.com.* Allison is the founder of *FreeZone,* a collection of youth-driven publications. In her free time, she writes middle grade fiction. E-mail her at *allison.ellis@comcast.net.*

Alex Estey is fourteen years old and lives in New Brunswick, Canada, with her family. She hopes to be a professional author someday. Her hobbies include basketball, drama, writing and spending time with friends and family.

Greg Evans discovered at an early age that he wanted to be a syndicated cartoonist. His exciting comic strip, *Luann,* chronicles the joyful discoveries and torturous experiences of adolescence. Syndicated by King Features from 1987 until March 1996, when Evans moved the strip to United Feature Syndicate, *Luann* has developed a loyal following of readers of all ages in more than three hundred newspapers. Evans has been praised for his amusing, insightful portrayals of the issues that teens face; and has held *Luann* up as a fine example of the positive power cartoons can have.

MacKenzie Exner is an eighth-grade honor student. She is an Irish dancer and hopes to become an animal trainer. MacKenzie enjoys camping, swimming, watching movies and babysitting.

Melinda Fausey received her bachelor of arts in 1995 and currently is a stay-at-home mom of three children. She enjoys writing and has made recent sales. Melinda is a Florida native and enjoys traveling, jet-skiing, surfing, swimming and spinning. She is currently working on several children's books.

Jill Helene Fettner is a writer and actor in classical and contemporary theater, film, TV and radio, living in New York City. She is a graduate of New York University's Tisch Drama program and a member of the Society of Children's Book Writers and Illustrators. Visit *www.JourneyBold.com.*

Jaime Fisher is fourteen years old and lives in Texas. She enjoys being with friends, talking on the phone and going to the movies. She plans to go to college at LSU and become a pediatrician.

Emma Fraser lives on the west coast of Canada and is currently in seventh grade. She enjoys soccer, surfing, reading and spending time with her many pets. She has competed in local surfing and distance running events. Emma dreams of one day being a writer and photographer.

Jared Garrett is a student at Mid-America Christian University in Oklahoma City, Oklahoma, pursuing a degree in secondary education. Jared works with fifth- and sixth-graders at Crossroads Cathedral Church and is an avid University of Oklahoma fan. He can be e-mailed at *ousport@cox.net.*

Kerry Germain writes and publishes children's picture books on the island of Oahu, Hawaii. She enjoys island activities with her son and his friends, telling stories of when she was a kid, surfing, shell hunting, sailing and diving with sharks. Check out her Website at *www.surfsupforkimo.com.*

Shannon Griffin is an experienced creative writing teacher and freelance writer. Her writing passion is young adult fiction that enlightens and empowers adolescent females. She is happy to report that her brother, Brian, from "I Wish You Were Dead" is a survivor in every sense of the word.

Nicolas Hall is a sixth-grader who likes PlayStation, Nintendo and watching movies. He is very interested in learning more about Jesus.

Cynthia M. Hamond has been writing for six years. She has numerous stories in Multnomah's *Stories for the Heart* series as well as the *Chicken Soup for the Soul* series and in magazines. She has received three writing recognitions and her story, "Goodwill" is a TV favorite. You can e-mail her at *candbh@aol.com.*

Elisabeth Haney is a twelve-year-old who has never been published, until now! She enjoys reading, playing basketball and playing outdoors. She has an eight-year-old little brother who drives her crazy. Her mom home schools Elisabeth and her brother, and her dad is a pastor at a bilingual church.

Hannah A. Heninger is a freshman in high school and an honor student. She takes voice lessons and partakes in the drama department at her school. She plans to go into medicine and hopes to inspire young people all over the world.

Brittany Nicole Henry is a fifteen-year-old who enjoys skateboarding, writing, drawing and hanging out with friends.

Bunny Hoest is one of the most widely read cartoonists today, reaching nearly 200 million diverse readers every week. She produces *The Lockhorns*, which King Features Syndicate distributes to 500 newspapers worldwide; *Laugh Parade,* featuring Howard Huge, for *Parade Magazine,* which is seen by more than 80 million people every Sunday; and the long-running *Bumper Snickers* for the *National Enquirer,* which has a circulation of more than 7 million. Known as "The Cartoon Lady," the dynamic and versatile talent has 25 bestselling anthologies and a host of exciting new projects in the works, including a Lockhorns TV pilot and a Howard Huge animated feature in development with Merv Griffin Entertainment.

Holly Howard has been writing and telling stories for as long as she has been able to talk. She loves to ride horses, read, write and serve in her church. Holly wants to help other kids work through their experiences of growing up with bipolar disorder.

Heather Hutson is a sixth-grader who likes snowboarding, horseback riding, barrel racing, swimming, skiing and gymnastics. She plans on becoming a veterinarian or physician's assistant.

Stephanie Ives, fourteen, lives with her parents and younger sister and enjoys reading, volleyball, writing, and history. Stephanie aspires to be a high school math and history teacher.

Janalea Jeppson was born and raised in Salt Lake City, Utah, and is a graduate of the University of Utah. She currently works as a customer service specialist for a major wireless carrier. Janalea enjoys spending time with her large extended family, working with children and serving in her church. Janalea writes short stories and poetry and especially enjoys writing for children. E-mail her at *giggles2263@juno.com.*

Lance Johnson is currently a sophomore in high school. His hometown of Mammoth Lakes provides a wonderful environment for skiing and mountain biking. He enjoys writing and hopes to be a professional author when he grows up to be an old wise man.

Alex Judge is an eleven-year-old who lives in Ontario, Canada. He likes reading, riding his bike and playing computer games with his friends. He has a green belt in Tae Kwon Do and enjoys swimming.

Jennifer Kerperien is a sixteen-year-old whose favorite subjects in school are math and history. She enjoys tutoring other kids in math after school and helping the elderly. Jennifer also likes writing, going to the movies and doing housework.

Sarah Kessler, thirteen, enjoys attending high school in Wisconsin. She loves basketball, acting, writing and reading. She thanks all of her family, friends and teachers who have encouraged and believed in her and feels blessed to have such incredible people in her life.

Hank Ketcham, American comic artist, was born in 1920 in Seattle, Washington. Tired of the normal studies at his university, he began a career in animation. Ketcham worked with Walt Disney Productions on *Pinocchio, Fantasia* and some *Donald Duck* shorts; and in 1948, he moved to Carmel, California, where his most famous creation, Dennis the Menace, was born. Ketcham drew *Dennis the Menace* with an irreverent yet affectionate pen for over forty years, and officially retired in October 1995. After suffering from heart disease and cancer, he passed away peacefully on June 2, 2001, at the age of eighty-one.

Mridu Khullar is a freelance writer from New Delhi, India. She is the editor-in-chief of *www.WritersCrossing.com* and has been published in hundreds of national and international magazines including *New Woman* and *Business World*. She is currently completing her studies in information technology from Delhi University.

Erin K. Kilby received her bachelor of science in education and English from Bowling Green State University in 1994. She teaches English at a high school in Texas and enjoys writing freelance, crochet and spending time with her husband, Michael, and son, Tyler. Please contact her at *erinkilby@hotmail.com*.

Nicole Koah is a thirteen-year-old who is close to her family and friends. She likes to read, write, use her computer, sing and hang out with friends.

Ashley Kopf was born and grew up in the Jersey Shore area, and has written hundreds of poems and short stories as well as having a few novels in the works. She's studying to be a doctor, but drawing and writing are her true passions, which come naturally to her.

Cheryl Kremer is married to Jack and is the mother of Nikki, twelve, and Cobi, nine. She is a "soccer mom" who cares for infants and toddlers in her home and church nursery. When she isn't watching her kids play soccer, she can be found crocheting, cross-stitching and writing inspirational stories of her everyday life as a wife and mother. She lives in Lancaster, Pennsylvania, and can be reached at *j_kremer@msn.com*.

Amber Kury, age twelve, is a poet who leads a physically active life and likes to help others. She handles difficult situations with a positive demeanor and fun attitude. To her sister, brother and father, she exemplifies hope, love and caring. Amber plans to attend a university and graduate in a field where she can use her knowledge to help others deal with life.

Carmen Leal is the author of six books including *The Twenty-Third Psalm* *for Caregivers.* A storyteller with a dramatic testimony, she is a popular presenter at women's retreats, church groups, conventions and conferences. To learn more about Carmen, please visit her Website at *www.carmenleal.com.*

Veneta Leonard lives in Crown Point, Indiana, and enjoys raising her family. She's an avid reader and plans to go back to college next year to get her teaching degree. Veneta also enjoys playing bunco, Skip-Bo, bowling and going to the show. She lives a happy and blessed life and wishes everyone lots of happiness and peace. God bless.

Lennox "The Lion" Lewis is a man who has made history. Capping an impressive amateur boxing career, Lewis earned a gold medal by knocking out future heavyweight champion Riddick Bowe as a member of Team Canada during the 1988 Olympics in Seoul, Korea. In 1993, only a few years after turning professional, Lewis was officially crowned WBC Heavyweight Champion of the World and went on to defend the title three times. His scientific approach to boxing along with a stiff jab and blistering overhand has secured his place as the preeminent boxer of his generation. Refusing to rest on his laurels, Lewis has consistently and vigorously defended all of his titles and in his quest to succeed at whatever he puts his hands to, "The Emperor of Boxing" continually grows from strength to strength.

Karen Lombard holds a Ph.D. in economics from the University of Chicago and has a broad range of consulting, research and teaching experience in the areas of antitrust, industrial organization, labor economics and applied microeconomics. Her current passion is writing for children and entertaining her two-year-old son, Geordie.

Amanda Macht is a seventh-grader who enjoys reading and writing, talking on the phone and spending time with her younger sister and brother. She hopes to someday work with abused children.

Colleen Mahoney got a scholarship from Take Stock in Children in the sixth grade. She is currently in the seventh grade and her hobbies include singing, acting and anything that involves performing. She would like to major in fine arts.

Lauren Maffeo, a fifteen-year-old, has been acting since the age of eleven and has appeared in numerous local films and theater productions. Her biggest role to date has been a voice-over in the independent feature *Little Erin Merryweather,* which was screened at the Hollywood Independent Film Festival. As a writer, she has been published in *Teen Vogue, Teen Ink* and *Spire* magazines. Lauren enjoys skiing, traveling, shopping, listening to music, and spending time with her friends and family. Being published in her favorite book series is a dream come true, and her poem is dedicated to her dad.

Amy Mallinder-Morgan, fourteen, was born in England and now resides in Windermere, Florida. She enjoys music, horses and her PC. Her volunteer activities inspired her writing and she was selected in the top ten for Disney Dreamers and Doers at her school for her piece on Give Kids the World.

Caleb Mathewson enjoys playing basketball and baseball. He is an avid fan of the St. Louis Cardinals and has an extensive collection of baseball memorabilia. Caleb appreciates playing catch and hoops with his dad, his brother, Jordan, and his sister, Allyse.

Molly McAfee is a seventh-grade student. She is involved in volleyball, softball and BETA. She also enjoys reading, writing and being with family and friends.

Heather McPherson was born and raised in British Columbia. The fifteen-year-old's hobbies include reading, singing, dancing, acting and doing volunteer work. In the future, Heather hopes to become a professional photographer or work in the performing arts.

Carol Miller is a freelance writer who lives in New Jersey with her husband, Jack; daughters, Stephanie and Lauren; and beagle, Tapper. Her work has appeared in *Chicken Soup for the Mother & Daughter Soul*, *FamilyFun*, *The Christian Science Monitor* and many other publications. Contact her at *miller_carol@usa.net*.

Marie-Therese Miller earned her M.A. in writing from Manhattanville College. She pens a humorous family life column for the *Taconic Press* newspaper and writes about family issues for the *Poughkeepsie Journal* and *Hudson Valley Parent*. She, her husband, John, and their five children live in Salt Point, New York. E-mail her at *thisisthelife@hvc.rr.com*.

Molly Miller is twelve years old and lives in Illinois. She enjoys writing, being on the computer and hanging out with friends. She wrote her story after her dog, Maddy, died when she was nine. She wants to become an author and a lawyer when she gets older.

Sydney Jane Miller is a sophomore from Southern California. She loves photo booths, sushi and receiving mail.

Sydney Milucky, age thirteen, lives in Southern California and loves a good story. She's always writing, drawing and watching movies. Her dream is to have a career in film. Sydney has a compassionate heart and cares about those who struggle.

Jordan Mitchell, fourteen, is the youngest of four and lives in California. She is a creative artist and passionate writer. Jordan enjoys playing soccer, watching movies and being with her friends and family.

Marisol Muqoz-Kiehne was born in Puerto Rico and lives in the San Francisco area. She is a clinical psychologist who works with children and families, teaches child psychotherapy, and is the host of *Nuestros Niños,* a radio program on parenting and child development. She can be reached at: *marisol@nuestrosninos.com.*

Colleen O'Brien, age thirteen, wrote her story for *Preteen Soul 2* after reading about other people's experiences much like hers. It is her hope that those who read about her experience of loss at a young age will find comfort. Colleen's hobbies include reading, writing and hanging out with friends.

Jennifer O'Neil has a master of fine arts in screenwriting and has over ten years experience in film. She is a writer, producer and director in San Francisco and creator of gala-event scripts for Columbia/Tristar, Sony, and Discovery Networks. Jennifer and her sister Kitty's first book, *Decorating with Funky Shui,* hits bookstores in June of 2004.

Jena Pallone, a junior in high school, has been homeschooled for eleven years. Her writings have placed in contests and been locally published in the *Jeffersonian Democrat* and *The Path.* Jena enjoys reading the classics, writing, hunting, and showing her horse in local and 4-H shows.

Tenna Perry has black belts in American Freestyle Karate and Bushido Kai. She has taught martial arts to students of all ages for ten years. Tenna focuses a great deal of her writing on self-defense, all forms of child abuse and rape. Please e-mail her at *midnightwriter@ev1.net.*

Victoria Perry is a high school freshman and a junior karate instructor who enjoys teaching other children the importance of self-defense. Victoria participates in as many karate tournaments as possible in her area where she has consistently won in both sparring and katas.

Kelsey Peters is an eleven-year-old who enjoys reading *Chicken Soup* books, writing and playing with her dogs, Lilli and Dottie. She is in fifth grade and loves to sing for her church.

Nathan D. Phung is a seventh-grader from California. His hobbies are reading, bowling, searching for cool jokes on the Internet and practicing magic tricks. He plays the piano for his school jazz band and the trombone in the marching band. Someday, Nathan would like to be a computer engineer or magician.

Michael T. Powers is a high school girls' coach, youth pastor, founder of *www.Heart4Teens.com,* and author of his own book, *Heart Touchers.* To read more about his writings, which appear in nineteen inspirational books, or to join the thousands of worldwide readers on his inspirational e-mail list, visit *www.Heart4Teens.com* or e-mail him at *Heart4Teens@aol.com.*

Rachel Punches grew up in Muskegon, Michigan, and is a soldier in the Army National Guard. She now lives in Kalamazoo, Michigan, where she is attending college. In her spare time, she enjoys movies, reading, singing at the top of her lungs and dancing when no one is around. She draws inspiration for her writing from family and friends. She dedicates her poem to her friend, Kerry, whom she loves and misses very much.

Lin Rajan received her bachelor's degree in electronics engineering from Goa University, India, with honors. She is settled in Virginia with her husband and loves writing, reading and cooking. She believes that an individual is "successful" when he/she is "happy." E-mail her at *lin_rajan@hotmail.com.*

John Reiner was born in 1956 and raised on Long Island. He met *Mad Magazine* artist Mort Drucker in 1974, who encouraged him to pursue cartooning as a career; and in 1984 hired Reiner to work on King Features' comic strip *Benchley.* In collaboration with Bunny Hoest, Reiner took over production of the classic comic panel *The Lockhorns,* created by the late Bill Hoest. They also took over *Bumper Snickers, Howard Huge* and *Laugh Parade.* Reiner won the 1994 National Cartoonists Society award for gag cartoons.

Alexandria Robinson, twelve, is an excellent writer who loves to express her feelings, thoughts, emotions and life experiences on paper. She likes to do normal girl stuff like hang out with friends and talk on the phone. She still can't believe that one of her poems was picked to be in *Chicken Soup for the Preteen Soul 2!*

Gwen Rockwood received her English degree from the University of Arkansas. She writes a humor column called "The Rockwood Files" for newspapers in Arkansas and Missouri and is currently working on a compilation book of her columns. E-mail her at *rockwood@cox-internet.com.*

Leigh Rubin, with his cartoon panel, *Rubes,* in hundreds of newspapers across the country and gracing millions of greeting cards, mugs and T-shirts, began his career in 1979, when he created a publishing company, *Rubes Publications.* After distributing his own greeting cards; Rubin went on to publish the popular *Notable Quotes* in 1981. Just three years later, *Rubes* began appearing in newspapers and is now distributed by Creators

Syndicate to more than 400 newspapers worldwide. Rubin is married and has three sons.

Jessica Sagers is in eighth grade in Utah. She is boy crazy, loves hanging out with her friends and enjoys seeing Orlando Bloom movies. Jessica likes writing poetry and fictional stories and plays tennis, water-skis and snow-skis.

Cassandra Scheidies is finishing her bachelor of organizational communications at Bellevue University. She received her associates in biblical studies from Grace University in Omaha, Nebraska. She enjoys kickboxing, basketball and reading. She is now working on an inspirational novel.

Jerry Scott started cartooning professionally in the mid-1970s by submitting gag cartoons to magazines and sold one from his first batch to the *Saturday Evening Post*. In 1983, he was asked to take over the *Nancy* comic strip, originally by Ernie Bushmiller, which he continued to create for twelve years. Scott went on to create the *Zits* comic strip in collaboration with cartoonist Jim Borgman that debuted in July 1997 in more than 200 newspapers—one of the strongest strip introductions in years. Jerry, his wife, Kim, and their daughter live in California.

Erin Shirreff is fourteen years old and enjoys swimming, horseback riding and most of all singing. When she grows up she plans to be on Broadway!

Jaimee Silber is an eighth-grade honor student from Michigan. Her interests include cheerleading, dance and, of course, writing. She has a dog, a cat and a sister, Alexis. This is Jaimee's first published work and she would like to thank her Nana for buying her her first *Chicken Soup* book.

Samantha Slaughter, age twelve, has been surrounded by people who read her entire life. She loves to write and includes her personal feelings in her pieces. Her favorite color is purple and she likes playing basketball and spending time with family and friends.

Allen Smith is currently a sophomore in high school. He enjoys hunting, fishing, camping and anything dealing with the outdoors. He is currently in Scouting and is working toward his Eagle rank.

Danny Stein enjoys hockey, golf and skiing, as well as playing guitar. He believes that you can do anything you put your mind to!

Michelle Strauss is a fifteen-year-old from Weatherford, Texas, who enjoys writing poetry. She has been entering and winning writing competitions since the third grade and often competes with her twin sister. Michelle is the editor of her school newspaper and plans to attend college to earn a degree in creative writing.

Craig Strickland is married with two kids. He likes bodysurfing and going to movies. He has had numerous stories published in magazines and anthologies. His two books for middle-readers are *Scary Stories from 1313 Wicked Way* and *Scary Stories for Sleepovers #8*. You can e-mail him at *Strickland-4@cox.net*.

Mark Tatulli drew his first published newspaper comic strip in 1988, for the *Burlington County Times* in New Jersey. His next strip, *Bent Halos* a comic about a couple of rambunctious angels, was nationally syndicated. In 1997 *Heart of the City* quickly caught the eyes of senior editors at Universal Press Syndicate and debuted in newspapers in 1998. An Emmy award winner, Mark is also an accomplished filmmaker and animator. He resides in New Jersey with his wife, son and two daughters.

B. J. Taylor now has a home of her own that she shares with three cats, one dog and a wonderful husband. She has been published in newspapers and magazines and is writing a book for dog lovers showing how a dog and its owner can make a difference in their community by helping others. E-mail her at *bjtaylor3@earthlink.net*.

Bob Thaves is a master of the twisted phrase and skewed outlook. A true innovator, *Frank and Ernest* was the first comic panel presented in a strip format. Thaves, who holds both bachelor and master degrees in psychology, began cartooning as a kid and never stopped. He has been honored with three Reuben Awards for Best Syndicated Panel in 1986, 1984 and 1983, and was given the Free Press Association's Mencken Award for Best Cartoon in 1985. He was also voted "Punster of the Year" in 1990 by the International Save the Pun Foundation.

Aidan Trenn is a nine-year-old girl who loves to draw, make crafts and play with her friends. She was born in Maryland and has lived in Florida, Oklahoma and New Mexico. Aidan also enjoys inline skating and boogie boarding. She is in Mrs. Jones' third-grade class and is a member of the Math Superstars Club.

Quinn Thomas lives in Georgia with her husband and one-year-old daughter. After a twelve-year career in social services, she is now a stay-at-home mother and loves spending time with her daughter and writing children's stories.

Mike Vallely, skateboard legend and East Coast rebel-punk-poet, changed the face of skateboarding in 1986 with his innovative and artistic approach to street skating. Eighteen years later he is still making an impact with his unflinching individuality and his aggressive and expressive skating. A touring machine, Mike V. has covered more ground than any other professional skater in the history of the sport, spreading the gospel of skateboarding around the globe. Lead singer of the hardcore punk outfit Mike V. and the Rats and star of ESPN's Tony Hawk's Gigantic Skatepark Tour and featured in the Tony Hawk Pro Skater video game series, he is on a mission to live his life to the fullest each and every day, which means plenty more relevant and impassioned skating and music is yet to come from this man.

Lauren Ashley Weilbacher is a high school freshman. Her hobbies are ballet, pointe, jazz and tap. She is a pom-pom girl and also teaches ballet and tap.

Ellen Werle, age twelve, is currently attending acting school. She likes swimming, biking, inline skating and playing with her friends.

Spencer Westcott was seventeen when he wrote "My Dad, the Superhero." He is currently studying political science at the University of California, San Diego. Spencer is the president of the Poker Society, the Secret Society of Pirates; a member of the Associated Students; and enjoys playing golf and guitar. You can contact Spencer at *spencer@ucsd.edu*.

Michelle Williams joined Destiny's Child, one of the bestselling female groups of all time, with steely determination to learn. That same fearless, faith-driven quality came in handy while jump-starting a solo career as an inspirational/gospel recording artist with her 2002 release, *Heart to Yours*. Her tireless work ethic motivated her to conquer a starring role on the Broadway stage as the love-crossed Nubian princess, *Aida*. And in January 2004, Michelle excitedly delivered *Do You Know*, an inspirational and contemporary urban-gospel style, set to everyday life-based testimonials of self-doubt, questions of faith and bad relationships.

Kristi Yamaguchi is skating's best and brightest; a dominant force and major star in the world of figure skating. Her professional career is marked by numerous major championship titles and critically acclaimed performances earning her accolades from major sportswriters as the "best female skater in the world." Following a tremendous amateur career, in 1992 Kristi won the U.S. National Championship, fulfilled a lifelong dream by winning the Olympic Gold Medal in Albertville and defended her World title in her hometown in Oakland. In 1998 Kristi returned to the U.S. National Championships to be inducted into the U.S. Figure Skating Hall of Fame. She has recently finished her tenth year of touring with Stars on Ice along with fellow Olympic medallists Katrina Witt, Ilia Kulik, Todd Eldridge and Tara Lipinski.

Julia Yorks is a fifteen-year-old high school freshman who loves to write, although her ambition in life is to be an actress or news commentator. Julia has appeared in M. Night Shyamalan's *Unbreakable*, and on the CBS television show "Hack," among others. Her favorite pastimes include singing, being with friends and playing sports.

Patty Zeitlin is an author, poet, playwright and songwriter with recordings for young people and adults and an M.A. from Pacific Oaks College in human development. She teaches classes in Compassionate Communication (NVC). Patty enjoys dancing, reading and Hawaii. She just finished writing a fantasy-fiction novel for young adults. Contact her at *patty@psncc.org*.

Christina Zucal is working on her GED and hopes to attend college in a year or two. She enjoys using her computer to play Counter-Strike and to chat online with friends.

Deep Inside. Reprinted by permission of Stephanie Ives and Joanna Ives. ©2003 Stephanie Ives.

More Than I Had Dreamed Of. Reprinted by permission of Lin Rajan. ©2003 Lin Rajan.

Welcome to New Hope, Pennsylvania. Reprinted by permission of Julia Yorks and Robert Yorks. ©2004 Julia Yorks.

Better Off. Reprinted by permission of Kirk Brandt. ©2004 Kirk Brandt.

No Place I'd Rather Be. ©1998 by Kristi Yamaguchi and Greg Brown. Published by Taylor Trade Publishing, an imprint of The Rowman & Littlefield Publishing Group, *www.rlpgbooks.com.*

Story Opener. Reprinted by permission of Brittany Hielckert and David Hielckert. ©2003 Brittany Hielckert.

Stay with Me. Reprinted by permission of Jaime Fisher and Sherri Hill. ©2003 Jaime Fisher.

A Loving Mother. Reprinted by permission of Holly Howard and Sheryl Chamness. ©2003 Holly Howard.

Story Opener. Reprinted by permission of Kristina Taskova-Zeese and Tatyana Taskova. ©2001 Kristina Taskova-Zeese.

The Worst Day of My Life. Reprinted by permission of Jennifer Kerperien and Richard Kerperien. ©2002 Jennifer Kerperien.

Lucky. Reprinted by permission of Molly McAfee and Shelly McAfee. ©2001 Molly McAfee.

Maddy. Reprinted by permission of Molly Miller and Caryn Borman. ©1998 Molly Miller.

A Halloween No One Will Forget. Reprinted by permission of Heather Hutson and Judy Hutson. ©2001 Heather Hutson.

The Sandals That Saved My Life. Reprinted by permission of Mallorie Cuevas and Ellen Gereau. ©2002 Mallorie Cuevas.

65 Roses. Reprinted by permission of Denise Marsh and Jodie Griffin. ©2000 Denise Marsh.

Klutz Dust and Puberty. Reprinted by permission of Cynthia M. Hamond. ©2003 Cynthia M. Hamond.

Jimmy, Jimmy. Reprinted by permission of Karen Lombard ©2003 Karen Lombard.

Staying True to Myself. Reprinted by permission of Michelle Williams. ©2003 Michelle Williams.

No, Really . . . Barney Ate My Report Card! Reprinted by permission of Jenn Dlugos. ©2003 Jenn Dlugos.

There's Always Someone Less Fortunate. Reprinted by permission of Amy Mallinder-Morgan and Mandy Morgan. ©2002 Amy Mallinder-Morgan.

Thirteen Candles. Reprinted by permission of Allison Ellis. ©2003 Allison Ellis.

Disabilities. Reprinted by permission of Heather Bradley and Amanda Bradley. ©1999 Heather Bradley.

The Helpful Stranger. Reprinted by permission of Alex Judge and Mary Judge. ©2003 Alex Judge.

Eclectic Wisdom Chapter Opener. Reprinted by permission of Lauren Maffeo and Deborah Ann Collins. ©2003 Lauren Maffeo.

Covered. Reprinted by permission of Tenna Perry and Victoria Perry. ©2003 Tenna Perry.

Pyramid Surprise. Reprinted by permission of Holly Cupala. ©2003 Holly Cupala.

Initiation. Reprinted by permission of DeAnna Doherty. ©2003 DeAnna Doherty.

My Dad, the Superhero. Reprinted by permission of Spencer Westcott. ©2002 Spencer Westcott.

Grandma's Pearls. Reprinted by permission of Catherine Adams. ©1997 Catherine Adams.

Preteen Wisdom. Reprinted by permission of Rachelle Carpenter and Christopher Carpenter, Emma Paradis and Susan Paradis, Sara Hess and Lynn Hess, Alexandra Mendoza and Jennifer Mendoza, Hamizatul Nisa and Mohamed Zabidi Bin Ramli, Louise East and Peter East, Nikollas Van Den Broek and Henry Van Den Broek, Ailene Evangelista and Marisol Berrios, Zainab Mahmood and Manzur Mahmood, Nicole Paquette and Bonita Paquette, Ambreen Hooda and Rasheed Hooda, Emily Craft and Jane Craft, Hayley Hunter and Steven Hunter, Sara Mangos and Carole Mangos, Jordan Rakes and Kristen Karr, Lauren Maffeo and Deborah Collins, Alexander Siu and Alan Siu, Emily Kent and Rebecca Kent, Alec Don and Jacqueline Don, Jenna Druce and Jolyon Druce, Jonathon Tracey and Shirley Tracey, Quinn Thomas. ©2003 Rachelle Carpenter, Emma Paradis, Sara Hess, Alexandra Mendoza, Hamizatul Nisa, Louise East,

Yuan Gao, Sun Zhong, Nikollas Van Den Broek, Ailene Evangelista, Zainab Mahmood, Nicole Paquette, Ambreen Hooda, Emily Craft, Hayley Hunter, Sara Mangos, Jordan Rakes, Lauren Maffeo, Alexander Siu, Emily Kent, Alec Don, Jenna Druce, Jonathon Tracey.

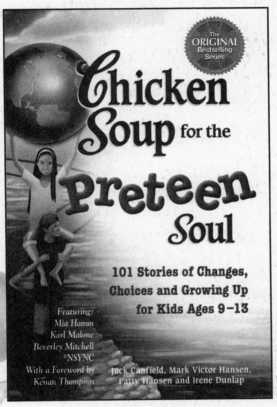

Awesome Reads

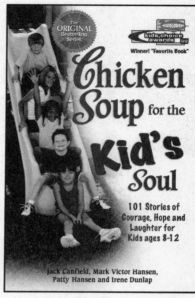

Code 6099 • $14.95

Code 4052 • $14.95

Fun Stories

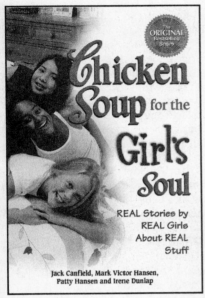

Code 3137 • $14.95

Code 2831 • $9.95

Also Available

Chicken Soup African American Soul
Chicken Soup African American Woman's Soul
Chicken Soup Breast Cancer Survivor's Soul
Chicken Soup Bride's Soul
Chicken Soup Caregiver's Soul
Chicken Soup Cat Lover's Soul
Chicken Soup Christian Family Soul
Chicken Soup College Soul
Chicken Soup Couple's Soul
Chicken Soup Dieter's Soul
Chicken Soup Dog Lover's Soul
Chicken Soup Entrepreneur's Soul
Chicken Soup Expectant Mother's Soul
Chicken Soup Father's Soul
Chicken Soup Fisherman's Soul
Chicken Soup Girlfriend's Soul
Chicken Soup Golden Soul
Chicken Soup Golfer's Soul, Vol. I, II
Chicken Soup Horse Lover's Soul, Vol. I, II
Chicken Soup Inspire a Woman's Soul
Chicken Soup Kid's Soul, Vol. I, II
Chicken Soup Mother's Soul, Vol. I, II
Chicken Soup Parent's Soul
Chicken Soup Pet Lover's Soul
Chicken Soup Preteen Soul, Vol. I, II
Chicken Soup Scrapbooker's Soul
Chicken Soup Sister's Soul, Vol. I, II
Chicken Soup Shopper's Soul
Chicken Soup Soul, Vol. I-VI
Chicken Soup at Work
Chicken Soup Sports Fan's Soul
Chicken Soup Teenage Soul, Vol. I-IV
Chicken Soup Woman's Soul, Vol. I, II

To order direct: Telephone (800) 441-5569 • www.hcibooks.com
Prices do not include shipping and handling. Your response code is CCS.